SHORT CUTS

SHORT CUTS

A Guide to Oaths, Ring Tones,
Ransom Notes, Famous Last Words,
and Other Forms of Minimalist
Communication

ALEXANDER HUMEZ

NICHOLAS HUMEZ

ROB FLYNN

OXFORD
UNIVERSITY PRESS

2010

OXFORD
UNIVERSITY PRESS

Oxford University Press, Inc., publishes works that further
Oxford University's objective of excellence
in research, scholarship, and education.

Oxford   New York
Auckland   Cape Town   Dar es Salaam   Hong Kong   Karachi
Kuala Lumpur   Madrid   Melbourne   Mexico City   Nairobi
New Delhi   Shanghai   Taipei   Toronto

With offices in
Argentina   Austria   Brazil   Chile   Czech Republic   France   Greece
Guatemala   Hungary   Italy   Japan   Poland   Portugal   Singapore
South Korea   Switzerland   Thailand   Turkey   Ukraine   Vietnam

Copyright © 2010 by Alexander Humez, Nicholas Humez, and Rob Flynn.

Published by Oxford University Press, Inc.
198 Madison Avenue, New York, NY 10016

www.oup.com

Oxford is a registered trademark of Oxford University Press.

Library of Congress Cataloging-in-Publication Data
Humez, Alexander.
Short cuts : a guide to oaths, ring tones, ransom notes, famous last words,
and other forms of minimalist communication / Alexander Humez,
Nicholas Humez, and Rob Flynn.
p. cm.
Includes bibliographical references and index.
ISBN 978-0-19-538913-5
1. English language—Terms and phrases—Dictionaries.
2. English language—Idioms—Dictionaries.
3. Figures of speech—Dictionaries.
I. Humez, Nicholas D.   II. Flynn, Rob.   III. Title.
PE1689.H86 2010
302.2'2—dc22   2009047667

1 3 5 7 9 8 6 4 2

Printed in the United States of America
on acid-free paper

For
Jean, Leslie, and Sharon

CONTENTS

PREFACE

A Quick Tour of the Park

OUR EVERYDAY LIVES ARE INEVITABLY TOUCHED—AND immeasurably enriched—by an extraordinary variety of miniature forms of verbal communication, most of them so familiar that we don't think of them as belonging to an extended family united by their characteristic brevity, if we think of them at all. We glance over breakfast at the headlines and the "News in Brief" column before turning to our horoscope or the personals, advice to the lovelorn, or the obits, depending on our age and the kind of newspaper we read. Billboards, posters, and street signs solicit our attention on the way to work, while the graffiti on the subway walls all but demand it. Once we're at work, we go online to check our e-mail and perhaps our favorite blogs or the cartoons that our local newspaper no longer carries. Moreover, at some point in our lives if not routinely, we are all obliged to sign somebody's yearbook, put our best foot forward in a résumé, or (in response to the timeworn interview challenge) describe ourselves in a single word. And who hasn't mentally attempted to compose the perfect epitaph or "famous last words?"

To live in what has been characterized both as "the age of information" and, just as aptly, as "the era of short attention spans" is to plunge daily into a personal universe of abbreviated discourse. *Short Cuts* is a guide to the geography of that universe and its cultural history. Organized thematically by location (both physical and figurative, as, for example, in the dictionary and in and out of trouble), *Short Cuts* examines a wide range of minimalist discursive genres as varied as the bank robbery note, the oath of allegiance, the sniglet, and the Facebook profile, focusing on some (e.g., the oath—both kinds—and the hobo sign), mentioning others only in passing (e.g., the pickup line and the protologism), and leaving others unmentioned (e.g., the elevator speech and the little card inside the glass case at the museum—*pace* Epimenides) on the assumption that these will elicit an aha! as the reader spots them independently.

These are the main stops on the tour:

- *In the Eye of the Beholder*—Icons and their relation to text: Western writing systems, the evolution of ideographic to alphabetic systems, and the return to graphics as a means of communication in such disparate realms as the computer screen and the highway, the cartoon page, the storefront, and the sky.
- *In the Dictionary*—The notion of "the dictionary" from its Babylonian origins to the Wiktionary and what a dictionary should (and shouldn't) contain: lemmas and glosses, ghost words, sniglets, and Mountweazels.
- *By the Great Crikes!*—Oaths (of both the pledge and curse word varieties), curses (of both the hex and swearword varieties), and the relationships among all of the above. Indeterminates (thingamajigs),

magic words, prayers and incantations, insults, snappy comebacks, and *esprit de l'escalier.*

- *On or About Your Person*—Our physical presentation of self says a lot about us, from the logo on our gimme cap to the name of the s.o. tattooed on our ankle. Do you have a driver's license or a Selective Service card in your wallet? Money in your pocket? A medical alert bracelet around your wrist or your boyfriend's class ring on a chain around your neck? And what about that substantial extension of self, your car? Does it have a vanity plate or a bumper sticker proclaiming that you heart your German shepherd's head? Taken together, these text-bearing personal accoutrements tell us a lot about who you are and the world you inhabit.

- *On the Lam*—Bank robberies, blackmail, kidnapping, and bomb threats typically involve a note (or notes) composed by the perpetrator and subsequently analyzed by the forensic linguist, while wanted posters, APBs, AMBER alerts, and the reading of the suspect's Miranda rights all call upon the verbal abilities of various officers of the law. Add the flier stapled to the phone pole asking for information about your missing iPod (no questions asked) and the milk carton featuring the missing child, and the world of crime turns out to be a fairly talky place.

- *In the News*—Newspapers historically have offered a wealth of interesting material in short format, from the headline to the classified ad. Read all about it.

- *On the Phone*—Since its contended invention in the second half of the nineteenth century, the telephone has undergone a number of refinements, which have fostered associated innovations in the use of

language (some of it wordless) and the etiquette
of remote communication. While the "telephone
voice," the standard verbal formulae marking the
beginning and end of a conversation, the language
of the answering machine and phone mail, and the
cold-caller's sales pitch have not yet been completely
replaced by the rituals of instant messaging, some
kind of signal telling us that someone is on the line
and wants to talk has remained an evolving constant,
from the bell to the ring tone, which can be any sort
of digitized sound, including speech.

• *In the Mail*—Silent telecommunication has taken
many forms over the ages, each reflecting a shrinkage
in the amount of time it takes for A to tell B
something when B is out of earshot. Between ancient
times, when you had to wait for your runner's hair
to grow back over the message you'd written on his
shaved head before you could send him off to deliver
your message, and today, with its instant messaging
technology, we have relied on the mail—letters and
postcards sent via "snail mail" and, more recently,
messages sent electronically via e-mail and Twitter.
Letters, of course, come in a number of flavors—Dear
John, job application, resignation, reference, crank,
and Holiday family-news-of-the-past-year, to name
just a few. Each has its own structure and component
parts, as do their more recent electronic progeny, all
of which we are here to read.

• *In and Out of Trouble*—Avoiding getting into trouble,
realizing that you are in trouble, and extricating
yourself from trouble are processes that all have
short forms of communication associated with them.
Warnings, disclaimers, weasel words, and the terms
of use agreement (including the prenup) may or

may not serve to keep you out of trouble. If not, the parking ticket on your windshield, the summons slipped into your unsuspecting hand, or the error message that flashes on your computer monitor just before the appearance of "the black screen of death" may all elicit the "uh-oh" of recognition (or some other emotive interjection). In the first two cases, there's not much to do besides face the music, perhaps with an accompanying apology. (If you're a reporter and you blunder in print, you may be able to publish a correction or retraction to get yourself off the hook.) In the case of a computer error, you may be able to access the online help system and read a message that explains the source of the problem and, if you're lucky, what you can do to restore your work, no apology required.

* *In the End*—Famous last words, suicide notes, farewells, and sign-offs—XXX, XOXO, "Hi-ho, Silver, away!"—bring all things to an end, generally in few words. Sometimes the farewell is temporary—see you later—but some, like the obituary notice, are final. These may be followed by prayers, eulogies, funeral home guestbook entries (now increasingly visible online), and the tombstone epitaph, all by their nature brief.

In the late fourth millennium B.C.E., the earliest known precursor of writing—clay tokens representing animals or other standard goods, pressed into the skin of a hollow clay vessel and then sealed up inside of it—employed an economy of symbolic content uncannily reminiscent of the icons on our computer screens today. In the intervening five thousand years, the tension has always been between clarity and brevity: Make it lucid, but keep it short. In today's world we are exposed to an astonishingly rich variety of ways in which these two opposing goals are reconciled. No surprise, then, that the forms of communication that best succeed at this are the ones that capture and hold our attention and are the subject of this book. Read on.

SHORT CUTS

1

IN THE EYE OF THE BEHOLDER

What's Your Sign?

I<small>F A PICTURE IS WORTH A THOUSAND WORDS, AND THE</small> old song urges us to let a smile be our umbrella, it should follow that a four-page spread of the Sunday funnies ought to keep the rain off our heads better than the rest of the newspaper combined—but no. Nevertheless, the ubiquity of comic strips has had a profound effect not merely on the popular culture and high art of the last century but on its verbal (and extraverbal) discourse as well.

Cartoons are arguably as old as writing itself (as historians of comics and sequential art are very pleased to remind us) if under "cartoon" we include pictographs. The two-stroke Chinese ideogram *ren*$_2$ 人 ('human being') *looks* like a walking person seen from the side; the Old Babylonian character for 'ox,' ⇨ (pronounced *gud*), is a plausible sketch of a bull seen from above; and the Egyptian hieroglyph ⬤ represented an eye and, by extension, the verb 'to see.' In their earliest stages of development, the first writing systems were all ideographic. Such a system has three obvious disadvantages: (1) An ideogram can represent a multiplicity of different words; (2) even if you lump semantically related words under the same sign and let context do some of the disambiguation, you still need unique signs for a large number of semantic mini-domains, a forbidding learning task for any would-be scribe, and (3) pictures are time-consuming to draw, which is fine for art but overkill for, say, a bill of lading. To cut down on writing time, ideographs became more streamlined (though less representational), and the problems of pictoral polysemy and the profusion of symbols were addressed by *pictograms* (or *pictographs,* also known as *logograms* or *logographs*) and *phonograms.*

A *pictogram* is a picture—possibly a composite of pictures—that represents an actual word or phrase, and a *phonogram* is a picture that represents a particular sound or series of sounds (a syllable) without regard to meaning. The Egyptian writing system developed into a mixture of pictograms and phonograms, a practice echoed by the modern-day *rebus* (an eye for an "I," a bee for a "be," a tree and a pan for "trepan," and perhaps a B plus some raindrops for a "brain"). Bumper stickers reading "I ♥ NY" are rebuses in mufti: They draw on the rebus tradition, which says "Interpret my pictures as words," but obviously "I heartnee" would be a naive pronunciation of the slogan. Instead, we know to read the word "love" as the contextually accurate meaning of the heart icon, in large part because a lifetime of exposure to it (especially in connection with the celebration of St. Valentine's Day) has conditioned us to do so.

More precisely, the Egyptian hieroglyphic ideographic writing system evolved into the decidedly more fluid hieratic script, which in turn spawned demotic (also known as enchorial) script, serving the interests of speed of production much as later cursive and shorthand scripts would appear as faster alternatives to block printing. As with block printing, cursive, and shorthand, hieroglyphics, hieratic, and demotic coexisted, each in its own sphere of usage.

All of these scripts used a combination of ideograms, pictograms, and phonograms. At some point, out of all of this
came the Proto-Canaanite script in which a small number
of pictograms did double duty, each representing both a
word and its initial sound. (Such a script is called *acrophonic*,
from Greek *ákros* 'outermost' and *phōnḗ* 'sound, tone') For
example, the Proto-Canaanite representation of the word
for 'house' (*bet*) was also used to represent the sound [b].
From there, it was only a matter of time before the notion
of "one sound: one symbol" (give or take) took off (thanks
to the Phoenicians), resulting in today's alphabetic scripts,
each a minuscule inventory of pictures, albeit abstract art.

The word *icon* (from Greek *eikṓn*, 'figure, image, likeness')
is literally 'an image or representation' and by extension 'a
symbol,' specifically one that stands for something by virtue
of its similitude to it. The logician C. S. Peirce wrote that "in
contemplating a painting, there is a moment when we lose
the consciousness that it is not the thing." Indeed, in the
Eastern Orthodox Church, icons are images of Christ and
the saints that are believed to be worthy of veneration precisely because, as St. Athanasios put it, the picture contains
both the *eîdos* (idea) and *morphḗ* (shape) of what it depicts;
hence the icon itself could say that its subject "is in me and I
in him; [we] are one," the distinction between the representation and what is represented all but collapsing to zero.

Of course, we do not take a heart icon to be intended
as an anatomically correct picture of an actual body part,
and a valentine that featured such a representation would
probably be received with a sentiment significantly at odds
with the one in which such cards are usually sent. Nor is an
icon consisting of an abstracted figure of a woman in a skirt
supposed to represent an actual woman; we correctly read it
rather as a sign that beyond the door it designates is a space
for women (and by convention a toilet that is exclusively so,

an exception being made for boys too young to visit the men's room on their own, with the proviso that their license to enter this feminized space is conveyed only by virtue of their being chaperoned by someone of the female sex).

It is no accident that we are surrounded by such signs in public places such as airports and parks; they have come to achieve something of the status of a universal language, thanks in large part to a determined effort by international commissions such as the United Nations Conference on Road and Motor Transport, as well as federal agencies such as the Department of the Interior's National Park Service. Thus we are all familiar with the stick figure in the wheel-chair for handicapped access, silhouettes of escalators or telephones to direct the traveler to these amenities, or the red circle with the slanting bar to indicate that whatever icon on which it is superimposed (e.g., a cigarette with smoke waves emanating from it) is forbidden. Indeed, the "No—" icon might better be called a "meta-icon," for it functions as a syntactic operator that can be applied anywhere, not just to other icons (e.g., over a capital L to form a Yuletide rebus for "Noël").

Trademarks are often quintessentially iconic, being an integral part of that function of publicity that advertising agencies call "establishing identity." A pervasive example of iconic signage as branding was the adoption by the Massachusetts Bay Transit Authority's T-in-a-circle logo in 1965 to replace the "MTA" signage of its Boston-and-vicinity predecessor, the Metropolitan Transit Authority. Whereas the latter was an abbreviation that at least had its roots in the actual name, the "T" logo bought easy recognition at the expense of ambiguity (it was short for Transit but could just as well have stood for Taxi). More ominously, some of its crit-ics saw the "T" logo as an example of a wider drift away from dependence on the written word as signifier, such signage tending to undermine literacy rather than to enhance it. (Nowadays, of course, we have all gotten quite used to cash registers at McRestaurants with icons of burgers and fries on keys to save the cashier the brain-work and time of punching in actual prices, so perhaps the doomsayers were on the money.) Nevertheless, the logo caught on, and the Transit Authority came to be widely referred to as "the T," just as the promoters of the identity campaign had planned—a case in which life was actively encouraged to imitate art.

Computer icons function much as the fast-food keys do. Thanks to the graphical user interfaces (GUIs for short) first developed at the Palo Alto Research Center by the Xerox Corporation and enthusiastically made a feature of both Microsoft Windows and the Macintosh operating system in the 1980s, it is now unnecessary to type, say, "run heehaw.exe" at a command line prompt when you can simply click on a little picture of a braying donkey's head on your screen instead. (Rather than "Back to the Future," this might arguably be termed "Forward to the Past," the alphabet yielding once again to the ideograph.) In the intermediate stage between the command line prompt of yore and today's icon-rich GUIs, interactive software programs for other than the specialized user first allowed you to specify what you wanted the software to do by choosing from a cascading text-based menu (Insert > Picture > From File), for which there were soon introduced shortcuts that allowed users to execute commands without navigating a menu tree, such as "IPF" to perform the operation.

GUIs made it possible to execute at least the most commonly used commands with a mouse click on an icon, and as the number of icons grew beyond the presumably self-evident ones (e.g., the Windows C-clamp squeezing a filing cabinet for its file compressor WinZip, or the Apple trash can for deleted files) and changes in the technology rendered even some of these archaic (e.g., floppy disk for "save file"), there has been a move toward providing a text string, explaining what the icon means, that pops up in a little box when your mouse holds the cursor ("hovers") over the icon. This move has been given a considerable push by paragraph 1194.22 of the 1998 amendment to the Rehabilitation Act of 1973, Section 508, which mandates that to assist in making Web-based applications with their GUIs accessible to the visually impaired, "[a] text equivalent for every non-text element shall be provided (e.g., via "alt" [hover help], "longdesc" [text in an external file reachable via a labeled link], or in element content)," which text-to-speech software will "read."

Despite such secondary aids, the principle of user-friendliness mandates that a computer icon be reasonably self-evident in spite of its small size—on a screen with a 13" diagonal, a half-inch in height for a screen icon and a quarter-inch for a toolbar one. This does not leave a lot of pixels to draw with, which is why one is unlikely to see icons that consist of a miniature version of the New York City subway map, or even of the much simpler Philadelphia one. Aspect ratio also plays a part: Icons cannot deviate too far from a square, so a representation of, say, Leonardo's Mona Lisa might be OK, but the Last Supper would be right out.

In medieval Europe and Japan, formal coats of arms relied on conventional heraldic signs that were easily associated with the house and lineage of the bearer. Japanese shoguns and warlords emblazoned their house crests (*mon*), often incorporating floral designs, on their banners, which functioned somewhat like the Roman army standards as highly visible rallying points; by contrast, the individual samurai would display his own *mon* on small roundels on his armor, which, as Peter Gwynn-Jones, Garter Principal King of Arms for the United Kingdom, writes, "could not have been identified until a close inspection was made after his death," much as with modern-day dog tags.

In France and England, however, according to officer of arms Francis J. Grant, "warriors adorned their shields with marks to distinguish one another, and decorated the tops of their helmets with crests" precisely so as "to be able to recognise each other as friend or foe in the *melée*," notwithstanding dust, distance, and the fast-paced action of the battlefield. Simple geometric shapes, such as bars (in heraldic language, diagonal *bends*, vertical *pales*, V-shaped *chevrons*) or checkerboard patterns, were combined with emblems such as the Plantagenet boar or the fleurs-de-lys of the French kings (a stylized depiction of the flowers associated with the originally marshy land on which Paris was built). The legibility of such devices from afar was a matter of no small importance when the bearer was engaged in combat on horseback and bearing down on his presumed adversary at full tilt.

SIGNING IN THE STREET

Nowadays, though the object has shifted to *avoiding* collisions with high-velocity others while encased in sheet steel, good road sign design still takes into account the distance at which meaning must be clear in time to process it at normal driving speeds. To address this issue, as well as to impose a coherent uniformity of discourse in American highway signage generally, the U.S. Department of Transportation publishes standards for road sign size and lettering in its *Manual on Uniform Traffic Control Devices* (MUTCD). These are given in as many as five different sizes, depending on the type of sign and the volume and speed of traffic on the road. Among the principles set forth by MUTCD is the underlying rule that "[w]ord messages should be as brief as possible and the lettering should be large enough to provide the necessary legibility distance. A minimum specific ratio, such as 25 mm (1 in) of letter height per 12 m (40 ft) of legibility distance, should be used." (In case you were wondering about other colors besides the standard federal red, black, yellow, orange, and green, USDOT is hedging its bets, since "coral, purple, and light blue are being reserved for uses that will be determined in the future by the Federal Highway Administration" [MUTCD section 2.11].)

Like billboards, signs can be "public" (managed by representatives of officialdom) or "private" (managed by you or your organization). Examples of "public" signage include warnings ("Danger," "Falling Rock Zone"), instructions ("One Way," "No Right on Red"), or information as to your location ("Entering Marion," "Centerville 6 mi (10 km)"), mileage markers being possibly the oldest form of public signage. Examples of "private" signage include such admonitions and warnings as "Private," "Keep Out," and "Beware of Strange Cat," and informational signs such as those that identify your dwelling ("The Gleasons," "Toad Hall") or shop ("Elegant Tailor," "From Beer to Eternity"), possibly the oldest kind of private sign. Here too belongs the personal plea for alms, typically handwritten on cardboard: "Homeless Vet/Sober/God Bless," "What if *you* were hungry?" or "Will Work for Food," appearing in slightly altered form as "Will Work For Fools" in a classic Dan Piraro cartoon.

People sometimes alter signs, especially public signs. "People" can be members of officialdom or random individuals. For example, the Massachusetts Department of Public Transportation altered the highway signs at the border cautioning visitors that the Commonwealth requires the use of seat belts, taping over the word "requires" with a sticker saying "suggests" after the 1986 repeal of the state's seat-belt law, thanks largely to the private crusade of talk-show host

Jerry Williams. Massachusetts, coming to its senses, put a new seat-belt law into effect in 1994, replacing the cautionary signs with ones reading "Click It or Ticket" accompanied by a graphic of an unfastened seat belt.

Private (i.e., unauthorized) alteration of a (usually public) sign is termed "defacing" or *détournement*, depending on your point of view. The term *détournement* (literally, 'diversion, turning away') was used to designate "the reuse of preexisting artistic elements in a new ensemble" by the Situationists, an informal collection of politically engaged artists who flourished in Europe in the 1950s and 1960s. Methods employed in *détournement* in which one "artistic" element is a conventional sign and the other is a bit of added, replaced, deleted, or otherwise altered text:

- Replacing text on a sign by pasting new text over it, as with the Massachusetts highway seat belt sign in which the word "suggests" was pasted over the word "requires").
- Altering a sign's text by changing one or more of its constituent letters (the judicious use of a laundry marker turns "No Parking" into "No Barking") or adding text (as in the "Stop" sign example below).
- Removing part of the sign's text (erasing the initial *Vehí* from *Vehículos entrantes* to change the cautionary "Vehicles entering" to "assholes entering," or, on the door at the end of the subway car, "No_assing __rough").

Note: Treating a sign as simply a canvas on which to display a graffito with no reference to the sign's original message doesn't count as *détournement*, whatever its sociopolitical content: It is *not* an example of *détournement* to paste your band's bumper sticker onto the map of the subway system in the Place-des-Arts Métro station. Roger Cohen ("Balkan

Road Signs: This Way to Chaos") puts a different spin on the idea of *détournement*, noting signs that point to places that no longer exist (because they have been destroyed) and what might be termed "phantom signs," places where signs to a town have been removed (because the locals no longer want to acknowledge the existence of that enemy town).

In the spirit of *détournement*, the sign shown in figure 1.1 was displayed in an otherwise unassuming store window in Somerville, Massachusetts. The canonical stop sign with its familiar octagonal shape and white lettering on a red background dates from 1954, though the original black-on-white version made its debut in Detroit, Michigan, in 1915. Considering that the first red-green traffic light in the United States appeared in 1912, it is a bit surprising that it took so long for the stop sign to standardize on the color red for its background, given the stop-light standard of red to mean "Stop" (though design by committee, never mind the adoption of a standard by the world at large, does tend to proceed with the speed of glacial advance). Indeed, Great Britain didn't adopt the red octagon until 1975, having until then used the red triangle with white background now widely used as the sign for "Yield" (and still in use by the Japanese for their stop sign).

The stop sign as we now know it poses a serious temptation, in the English-speaking world at least, to *détournement* (see figure 1.2). This example combines the artistic elements of the original stop sign, painted text, and bumper sticker (whose original meaning "Vote for Bush" is completely subverted by the text of the sign). This kind of *détournement*, involving the addition of a noun as the direct object of the verb "stop," is possible in English because English *stop* can function grammatically as a transitive verb (Stop the car), an intransitive verb (The car stopped), or a noun (The car

Figure 1.1

came to a stop). "Stop rape," "Stop Bush," "Stop pollution" all construe the "Stop" of the stop sign as a transitive verb and fair game to take a direct object. Stop signs in other languages do not always present this option: Depending on the part of the world, Spanish signs say *Alto* (an interjection, 'Halt'), *Pare* (the intransitive verb 'Stop'), or *Stop* ('the word on the sign that tells you to come to a halt,' pronounced *eh-stop* and of dubious grammatical status).

In Canada, it would be possible, if a stretch, to argue that the French rendering of English "Stop"—*Arrêt*—is a verb (the informal *tu* form of the imperative of the verb *arrêter*) rather than a noun, but the evidence is against this, exhibit A being that Canadian French signage of this sort tends to use the polite *vous* form (which in this case would be *arrêtez*). Consequently, if you want to use a stop sign in francophone Canada as a vehicle for stopping the war, the text of the sign is not going to be of much help: French grammar won't cooperate, and bilingual signs don't leave enough room to add much text.

Figure 1.2

Canada sports two flavors of English-French bilingual stop sign, with the words "Stop" and "*Arrêt*" one atop the other. The federal sign has the English above the French, and the provincial sign favored in New Brunswick (and formerly in Québec) has French over English. Since the 1977 passage in Québec of Bill 101, mandating that all public signage be in French, stop signs in that province have become monolingually French (except where the federally erected *Stop-Arrêt* sign trumps the provincial or in certain predominantly Anglophonic neighborhoods; see figure 1.3). True, the sign still has the internationally recognized red octagon with white lettering, and it is apparently not considered remarkable that stop signs in France all say "Stop," not "*Arrêt,*" the word on the continental sign being parsed as an interjection, if parsed at all. After all, who looks at the text now anyway? The octagon (recognizable both from the front and the back) and the color pretty much say it all. The text could just as well be an icon, or absent altogether.

Figure 1.3

In any case, the worldwide trend in public signage is away from text in favor of icons. While it is unlikely that this will seriously discourage the creative private alteration of public signage, it will have the advantage of eliminating such linguistic contortions as the "Fin de CONSTRUCTION ends" signs posted at the end of road work on officially bilingual New Brunswick's highways and, in multilingual communities, the wrangling over whose language should come first and in what font size. The Israeli stop sign offers one solution (figure 1.4). The ready recognition of the red octagon allows it to function as a signifier that is independent of its text: Shape and color tell us what sort of legend to expect, even before the traveler draws within a range to read the actual contents. Thus, "Yield" signs are triangles, point down (appropriately emblematic

Figure 1.4

of the meeting of three ways); yellow diamonds tell us to exercise caution because of such hazards as the curve/ deaf child at play/bump/slipperiness-when-wet ahead of us. (When the legend requires long words, however, a yellow cautionary sign may be rectangular instead, such as the three-liner "Breakaway Truck Lane 500 Feet.") As with the stop sign, the shape and color lend themselves to parodic alteration, as when a church has availed itself of the "your legend here" option offered by canonical road sign companies by marking, for example, the pastor's spot in the parish parking lot with a custom "Thou Shalt Not Park" imprinted on the usual 18″ × 24″ white template for a "No Parking" sign.

Mies Hora, whose design firm compiled and publishes *Official Signs and Icons 2*, a widely used sourcebook for public-space icons, has scolded American road signs for containing "far too many word messages, like 'exit closed,'" which is problematic for non-English-speaking foreign travelers, and thus approves of the trend in developing countries toward signage that can "rely more on pictorial symbols to navigate" as a means "to avoid such confusion and misapprehension." The red-bordered white triangle of the (formerly yellow) "Yield" sign is a step in this direction; following European practice, it is now also being used point side up to enclose graphics indicating such hazards as railroad trains, moose, and the proverbial long drive off a short pier (the water at its end being indicated here, as in ancient Egypt, by a wavy line; *plus ça change*...).

MAKING YOUR MARK

In his *City Signs and Lights,* Steven Carr notes that "[s]igns and lights do not 'communicate' with people in the usual sense of exchange; rather they inform people about rules, activities, and occurrences of various kinds. Of course, when informing does become communication, it is particularly valuable." This is as true of hobo signs as it is of "official" signs and their derivatives (parodic or serious). On their face, these chalked or penciled marks, whether in public thoroughfares or on the side of private houses, might be dismissed as mere graffiti; but like official signage they serve as a visual code to enable their target readership to navigate the landscape by conveying more about its perils and payoffs than is obvious to the uninformed onlooker (e.g., 'safe camp,' 'fierce dog,' 'kindhearted lady,' 'man with gun,' 'stop here,' 'food for work,' 'bad water,' 'tell pitiful story').

Hobo signs resemble airport icons in their lack of text, literacy being by no means universal among the population in which they originated. While many of these signs attained widespread currency in America during the Great

Depression of the 1930s, some had been in use long before that by "knights of the road" on both sides of the Atlantic; facing the frontispiece of an anonymous English *Slang Dictionary* of 1873 is a sample map of a town with "cadgers' hieroglyphics" deciphered (including the same crossed-handle sickle mark for 'stop here' current in America today), and its editors cite earlier mentions of such signs both in Snowden's *Magistrate's Assistant* (1853) and Henry Mayhew's *London Labour and the London Poor* (1851).

Some of the symbols are more or less self-evident: 'Kind woman' is a drawing of a cat lying on its side, and 'man with gun' a triangle with two raised stick-figure hands; others are apt to be meaningless to those unfamiliar with the conventions, such as a horizontal rectangle with a dot in the middle for 'danger,' or two overlapping rectangles for 'afraid.' Degree of literacy aside, this sort of iconography functions as a channel of covert communication, an in-group language opaque to, or even overlooked by, the general public. On the other hand, different sources report variants on some of these signs, indicating that there is still some fluidity in this iconic language across time or space or both. A "Homeless City Guide" has been recently published in Britain that attempts to promulgate a uniform set of signs for "chalking" by street people, though how successful this will be in stabilizing the inventory remains to be seen.

Up until the 1980s, railroad yard workers commonly would make chalk marks on cars, sometimes mistaken for hobo signs (no surprise, given the legendary popularity of freight trains as a mode of free long-distance migration). "Dave1905," in a posting to an Internet model railroaders' newsgroup, reports that

> they were marks used for car routing and switching, so some were letter or number block, track or

destination codes. The carmen would chalk the cars to mark that they had inspected the car and oiled the journals. A typical pattern was a '+' sign with a letter or number code for the location, shift, carman and 'ok' for work done in each of the [four] quadrants. The carmen used chalk or lumber crayons.

Meanwhile, in imitation of hobo practice, chalked signs on sidewalks and walls adjacent to computer wireless nodes began appearing in the summer of 2002. These "warchalking" symbols denoted "open," "closed," and "WEP" nodes along with their SSID and bandwidth (and, where applicable, access e-mail address). Originally the handiwork of creative hacker Matt Jones, the symbols allowed Wi-Fi users opportunities to piggyback onto existing nodes at a time when access was still relatively rare and usually restricted; other symbols were soon added indicating service that was encrypted, down, gone, or logged/sniffed.

Another variant on hobo signs, reportedly current in California a generation ago and perhaps still in use, was a set of marks chalked at the end of driveways by children on Halloween to let other trick-or-treaters know what sort of reception and goodies to expect at a given house, from a house icon with a slash across it (for 'no one home') and a horizontal zigzag (identical to and meaning the same as the hobo 'bad dog' sign) to an infinity sign in a rectangle for Reese's peanut butter cups, four diagonal lines for Twix bars, and an inverted parabola with two eyes for 'Be scared here for extra candy portion.'

As already noted, American hobo signs do not require literacy, or even fluency in English; they constitute an adequate sign language in their own universe of discourse, albeit one with severe grammatical restraints, consisting mostly of nouns. Graffiti throughout history have run the gamut of forms conveniently frozen in time at Pompeii when Vesuvius erupted in 79 C.E.: a single name hurriedly scribbled onto a wall; political slogans; poems; elaborately calligraphed advertisements for upcoming spectacles. The one thing all of these have in common is text, and it usually is short.

Pompeii, for all its fine frescoes in private homes, lacked the public-space equivalent of the extravagant polychrome picture-and-text paintings on walls and subway cars that twentieth-century New York City could boast or complain of, take your pick. Critics of graffiti in contemporary urban America generally adduce the "quality of life" argument: that it's an invasion of our visual territory, just as loud music with profane lyrics blasted from a moving car invades our sonic space. Moreover, they point out, gangs use graffiti to give notice of neighborhood primacy, perceived (often correctly) as the sign of a threat to the general peace. But even the individual just "getting my name up" is making a spatial claim subversive of the dominant social order in its assertion of an ability, and even a right, to alter the character of public space by literally putting one's signature upon it.

In the early 1980s, Paul Theroux described the sensation of riding in a New York City subway car with sprayed-over windows and defaced safety instructions as "a nightmare, complete with rats and mice and a tunnel and a low ceiling....manifest suffocation, straight out of Poe." Harvard sociologist Nathan Glazer offered a slippery-slope argument connecting graffiti with the subway rider's fear of crime, "the sense that all are part of one world of uncontrollable predators....Even if graffitists are the least dangerous of these, their ever-present markings serve to persuade the passenger that, indeed, the subway is a dangerous place."

Under Mayor John Lindsay, the city began a concerted effort to crack down on subway graffiti that would outlast his administration by almost two decades. But meanwhile, graffiti blossomed into an art form that would encompass elaborate paintings of whole subway cars and even entire ten-car trains, often informed by popular art forms such as comics and Pop Art. The scale of these elaborate artworks meant that they could be seen from a great distance, in particular wherever trains emerged from the tunnels to run on elevated tracks. Moreover, the designs still read coherently even when tagged by someone just getting his name up (especially when the tagger used "wild style" writing that deliberately defied easy legibility, such tags in effect becoming merely a textured patch of the larger piece).

Even as the crackdown escalated, with dogs in the yards and acid-wash baths to scrub the cars down, artists such as LEE (Lee Quinones) and SAMO (Jean Michel Basquiat) were getting recognized in the above-ground New York art scene and showing their work, not just at "progressive" exhibition spaces but in well-respected upscale venues as well. The art form was also legitimated by such books as *Subway Art*, a collaboration by two photographers, Martha Cooper and Henry Chalfant, published in 1984 and packed with striking photos of pieces by LEE, DONDI, SKEME, LADY PINK, the brothers MAD and SEEN, and many others, whose depictions of pop-culture icons such as Mickey Mouse, Santa Claus, Daffy Duck, Sherlock Holmes, Mario Bros., the Teenage Mutant Ninja Turtles, and so on, were interlaced with text, often explicitly political, commenting on contemporary urban life.

In general, the more controversial the graffito, the less time to get it up. Folk wisdom from the turbulent late 1960s favored keeping this short form even shorter, because there would be just so many minutes to put it on the wall before the police arrive, and nothing looks more pathetic than a slogan beginning with a right-on "ALL POWER TO THE..."

only to trail off unfinished because the writer was forced to hotfoot it out of there.

For some, skywriting is simply aerial graffiti; but most of us will look up at it just the same, in part because it is ephemeral: We see letters being slowly formed in front of us in clear white smoke (made by the burning of paraffin-laced machine oil sprayed onto the airplane's engine's hot exhaust manifold) even as the previous ones begin to disperse and fade. Brevity is of the essence. The invention is attributed to an Englishman named John C. Savage, and its first use to Capt. Cyril Turner, who in 1922 wrote the name of the newspaper *Daily Mail* in the British skies. That same year, either Turner or an American flyer named Allen J. Cameron wrote "Hello USA" over New York. Throughout the years since then, skywriting has conveyed all sorts of short messages to millions of viewers, from marriage proposals to apologies to smiley or heart emoticons to aeroevangelism.

Skytyping is to skywriting as dot-matrix printing is to handwriting. It is done by sending up a squadron of five or more planes to fly in close formation and at a uniform distance from one another, with computer-generated release of simultaneous puffs of smoke to form letters in the aggregate. Even with the new technology, though (as Texas pilot Paul Sampson told us), "the sky is almost never totally calm; the air mass you fly in is almost always moving in some way relative to the ground. And the smoke decays fairly rapidly. All art is fleeting, but this is getting to the point of absurdity."

CARTOONS AND SIGN(ING) GAGS

Signs, however ephemeral, imply both a signifier and a thing signified, and they can be natural or conventional, as Aristotle observed over two millennia ago. A cat's cry can tell us that Kitty is on the other side of the door; this is a natural sign, as are the deer droppings from which we can read not merely that the animal has passed this way but also how recently. On the other hand, when we call *"Heeeere*, kittykittykittykitty!" and Kitty has learned to come in response, this is arguably a conventional sign. Words in general are conventional signs: We say *potato* and our French cousins say *pomme de terre*, but both signify the same spud. On the other hand, while a picture of a pipe may not be a pipe, as the French surrealist Magritte correctly observed, the humor in this painting lies in its being as close to a natural sign of a pipe as one can get with paint and canvas.

An in-depth discussion of semiotics—the study of how signs and sign systems work—is utterly beyond the scope of this chapter. But for our purposes the important thing to remember is that certain types of abbreviated discourse work as well as they do because we all have a rich inventory of acquaintance with natural signs through experience, and with conventional signs through acculturation. Perhaps nowhere is this so telling as in the funny papers: Cartoons and comics (as well as other forms of sequential art) draw on a wealth of cultural assumptions and conventions, both verbal and nonverbal, to convey meaning, and the persistence of these forms of communication is a testimony to how successful this attempt can be.

Satirical drawings in print date back almost to the dawn of printing itself, such as the scurrilous German engraving of the pope riding a pig that Sir John Harington approvingly described at the end of the sixteenth century in his *Metamorphosis of Ajax*. Speech had already been represented in medieval and Renaissance paintings: In Jan van Eyck's *Annunciation*, the Angel Gabriel's salutation *Ave, gratia plena* ('Hail [Mary], full of grace') is lettered in gold next to his smiling face, as is the Virgin's reply, *Ecce ancilla Domini* ('Behold [I am] the handmaiden of the Lord')—only upside down, so that it goes from her (closed!) mouth toward the angel instead of away from him.

Another solution was to inscribe speech on scrolls next to the speakers' heads, from which it was a short step to putting the speech in plumes issuing from the speaker's mouth, the usual practice in satirical engravings of the eighteenth and early nineteenth centuries. In this fashion, "An Attempt to Land a Bishop in America," published in London's *Political Register* in 1769, shows a man on a quay declaring "No Lords Spiritual or Temporal in New England" as he and his fellow pole-wielding colonists shove off a boat with a bishop in cope and stole climbing the rigging and declaring "Lord, now lettest thou thy Servant depart in Peace" (an ironic allusion to the Anglican evening canticle *Nunc Dimittis*). An alternative was to print the dialogue beneath the drawing, particularly when the cartoon was in effect an "illustrated joke" (e.g., the *Punch* cartoon of two gentlemen, one standing in the street in knickerbockers and trilby, the other in frock coat and top hat, running past: "Halloa, Charlie! What's the matter? Training for a race?" "No, Tom, racing for a train!").

But it was not until the twentieth century that speech balloons as we know them were developed by cartoonists, along with other conventions we now take for granted: dashed-line balloons for whispers, clouds for the text of thoughts, and so on. (Sociologist Erving Goffmann observed that soliloquy, once common in dramaturgy but now fallen out of favor, is nicely preserved "in comics where the author has the right to open up a character's head so the reader can peer into the ideas it contains," similar to the effect produced by movie and television voice-overs.) Variants include the wavy balloon (for such text as "The murderer's...name...is...*aaarghh*"—a type of exclamation often ending in a breath mark, also called "cat's whiskers," "fireflies," or "crow's feet"), burst balloon (indicating screamed text: "No, NO! *Not* the leg…!"), balloon with icicles ("I told you, Claudius, I'm *not in the mood!*"), "electric" balloons with jagged edges and spark-like tails to indicate radio or telephone transmission (*"Apollo, this is Houston. Can you read me?"*—according to Nate Piekos's "grammar" of comics text, the contents of such telecommunications balloons are always in italics to heighten this effect), balloons with notes in them to indicate song (often with syllables hyphenated, and italics and/or attenuated vowels on the long notes: "And did those *feeeeet* in an-cie-hent *tiiii-imes…?*") and even telepathic balloons, made by puncturing the edges of thought clouds with three or more sets of breath marks ("I am your spirit guide, Sananda, a Higher Being from the planet Clarion").

Here the balloon itself functions iconically to convey something about the tone and affect beyond the bare semantic content. Icons may be a feature of that speech itself: the rebus-like picture of a saw cutting a log that indicates snoring; the *jarns* (square and round spirals), *quimps* (little crescent moons or Saturns), *nittles* (asterisks or stars, mimicking the real-world retinal-excitation effect called *phosphene,* colloquially known as "seeing stars"), or *grawlixes* (horizontal squiggles) of a *maladicta balloon,* standing in for language too strong to be accurately rendered in a family newspaper; the *boozex,* or three-X inscription on a bottle's label to show that it contains alcohol; even the lightbulb in a thought balloon showing that the thinker has just attained an "Aha!" insight. Other symbols reveal the mental or physical state of a character, such as *squeans* (the centerless asterisk-like burst marks in the air around the head of a drunk), *spurls* (the corkscrew line above a character who is passing out), *crottles* (the crosses on the eyes of someone out cold), or *plewds* (the teardrop-shaped indicators of sweat and/or stress)—these last classified by Mort Walker, creator of the long-running Beetle Bailey comic strip, as a subcategory of what he calls *emanata,* along with the *waftarom* (the doubled curved line emanating from savory food) and the *solrads* and *indotherms* (wavy lines indicating that the sun or other object is radiating heat—strictly speaking, these should probably be called *exotherms,* but why quibble?).

Still other essentials for cartoonists are *briffits* (the clouds of dust behind a fast-moving person or object) and *lucaflects* (the little window to indicate a highly reflective surface such as a clean glass or a brand-new apple), both of which rely upon our internalized stereotypes about the way things are while simultaneously reinforcing them: Few apples are so felicitously placed or as shiny as to reflect an actual window, and to depict, say, Mercury in orbit around the sun with briffits to suggest its speed would require studiously ignoring how little dust there actually is in the near vacuum of interplanetary space. Likewise, no real bomb nowadays is a black sphere with a sputtering fuse—the actual image depicts a type of cannonball, obsolete by a century and a half along with chain and bar shot—yet so recognizable is this icon that it has found its way onto our computers in the standard set of funny TrueType characters called Wingdings (its keystroke being capital M).

Nor are these iconic features the only way in which a comic strip can signify; the very name "strip" reminds us that with the exception of the one-panel cartoon, comics are a form of *sequential* art. As such, their frames divide up a story, representing the relationships of time and space in ways that can be enhanced by how the frames themselves are used, from a comic-book story's opening splash page (which functions much like a movie's establishing shot) to the horizontal lengthening of a panel to express a corresponding expansion of elapsed time. Moreover, as Will

Eisner (of *The Spirit* fame) points out in his classic *Comics and Sequential Art,* "The frame's shape itself (or the absence of one) can become a part of the story itself…as well as contributing to the atmosphere of the page as a whole."

Here the process has come full circle: Iconic representation expresses thought while simultaneously conditioning the imagery in which we think it. This can be seen at perhaps its most elegant in puns from American Sign Language, in which not merely letters but whole words can be represented using one's hands and their position and motion relative to one's face and body. Thus the sign for 'hard' made against the nose rather than the passive hand means 'strict' (i.e., 'hard-nose[d]'); making the sign that means 'milk' while moving it across the eyes makes it 'past-your-eyes[d] milk.' In a silent world, sight-gags rule, and icons speak louder than words.

2

IN THE DICTIONARY

The Lexicographers Have Spoken

AT ONE TIME OR ANOTHER, EVERY LITERATE PERSON has consulted a dictionary, whether an actual bound volume, an electronic spell-checker, or what sociolinguist and lexicographer Rosamund Moon has termed "the UAD: the Unidentified Authorizing Dictionary, usually referred to as 'the dictionary,' but very occasionally as 'my dictionary'"—in other words, a collection of words, phrases, and usages that "ought" to be found in any general-purpose lexicon available to all, but actually residing in one's head. (A poor speller before the days of spell-checkers might have used Mom's UAD as the dictionary of choice until Mom, her patience wearing thin, told the struggling author to "go look it up in the dictionary.")

It was said at one time that every home owned, if no other books, a Bible and a dictionary, the Bible serving as the authority on matters spiritual and the dictionary serving as its secular counterpart, a repository of shared social values as revealed in both the selection of the words it enshrines (and, by implication, those it excludes) and the meanings that it assigns to those words (and those it ignores).

"IN THE BEGINNING WAS THE WORD..."

It has been commonly held that the first dictionaries were the bilingual Sumerian-Akkadian word lists of the twenty-seventh century B.C.E. and that the monolingual dictionary is a later arrival. Boisson et al., however, have argued that a case can be made that in fact the earliest "dictionaries" were monolingual word lists, such as those created as learning aids for the benefit of Sumerian and Egyptian scribes entering the profession. They maintain that it makes sense that a literate society would be concerned first with its own language and only later with somebody else's. In the case of the Akkadians and Sumerians, the former conquered the latter but were generally considered their cultural inferiors, and so found it expedient to make at least a stab at learning to get by in the language. It has been estimated that you need a vocabulary of at least 500 words in order to achieve a minimally functional level of communication in a second language, and presumably the bilingual word lists were helpful to both the conquerors and their subjects, at least those with jobs in the civil service.

Ultimately, though, as the authors suggest, what distinguishes a monolingual from a bilingual dictionary can boil down to a question of purpose and usage: A dictionary whose purpose is to encompass [*comprendre*] a foreign language can be called bilingual, and a dictionary whose purpose is to describe a language from the inside [*de l'intérieur*] can be considered monolingual. This would technically make the medieval Latin-Latin glossaries aimed at nonnative speakers of Latin bilingual, and likewise the contemporary translation of an English-English dictionary into, say, Russian (the subject of an interesting discussion by Rosamund Moon in the paper quoted earlier), not to mention the case of the adolescent native speaker who, hand in hand

with the nonnative language learner, searches the dictionary for dirty words (a practice, according to a study by Jerzy
Tomaszczyk, that 45 percent of his subjects, both native
and nonnative speakers, gave as a reason for consulting the
dictionary).

In any event, both bilingual and monolingual dictionaries have continued to evolve along somewhat overlapping
but ultimately distinct tracks. From the tenth century, Latin
texts began to appear in England with Latin glosses written
over "difficult" words, much as we might pencil in the English for the words we had to look up in a passage assigned
as homework in Latin 101, except that the glosses were
in Latin. Subsequently, the glosses were extracted from a
text and listed in order of appearance at the back of the
book. Still later, glossaries began to appear consisting of
Latin words with English definitions (if we can use "English" somewhat loosely). Typically, these were organized
by semantic domain—names of flowers, tools, and so on.
Still later, there began to appear English-Latin word lists,
the first generally held to be the fifteenth-century *Promptorium Parvulorum sive Clericorum* ["Young People's or Clerks'
Store-Room"], a dictionary written by the cleric Galfridus
Anglicus (also known as Galfridus Grammaticus, or Geoffrey the Grammarian)—clerks tended to be clerics, the two
professions becoming more distinct as literacy grew among
the general population.

The *Promptorium Parvulorum* was remarkable partly as
a feat of reverse engineering—Geoffrey came up with the
Latin words first, then their English translations, then listed
the English words in alphabetical order, giving the Latin
words as their glosses—but for two other reasons as well:
First, the author listed the sources from which the corpus
was drawn, and second, he made explicit the intended purpose of the work (namely, to help writers whose command

of the language might be shaky to write reasonably presentable Latin, free of the "barbarisms" that the compiler bemoaned on the part of some of his contemporaries in the decidedly utilitarian preface to the work).

English-English dictionaries of "hard words" began to appear toward the beginning of the seventeenth century, and by the end of the century, these had become fairly compendious—John Kersey's "revised, corrected, and improved" 1706 sixth edition of Edward Phillips's *The New World of English Words, or, Universal English Dictionary*, claimed to have added some twenty thousand words to the previous edition, which offered not only "An Account of the Original or Proper Sense, and various Significations of all HARD WORDS derived from other languages…as now made use of in our English Tongue" but "A Brief and Plain Explication of all Terms relating to any of the Arts or Sciences, either Liberal or Mechanical, viz. Grammar…Fishing, &c," in which the ellipses represent the names of fifty-two individual "Arts and Sciences," to which were added the derivations of men's and women's proper names, Greek and Latin terms for various animals, plants, and minerals, "and several other remarkable Matters more particularly express'd in the *Preface*."

The appearance in 1721 of Nathaniel Bailey's *An Universal Etymological English Dictionary* aimed to go Phillips/Kersey one better, promising to cover the same ground with the value added of "many Thousand Words more than either *Harris, Philips, Kersey,* or any *English* Dictionary before Extant." Bailey's work differed from those of his predecessors (and many of his followers) in at least one notable respect. Like Phillips/Kersey's, Bailey's title page is explicit about the work's purpose and intended audience:

The whole WORK compil'd and Methodically digested,
as well for the Entertainment of the Curious, as the

Information of the Ignorant, and for the Benefit of young Students, Artificers, Tradesmen, and Foreigners, who are desirous thorowly to understand what they Speak, Read, or Write.

However, aside from suggesting that one might read the dictionary for fun, the really important innovation was in what was left unsaid: The corpus is not explicitly restricted to words found in the "best authors" or print at all. In other words, Bailey largely dodges the issue that has plagued lexicographers ever since: how to explicitly delimit the corpus of data from which the dictionary entries are to be drawn to the exclusion of others.

Dr. Johnson, in the introduction to his *A Dictionary of the English Language,* first published in 1755, subsequently revised and reissued over the years, and long held as the ultimate authority, spends several pages backing and filling about criteria for inclusion and exclusion of entry words. His aim was, in essence, to regularize the orthography; to weed out creeping Gallicisms, slang, and cant; and to provide for the benefit of natives and foreigners wishing to master the language a snapshot of the "best" usage based on texts of past authors (or on his own experience when he couldn't find a locus for a word he thought should be in the dictionary), while acknowledging that no dictionary of a living language can hope to be definitive or truly all-inclusive and that the lexicographer's lot is not a happy one. In 1828, on the other side of the Atlantic, Noah Webster published the first edition of his *American Dictionary of the English Language,* modeled on Dr. Johnson's but substituting American authors where possible, proposing somewhat different orthographic conventions, and noting that British and American usage differed in places, both in their stock of vocabulary and in some of the meanings they assigned to words shared in common.

We may perhaps forgive Dr. James Murray, father of *The Oxford English Dictionary* (the OED, originally named *The New English Dictionary*, or NED), for failing to mention the controversial Mr. Webster in his 1880 President's Address to the Philological Society, in which he summarized the history of the development of the dictionary up to that time before going on to delineate his criteria for inclusion in what he saw as the culmination of that history, the NED. Taking as given that all entries had to be attested in print, Murray classifies candidates for supporting quotations as belonging to one or another of five classes, from most to least desirable, the most desirable being "those which show the word actually used in connected narrative to express thought, without being referred to *as a word* at all." Next best are texts containing words provided as a name or synonym, "as where a writer says, *e.g.,* 'this process is termed *acetimetry*,'" or "in explaining Foreign words, in French, Spanish, Italian, or other Dictionaries; they are not first-class witnesses, but often the best we can get…" The technical glossaries added to treatises and, even less desirably, specialized dictionaries (where words included for exhaustiveness may be obsolete or may never have been used) approach the bottom of the ladder, where Murray lists "General Dictionaries, especially those which profess to give all the terms used in the Arts and Sciences. The authority of these is to us almost *nil.*"

Over a century has passed since Murray's Address, during which time English has evolved (as have the media in which dictionaries could be served up to their users), and the criteria for selection among the ever more numerous candidates for inclusion in a "general-purpose" dictionary have loosened a bit. The OED Online, in its explanation of "Choosing which words to include," explains that

> Oxford's reading programmes pick up thousands of
> new words each year, but a new word is not included

IN THE DICTIONARY • 33

in the *OED* unless it has "caught on" and become established in the language. Words that are only used for a short period of time, or by a very small number of people, are not included.

To this may be compared the user-authored online "general-purpose" Wiktionary's "Wiktionary: Criteria for inclusion," which begins as follows:

General rule
A term should be included if it's likely that someone would run across it and want to know what it means. This in turn leads to the somewhat more formal guideline of including a term if it is **attested** and **idiomatic**.

The subsequent "Attestation" section provides the following definition:

"Attested" means verified through

1. Clearly widespread use,
2. Usage in a well-known work,
3. Appearance in a refereed academic journal, or
4. Usage in permanently recorded media,
   conveying meaning, in at least three
   independent instances spanning at least a year.

Most notable of these criteria is the first, which frees the would-be lexicographer from the restriction to print as a source for an entry. (While one might think that it was such a constraint that for so long mandated the exclusion of taboo, i.e., "dirty," words from mainstream dictionaries, this was actually not so, as most of the old standards have been attested in print for centuries—and, indeed, a few may be found in Bailey's dictionary.) The other three criteria (including the fourth, the so-called "rule of three") are not particularly novel, though the clarity of their statement is refreshing.

THE GOOD, THE BAD, AND THE BOGUS

Sidestepping the minefield surrounding exactly what is meant when lexicographers speak of a "general-purpose dictionary," assuming that the definitions in our individual UADs are probably reasonably similar, it might be useful to identify the basic components of such dictionaries.

Most begin with some sort of preface, often noting that this dictionary is a descriptive rather than a prescriptive work that aims to reflect reasonably current usage (but may include usage notes to warn you that, say, this is not a word that you should use in front of Grandma). There is usually a claim to an attempt at exhaustiveness (whether of the printed or both the printed and the spoken word), with the disclaimer that a living language is a moving target, so no dictionary can ever be definitive. Other front matter typically includes a list of abbreviations used in the work and the names of the various editors and subject authorities that contributed to the work. Then comes the main course, the entries themselves, in alphabetical ("dictionary") order.

This brings us, finally, to the short form of speech that is the true focus of this chapter, the dictionary entry, which consists of a really short form—the *lemma*—and the text that follows it. The OED gives as the relevant definition of *lemma* "The heading or theme of a scholium, annotation, or gloss." (The word "lemma" comes from Greek *lémma*—'something taken, taken as given; premise; title'—and "gloss" is from Greek *glôssa*—originally 'tongue,' hence 'foreign tongue,' hence 'foreign word needing an explanation.') More precisely? Here the going gets a bit rocky. Henri Béjoint gives it as good a shot as any:

Every single paragraph that constitutes an entry in a dictionary is headed by a short graphic sequence, the entry-form, which is generally—but not necessarily—the object of the information contained in the entry. In the prototypical dictionary, this sequence is usually a word, in the sense of 'any uninterrupted sequence of graphemes that is commonly felt to correspond to a concept.' In many modern dictionaries, some entries are also headed by morphemes, mostly prefixes and suffixes. Dictionaries of idioms may have longer strings of words, but there is one word in each string which is used as the classifying unit.

So, is a lemma a minimal meaning-bearing lexical unit? Yes, but not all such units are candidates for inclusion (the *–s* that marks the plural of a noun, for example, or the *–ed* that marks a past tense may or may not be present, though plurals and parts of the verb often appear within the entry for the root to which they apply, and some dictionaries list as separate lemmas the past-tense forms of irregular verbs). Let's say that "words" are what's in the dictionary, with the understanding that "word" is being used rather loosely.

That said, an entry nowadays in a standard, general-purpose dictionary consists of the lemma (which may appear with a superscript to distinguish it from its homonyms), followed by a phonetic rendering of its pronunciation, followed (often) by its etymology, followed by an identification of its grammatical part of speech plus any other relevant grammatical information (such as its plural, if a noun, or its tense forms if a verb), followed by one or more definitions (possibly with citations, possibly with usage notes, possibly with examples of use, possibly with synonyms, antonyms, or related forms). The order of definitions may be historical (as in the OED) or in ascending order of specialization.

Sometimes the entry may have an associated illustration. As for which sorts of actual "words" get to be lemmas and which do not, mileage continues to vary with a work's intended audience and the lexicographer's best guess as to what that audience hopes to find—or, in the case of some target audiences, not find, or have their children not find, as with, for example, Microsoft Word's spell-checker, which uses as its base the American Heritage Dictionary: Spell the f-word or c-word correctly, and the spell-checker gives you a pass (because those words are in fact in the dictionary, or at least the version sold outside of Texas), but if you deliberately misspell either of these words in the hope that the spell-checker will offer the correct spelling in its list of suggested replacements, you (or your adolescent) are out of luck.

Lemmas and Dilemmas

Still, there will always be words that aren't in the dictionary that someone will argue should be, and there will (less frequently) be words in the dictionary that really shouldn't be there at all. The former fall into two basic categories: Words that could be argued to have a legitimate claim to inclusion in a general-purpose work, and words that aren't really serious candidates for inclusion but are offered to the public as a form of linguistic entertainment. Typically, it is the useful neologism—the recent coinage with serious semantic content—whose supporters are clamoring at the gates, and often time and spreading usage win the day. (One such neologism is the Wiktionary's *protologism,* a term invented by Mikhail Epstein of Emory University to refer to a newly created and proposed word which has not yet gained acceptance.) The relaxation of certain linguistic taboos and changes in the social order have their influence as well. Words that appear in a general-purpose work but shouldn't are also of two types—accidental intruders and deliberate traps for the unwary—but all involve a fiction, something unreal, at least in the universe described in the work in which they appear (what we like to call "the real world," as distinct from fictional universes, the subject of whose documentation the Wiktionary's "Criteria for inclusion" handles with admirable skill and grace).

Sniglets and Other Wild Inventions   Coined by performer Rich Hall on the TV comedy series *Not Necessarily the News*, a *sniglet* is said to be "a word that doesn't appear in the dictionary but should," it being understood, however, that the reason the word doesn't (and in all likelihood never will) appear in any dictionary other than a dictionary of sniglets is that, well, it's silly. Serious lexicographers would exclude the sniglet on the criteria of current extent and length of history of use, leaving aside the issue of silliness; and, indeed, the very word "sniglet" itself has yet to appear in such standard dictionaries as the OED or the *American Heritage Dictionary*, though it has a solid presence on the Internet and has been in use since the 1980s. A couple of examples should be sufficient to give a sense of what a sniglet is and what is appealing about it:

furnidents: Indentations left in the carpet after moving heavy furniture.

nurge v. To inch closer to a stoplight thinking that will cause it to change quicker.

The phenomenon described by a sniglet is typically one with which we are all familiar but for which it has never occurred to us to require a name; the form of the sniglet is both phonetically plausible and, at its best, an original juxtaposition of disparate lexical items ("furniture" and "dent" in the first case and "nudge" and "urge" in the second). Sometimes, though, there is a fine line between the thing for which there doesn't really need to be a name and a thing for which a name would actually come in handy (and which may in fact already have one). For example, Hall proposes *profanitype* as a sniglet designating

> The special symbols used by cartoonists to replace swear words (points, asterisks, stars, and so on). It is yet to be determined which specific character represents which specific expletive.

Come to find out that the term *maladicta* had already been coined by cartoonist Mort Walker for these very symbols and was bidding to gain traction, at least in the specialized world of cartooning. Obviously, an idea whose time had come, though one for which neither of the proposed terms has appeared to date in a general-purpose dictionary.

Actually, the sniglet as a linguistic form is not new—witness, for example, Gelett Burgess's 1914 *Burgess Unabridged,* a collection of fanciful coinages, one of which (*blurb*), defying the usual trajectory of the sniglet, eventually managed to insinuate itself into respectable lexicographic society (along with *bromide,* an existing term for which he elsewhere coined the meaning "platitude"). Burgess, best known (much to his annoyance) as the author of the quatrain about the purple cow, credited Edward Lear and Lewis Carroll as his forebears in the creation of fanciful terms for fanciful ideas, but like theirs, Burgess's neologisms have mostly evanesced: *Bleesh* ("an unpleasant picture; vulgar or obscene"), *critch* ("to array one's self in uncomfortable splendor"), and *jirriwig* ("a traveller who does not see the country") continue to exist only in the pages of Burgess's book (or in books like this one), as linguistic mummies.

Ghost Words   The mirror image of the entry that should be in the dictionary but isn't is the entry that appears in a standard reference but shouldn't. We owe the term for a bogus dictionary entry to the eminent lexicographer Walter Skeat who coined it in his "Report upon 'Ghost-Words,' or Words which have no real Existence," a section in "The President's Address for 1886," which he delivered to the Philological Society:

> Dr. Murray, as you will remember, wrote on one occasion a most able article, in order to justify himself in omitting from the Dictionary the word *abacot,* defined by Webster as "the cap of state formerly used by English kings, wrought into the figure of two crowns." It was rightly and wisely rejected by our Editor on the ground that there is no such word, the alleged form being due to a complete mistake. There can be no doubt that words of this character ought to be excluded; and not only so, but we should jealously guard against all chances of giving any undeserved record of words which had never any real existence, being mere coinages due to the blunders of printers or scribes, or to the perfervid imaginations of ignorant or blundering editors...As it is convenient to have a short name for words of this character, I shall take leave to call them "ghost-words."

Note: "ghost word" should not be confused with "ghost entry," an entry appearing in earlier editions of a reference work but eliminated from later ones, an ironic example being "Ghost-word," which appears in the fourteenth edition of *Brewer's Dictionary of Phrase and Fable* but is nowhere to be seen by the sixteenth—*sic transit.*

So how do ghost words of the sort described by Skeat actually work their way into a dictionary? Two classic examples are offered by *dord* and *adventine*. *Dord* was an overzealous employee's misreading of "D or d," glossed as an abbreviation of the word "density," that made its way into Webster's *New International Dictionary* (second edition). *Adventine* was a misreading, according to Murray, of *adventive* in Francis Bacon's *Natural History*, which led to its mangled appearance in Dr. Johnson's dictionary. Theoretically, then, "dord" and "adventine" should be banished from the reference shelf, right? In fact, while even the most careful reader will not find *dord* in the latest *OED Online* (or, in all likelihood, in any other contemporary dictionary), *adventine* puts in an appearance as "[**adventine** in Johnson, copied by subseq. Dicts., from Bacon's *Nat. Hist.*, is a misprint for *adventiue*: see ADVENTIVE.]," whose brackets signal that the entry is "spurious," a typographical convention explained on the "Key to symbols and other conventions" page, which includes a link to another page ("Special types of main entries") that has the following to say about "spurious entries:"

> **Erroneous, spurious, or ghost words**
> Occasionally 'ghost' words find their way into print and into dictionaries. Typically these are the result of misreadings of manuscripts or of typographical errors by printers. The Dictionary includes a number of these, labeled as 'spurious' entries, when the words have been used incorrectly in former editions of texts or have otherwise achieved some spurious existence.

Murray was somewhat less diplomatic in his 1880 President's Address:

> It is marvellous, and to the inexperienced incredible, how Dictionaries and Encyclopædias simply copy each other, without an attempt either to verify quotations

or facts. Having beside us the chief works of this kind in the language, we are enabled to trace the whole career of such entries from their appearance in Cockeram, Blount, Phillips, Bailey, or Chambers, to their *rechauffées* in the publications of the current year.... So entries which are mere blunders are ignorantly handed down from Dictionary to Dictionary, each writer entering them as boldly and authoritatively as if he really knew of their existence.

It has been left to others to suggest that someone might "salt the dig," so to speak, by deliberately planting a fake entry in a reference work, a practice that presumably Murray and company would have denounced in no uncertain terms had they been aware of it: We live in what are perhaps more cynical times, in which commercial cartographers display "trap streets" (nonexistent streets) in their maps, the telephone directory lists the occasional nonexistent person and phone number, companies include *honeytokens* (fake entries in a corporate database or mailing list, for example, that trigger a notification to the owner when the entry is accessed), and dictionaries include deliberate ghost words. In all such cases, the idea is to set a trap for the plagiarist or unauthorized user. One such trap, first publicized by Henry Alford in an article in *The New Yorker,* was the ghost word *esquivalience,* which was planted in the second edition of *The New Oxford American Dictionary* (published in 2005). As Alford tells it,

> She [Erin McKean, editor-in-chief of the dictionary] said that Oxford had included [esquivalience] in NOAD's first edition, in 2001, to protect the copyright of the electronic version of the text that accompanied most copies of the book... The word has since been spotted on Dictionary.com, which cites Webster's New Millennium as its source. "It's interesting for us that

we can see their methodology," McKean said. "Or lack thereof. It's like tagging and releasing giant turtles."

Alford's article is memorable not only for his exposition of *esquivalience* but for his coinage of the term *Mountweazel,* a sort of ghost word on steroids.

Mountweazels   A *Mountweazel* is a bogus entry in a reference work (also known as a *Nihilartikel*), the original in question being the entry for the fictitious Lillian Virginia Mountweazel in the fourth edition of *The New Columbia Encyclopedia* (1975).

Like the NOAD's more straight-faced *esquivalience,* the "Mountweazel" entry in the NCE was supposedly slipped in as a control against copyright infringers, though it is hard to imagine that anyone who troubled to read the entry would not have spotted it as completely fanciful:

> **Mountweazel, Lillian Virginia,** 1942–73, American photographer, b. Bangs, Ohio. Turning from fountain design to photography in 1963, Mountweazel produced her celebrated portraits of the South Sierra Miwok in 1964. She was awarded government grants to make a series of photo-essays of unusual subject matter, including New York City buses, the cemeteries of Paris, and rural American mailboxes. The last group was exhibited extensively abroad and published as *Flags Up!* (1972). Mountweazel died at 31 in an explosion while on assignment for *Combustibles* magazine.

While an Internet search reveals that there actually *is* a Bangs, Ohio (it's in Knox County), citing it as the birthplace of someone blown to bits might have been a tipoff that someone was pulling the reader's leg. But identifying an entry in a reference work as a ghost word or Mountwea-zel presupposes that you've happened upon the entry in the first place, the question of how ghost words (and Mountwea-zels) get discovered once they've made it into print being at least implicit in Alford's article. If you were to read a refer-ence work cover to cover (as A. J. Jacobs claims to have done with the *Encyclopedia Britannica* in *The Know-It-All*), you might spot the phony (though, as David Fallows points out in his "Spoof Articles" entry in *The New Grove Dictionary of Music and Musicians,* "there are plenty of *bona fide* musicians whose names and lives look like outrageous fiction. One need only mention Gnocchi..."), but you're more likely to correctly identify an illegitimate entry either serendipitously—you were looking something else up on the page containing the entry and noticed it because who can read just one entry without at least glancing at its neighbors?—or by somebody's having tipped you off, as in the case of Heinrich Besseler's unmasking of Ugolino de Maltero.

Ugolino de Maltero was the surreptitious creation of the renowned German musicologist and theoretician Hugo Riemann (1849–1919), who claimed to have discovered a treatise by the "obscure" early fourteenth-century music theoretician, Magister Ugolino de Maltero Thuringi, enti-tled *De cantu fractibili brevis positio pro rudibus decem capitibus digesta,* which he published together with a German trans-lation, *Lehre von der Verzierung der Melodie für Anfänger in zehn Kapiteln* (splitting the Latin-German difference, 'Brief Instruction on Melodic Ornamentation for Beginners in Ten Chapters'), in the third volume of his collection of essays, *Präludien und Studien: Gesammelte Aufsätze zur Aes-thetik, Theorie und Geschichte der Musik.* The purpose of this elaborate hoax, which was undertaken in (fairly) dead seri-ousness, was to offer substantiation of some of Riemann's theories concerning the development of ornamentation in

Western music that had come under fire from various of his detractors. The historical precedent revealed by Ugolino's treatise was intended—and was taken—as solid vindication of Riemann's theories.

Riemann's creation was generally accepted, cited in learned articles, and even translated into French by an apparent true believer (René Leibowitz), who remarks at the end of his commentary that it's a shame that even today more of Ugolino's ideas aren't more unanimously shared. But eventually the truth came out—twice, actually, first in a footnote in the musicologist Heinrich Besseler's *Bourdon und Fauxbourdon: Studien zum Ursprung der niederländischen Musik,* in which the author remarks that Hugo Riemann's "Treatise" belongs in the category of humor rather than the fourteenth century, and second in a note by Besseler in *Acta Musicologica* in 1969, a mildly annoyed response to a recent article in the same publication by someone who, having evidently missed Besseler's 1950 footnote, was among those who took Ugolino's work to be genuine. The fact that the single sentence devoted to Ugolino in the twelfth edition of Riemann's widely respected *Musik Lexikon* (edited by Wilibald Gurlitt, published in 1961 after Riemann's death) stops just short of saying that Riemann made the whole thing up and then goes on to cite Besseler's footnote as the sole entry under "Documentation" does not seem to have caused a stir. Nor, apparently, did the entry in the supplement to the *Musik Lexikon* published in 1975, which says in effect that the discussion continues, citing Besseler's *Acta Musicologica* article.

The moral of the story is twofold: Street cred and a straight face can often convince people who ought to know better to accept a counterfeit bill of goods unquestioningly, but sooner or later somebody will spot the inevitable clues to the deception and blow the whistle. The clues in the case

I.

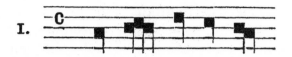

Figure 2.1

of Lillian Virginia Mountweazel were fairly glaring. Those in the case of Ugolino de Maltero were perhaps less so, though Besseler didn't seem to think so, and, once it was pointed out, the musical example that Ugolino/Riemann had picked as the theme to ornament should have sent up an immediate flare (see figure 2.1). As Besseler points out, in Riemann's time this tune would have been familiar as "Gott erhalte Franz den Kaiser," the Austrian national anthem, later as the Deutschlandlied ("Deutschland, Deutschland über Alles"), the national air of the Weimar Republic (and of today's reunited Germany, though now using only its kinder, gentler third verse, "Einigkeit und Recht und Freiheit..." ['Unity and justice and freedom..."]). The various other clues that Besseler identifies (not the least being the paucity of details of Ugolino's life) pale by comparison.

Typically, of course, once a Mountweazel is "outed" as a fake, it tends to disappear quickly, disowned by its original publisher and shunned by others (with the possible exception of metalexicographers). Not always, however: Sometimes the identity of a Mountweazel becomes a semi-open secret, known to some but not others, and subject to elaboration. Guglielmo Baldini (the Mountweazel, not the famous soccer player) is an illustrative case in point.

First appearing in the twelfth edition of Riemann's *Musik Lexikon* in 1959, Guglielmo Baldini entered the ordinarily staid world of Western musicology with the following biography:

Baldini, Guglielmo, born ca. 1540 in Ferrara; Italian composer, whose *Il primo libro de' Madrigali a cinque e sei* (Venice 1574) is known. The madrigals, dedicated to the then nuncio G. A. Facchinetti (later Pope Innocent IX), are permeated by homophonic passages and characteristics of the villanelle. Whether Baldini was related to the Ferraran printer Vittorio B. is unclear.

Plausible enough on the face of it—Facchinetti was indeed a nuncio who became Pope Innocent IX, and Vittorio was indeed a printer of the period. Failing to get a rise from the musicological community, the editors of the 1972 supplement to the *Musik Lexikon* included an addition to the original entry:

Baldini, Guglielmo, *circa 1540, [suppl.] traces of his life are lost after 1580. In the recently discovered correspondence of the Cardinal G. A. Facchinetti (who later became Pope Innocent IX) a heretofore unknown *Secondo libro de' madrigali* is mentioned. It is to be conjectured that at the Benedictine monastery of Santa Maria di Pomposa in Ferrara, where the Ferraran court printer Vittorio B. lived out his twilight years, B's fragmentary notes and compositions were to be found.

Apparently, this was the necessary spark, inspiring the following entry in the 1980 release of *The New Grove Dictionary of Music and Musicians:*

Baldini, Guillermo (*b* Ferrara, *c*1540; *d* in or after 1589). Italian composer. He may have been a relation of Vittorio Baldini, printer to the court of Ferrara from 1575. The pieces in his *Primo libro de' madrigali a 5–6 voce* (Venice, 2/1574), dedicated to the papal nuncio G.A. Facchinetti (later Pope Innocent IX), closely resemble those in Philippe de Monte's first book of six-part madrigals (1569) in their extensive use of homophonic writing and inclusion of traits typical of the villanella; the work is eclectic in its choice of texts (Ariosto, Sannazaro, Luigi Tansillo) and includes three sacred madrigals. A letter from Facchinetti to the Bishop of Freiburg, dated 1 March 1589, mentions a second book of (spiritual) madrigals, which does not survive.

The author included a couple of tip-offs: He lists the *Musik Lexikon* and a nonexistent article in a nonexistent periodical as sources. The entry was quickly removed and is absent from the follow-up edition of *Grove* later in the same year. (Not everybody got it, though: Alfred Baumgartner's encyclopedic *Alte Musik* in 1981 contains a serious entry for Baldini, with sections on his times and social milieu, his life, and his work, largely based, it would appear, on the two *Musik Lexikon* entries.) End of story?

No. The entry for Baldini appearing in the 1999 edition of the MGG (*Die Musik in Geschichte und Gegenwart: Allgemeine Enzyklopädie der Musik*), after remarking that outside of Riemann's work nothing is known about Baldini's life, helpfully offers that we have learned from the research of Budde and Stroux (contributing editors to the twelfth edition of the *Musik Lexicon,* as it happened) that Baldini's second book of madrigals had been destroyed in a fire. This entry is summarized and further elaborated upon in a peculiar posting (http://home.graffiti.net/hidemann/texte/guglielmo.htm) to the Internet, where, on eBay, one may also be tempted to try to purchase a CD of Baldini's second book of madrigals.

There is, as one might expect, a flip side to the Mountweazel, as there is to the ghost word: A fictitious biography can become attached to a real person, as a bogus meaning can be assigned to a legitimate word, though both of these phenomena are most likely to be found at a remove from the shelves of the library's reference room.

Anti-Mountweazels can take a number of forms. One is the real person whose public biography includes sometimes deliberately inaccurate information (a commonplace of the Internet), as revealed in the following interchange between an interviewer and the rock star, Meat Loaf:

> [T]here are several dozen stories for how you got your name, including one in Wikipedia that says you got run over by a car or something.
>
> Yeah, I made them all up. I'm serious. Once I realized that I could mess with people messing with my name, I just kept making up different histories. Every time. But I'm telling the truth when I tell you that I've been called Meat Loaf my whole life practically.

A variation is the real person who incorporates possibly fictitious personal information from somebody else's biography into his own, the subject of an article by Jennifer Saranow ("The Cut-and-Paste Personality") in the *Wall Street Journal*. Noting the high incidence of unattributed appropriations—well, plagiarism—of Hugh Gallagher's famous spoof college admissions essay ("I am a dynamic figure, often seen scaling walls and crushing ice...") in online presentations of self, Saranow recounts the tales of several real people whose biographical information (presumably accurate) has been borrowed from their online profiles on one or another of the Internet's social networking sites, an original take on the self-help movement's notion of "reinventing" oneself. Compare identity theft, impersonation or assuming a theatrical role, and writing under an assumed name, all but the first of which may be, like the identity of Baldini, an open secret: Everybody knows that P. D. Q. Bach is Peter Schickele's alter ego, and many are aware that Ellery Queen was (were) really two people joined at the literary hip. And in the days when you had to pay to have an unlisted phone number, you might, as a friend did, list your number under your dog's name (Daniels, Godfrey).

As mentioned earlier, anti–ghost words—real words that have been assigned bogus meanings—are the stuff of, at best, specialty dictionaries, such as Ambrose Bierce's *The Devil's Dictionary,* a wry collection in which words with whose conventional meanings you are assumed to be familiar are given a gloss that puts a spin on them. For example,

> **Pillory,** *n.* A mechanical device for inflicting personal distinction—prototype of the modern newspaper conducted by persons of austere virtues and blameless lives.

> **Piracy,** *n.* Commerce without its folly-swaddles, just as God made it.

and, of course,

> **Dictionary,** *n.* A malevolent literary device for cramping the growth of a language and making it hard and inelastic. This dictionary, however, is a most useful work.

Among the more recent in the genre is Douglas Adams's and John Lloyd's *The Deeper Meaning of Liff,* in which actual place names in England are treated as though they were common nouns, adjectives, or verbs with fanciful meanings supplied by the authors. For example,

> **Liff** (lif) *n.* A common object or experience for which no word yet exists.

3

BY THE GREAT CRIKES!

Oaths Both Sacred and Profane

"DASH BLAST THE GOSH-DARNED BLANKETY HECK!" exclaims the protagonist in *MAD Magazine*'s "Book! Movie!" satire showing corresponding scenes from a work of hard-boiled fiction and the sanitized 1950s Hollywood film made from it. Oaths are a deeply entrenched part of any language and the culture in which it is embedded, persisting in spite of pervasive taboos and conscious regulatory efforts to restrict their use in music, film, literature, and everyday speech: Junior gets his mouth washed out with soap for saying the f-word in Mom's hearing; in 1948, even as the Supreme Court is promulgating its "redeeming social importance" standard for determining that a work is not obscene, Norman Mailer is arm-twisted by his publisher to render that same word as "fug"; and in the 1960s, George Carlin's "Seven Dirty Words" comedy routine results in the explicit banning of the offending septet from the airwaves, a phenomenon lampooned by Monty Python's Flying Circus in their song "I Bet You They Won't Play This Song on the Radio," which bleeps the supposedly naughty bits by drawing on a cornucopia of funny noises that would have done Spike Jones proud.

Such taboo words fall into two main categories, the blasphemous and the obscene and/or scatological. These can be mixed, of course, as in *Jesus effing Christ,* a strong oath intensified by its quasi-gerund infix, or *holy shit,* whose noun mocks the conventions of euphemism by replacing the first kind of naughty word with the second. The force of either of these utterances is owed at least in part to the fact that they *are* hybrids: What makes a stream of profanity so colorful is its tendency to combine both types. In contrast, a mere eruption of "dirty talk" cloys, while a string of purely theologically based oaths begins all too soon less to resemble swearing than to evoke an exorcism or incantation.

The overloading of the words "oath" and "swear" reflect this duality. The OED gives as its first citation for "oath" Hrothgar's recounting in the Old English epic *Beowulf* of how he resolved the feud between Beowulf's father (Ecgtheow) and the Wulfings: "I sent the Wulfings old treasure over the water's back; he [Ecgtheow] swore me oaths [*hē mē āpas swōr*]," presumably of allegiance or alliance. It isn't until somewhat later that "oath" and "swear" are attested in the sense of "cuss," or as the OED puts it, "a casual or careless appeal invoking God (or something sacred) in asseveration or imprecation, without intent of reverence... a curse."

The kind of oath that Hrothgar is talking about corresponds to what the Romans referred to as a *sacrāmentum,* which, according to Varro's *De lingua Latina* (first century B.C.E.), was a sum of money that the plaintiff and the defendant deposited with the court as "earnest money" against the eventual outcome of their case, the word itself being derived from *sacrō* 'consecrate, set aside as holy.' According to Ernout and Meillet, *sacrāmentum* came to take on the sense of "oath" (*serment*) because the money "was accompanied by the swearing of an oath (*iūsiūrandum*)" and later came to refer specifically to a military oath (as distinguished from the more generic *iūsiūrandum,* the root of which gives such English terms as *justice* and *jury* and French *juron* 'swearword').

Among the most notable such oaths to come down to us from early Europe are the *Sacramenta Argentaria* (French *Serments de Strasbourg,* German *Straßburger Eide*), the Strasbourg Oaths sworn in 842 C.E. by Charles the Bald and Louis the German, two sons of Louis the Pious, pledging to stand up for each other against Louis's third surviving son, Lothair, in a territorial family squabble of epic proportions and Byzantine complexity. Charles and his half brother uttered the identical oath (switching the names), each in the language spoken by the other's troops, Charles in a dialect of Old High German and Louis in Gallo-Romance:

> For the love of God, and for the Christian people and our common salvation, from this day forward, to the extent that God give me the wisdom and the power, I will help my brother...

SWEARING SACRED

Oaths of this oldest sort generally invoke some sort of divine sanction as guarantee against oath-breaking. The Hippocratic oath, beginning "I swear by Apollo...," ends with "Now if I carry out this oath, and do not forswear it, may I acquire an eternal reputation among all people for my life and art; but if I stray from it and break it, may the opposite be my lot." Since Apollo was the sender of pestilence as well as the god of healing, "the opposite" is a very tactful way of saying "Go back on this and Apollo will see to it that not a one of your papers gets published in *JAMA,* and forget about getting a syndrome named after you, plus he'll zap you with the plague, all of which will serve you effing well right." The wish oath-takers express that some sort of bad consequence shall follow if they go back on their oath has a very long pedigree, well over three thousand years (e.g., Hittite military oaths, which called upon the gods to change the forswearer into a blind and deaf woman with abdominal dropsy, or Anglo-Saxon wills ending in such imprecations as "And whatsoever man shall and corrupt and violate [the terms of the will], may God Almighty corrupt his worldly honor, and also his soul's happiness"). Even our childhood "Cross my heart and hope to die" embodies the same theme, and while we may never have thought at the time that we were actually pledging our lives as hostages for our fidelity to truthfulness and promises (though well aware that we were at least putting our future reputation for honesty on the line), it is not too long ago that the oath "May God strike me dead if I lie" was commonly uttered by adults, attesting to a widespread and persistent belief in divine vengeance (satirized by George Price's cartoon of a witness in court being struck by lightning as the district attorney cries out "Aha! Fibbing, weren't you?")

Thunderbolts or no, as jurors or witnesses in court, we do take seriously the promise we make under oath to "tell the truth, the whole truth, and nothing but the truth"— a moral commitment to which the legal penalties for perjury add some secular teeth, to be sure, but which is also equipped with the escape hatch of our constitutional protection against self-incrimination (though offers of immunity from prosecution are sometimes proposed as an end run around the latter). After all, our self-image is at stake: We want to think of ourselves as reasonable persons of good faith, not the sort who'd get on the stand and lie like a rug. Apart from any abstract belief in the rightness of justice and judicial process, we endeavor to honor our oath, to which the formula, with its repetition of the word "truth," adds solemnity, majesty, and even a touch of preternatural awe.

That even oaths without allusions to the divine can be considered invalid if not spoken in the canonical form attests to their residual supernatural cachet: Just as an incantation isn't supposed to work unless you say the right magic words in just the right order, so flubbing the oath of office when swearing in a president on the Capitol steps can move both participants to repeat the same swearing-in correctly next morning at the White House, if only for form's sake. "Exact repetition of formulaic phrases," writes legal historian and linguist Peter M. Tiersma, "evokes an age when people believed in magic and divine intervention," adding that "[s]omeone who believes that God might strike him dead for lying, or that he might be condemned to hell, will become very nervous if he is swearing falsely," even as a stammer or omission of words might be perceived (correctly) by the court as a sign of perjury to come.

Such formalism is characteristic of legal language in general, serving for centuries as an inexhaustible source of innocent merriment for satirists and their audience. (Indeed, one might argue that the repetitions and restatements characteristic of "legalese" offer prima facie evidence for excluding it from a book dedicated to discussing *short* forms; but that would be quibbling.) In fact, the language of English and American law derives from three distinct sources: indigenous Anglo-Saxons, their Norman conquerors, and the Romans.

Roman oaths, like much of Roman religion, rested on a matter-of-fact relation between deity and worshipper: I give you this in order that you may give me that (or in Latin, *dō ut dēs*). So if a commander on the Rhine frontier facing a crucial battle vowed to build a temple to Mars or Jupiter if he won the battle, and his army was victorious, as soon as he got back to Rome groundbreaking would begin for a brand-new temple of "Mars Silvaticus" or "Jupiter of the Bogs," a deal being a deal. On the other hand, oaths as mere interjections were common as well, and among both sexes, *herclē* ('by Hercules!') being used mostly by men, while *edepol* ('by Pollux!') seems to have been confined almost entirely to women. This dual role of oaths as pact with heaven and as casual interjection would persist under Christianity, despite the strictures on oath-taking and use of the divine name inherited from Judaism.

It is from Christianized Rome that much of the language of canon law derived. In our secular society, it is easy to forget how widespread the influence of church courts was in the medieval world, regulating all matters relating to marriage and divorce, with important ramifications for the transfer of property. (Hence, as legal historian Charles Donahue has shown in his painstaking study of how medieval marriage law played itself out in the courts, a divorce in fourteenth-century Cambridgeshire, where only the eldest son inherited, was markedly more likely to be granted than it was in Paris, where bequeathed property might be divided up among multiple siblings.) Canon-law testimony and findings were as a matter of course recorded in Latin, this being the lingua franca of the church throughout Christendom. As Tiersma writes, "Use of Latin as a legal language introduced terms like *client, conviction, admit, mediate,* and *legitimate* into the English lexicon," as well as *clerk* (a doublet with *cleric*), since "[p]eople with religious training were among the few who could write in those days."

Modern English also preserves some Anglo-Saxon legal terms predating the Conquest, including *oath* and *swear, murder* and *manslaughter, steal* and *thief, ward* and *bequeath* (not to mention *will*), and the all-important *guilt* (though *innocence* is Latin via French; see below). Anglo-Saxon law also passed on its rhetorical habits of pairing and alliteration (a significant feature of its poetry as well: The hero Beowulf is described after his death as *manna mildust ond mon-ðwǣrust / lēodum līðost and lof-geornost* [roughly, 'that gentlest man, of all men most gracious, / kind in his kingship, most covetous of fame']). Expressions such as *devise and bequeath, without let or hindrance, to have and to hold, safe and sound, part and parcel, aid and abet,* and *rest, residue, and remainder* are all echoes of a legal tradition with a strong oral component, going back at least to 600 C.E., when a set of laws was compiled under King Æthelbert. (The primacy of speech over writing was also true of Iceland, whose annual assembly, the Althing, included a cyclic oral recitation of the law code, a third every year.)

One might think that French, the language of the new Norman ruling class, would have become the standard vernacular for non-ecclesiastical court proceedings in short order after 1066, but in fact it took nearly three centuries before "Law French" supplanted Latin even in writs sent to sheriffs and magistrates (many of which are still referred to by their Latin names down to the present, e.g., *mandamus, certiorari, subpoena,* and *habeas corpus*), let alone the court transcripts themselves—by which time the use of French by the gentry had virtually died out.

Remnants of Law French persist today in such expressions as *voir dire* ('tell the truth'—compare primary school's *show and tell*), *oyer and terminer* ('to hear and determine,' the kind of court, forerunner of today's grand juries, that returned indictments in the Salem witch trials), and of course the bailiff's cry of "*Oyez!*" ('Hear ye!'), as well as in a wealth of absorptions into English such as *marriage, estate, easement, tort, misdemeanor, trespass, larceny, arson, arrest,* and *bailiff* itself, just to name ten. From Law French also come those constructions in which the adjective comes after the noun (as usual in French) instead of before it: *letters patent, court martial, fee simple, accounts payable, notary public, malice aforethought,* and so on.

SWEARING PROFANE

In the Middle Ages, casual oath-swearing in everyday speech was common enough to provoke reprimands from preachers and poets alike. "At the end of the Middle Ages blasphemy is still a sort of daring diversion which belongs to the nobility," wrote Jan Huizinga, but like other customs of the gentry, it begins to be imitated all the way down the social scale until (as the poet Eustache Deschamps complains at the end of the fourteenth century) "There is no caitiff but says,/'I deny God and His Mother'" (*je renie Dieu et sa mère*). And there were plenty of euphemisms for the stronger stuff: *je renie Dieu,* contracted in familiar talk to the single word *jarnidieu,* could be replaced by *je renie des bottes* ('I deny some boots') or *jarnibleu* ('...blue'), while *jarnicoton* ('I deny cotton') would cover for *je renie Christ, palsambleu* for *par le sang de dieu* ('by God's blood'), and so on. The late chansonnier Georges Brassens built a lengthy song refrain from such expressions (his "Ronde des Jurons," or "Ditty of the Swearwords"), many of which are still a vibrant part of the vocabulary of modern standard French.

Related to *jurons* are *sacres* (compare *sacré* 'holy'), a category of profanity in broad use by the francophone inhabitants of the Canadian province of Québec. *Sacres* include names of sacred people—*crisse* ('Christ'), *viarge* (i.e., *Vierge,* 'Virgin Mary'), *mozusse* (the quasi-English variant of standard French *Moïse,* 'Moses')—but other ecclesiastical terms as well, such as *tabarnac* ('tabernacle'), *ciboire* ('ciborium, pyx'), *câlice* ('chalice'), *sacrament* ('sacrament,' presumably the Eucharist), *ciarge* (i.e., *cierge,* 'Paschal candle'), (*h*)*ostie* ('host, communion wafer'), and *baptême* ('baptism'). The verb *sacrer* has come to mean 'swear using *sacres*,' and, interestingly, is used as a substitute for the obscenity *foutre* in the expression *sacrer le camp* ('to get the hell out'). Most *sacres* have euphemized forms as well, such as *câlif* ('caliph') for *câlice*, *crimpuff* ('cream puff') for *crisse*, *tabarouette* ('wheelbarrow') for *tabarnac*, and so on.

The use of *sacres* by the Québecois has been traced to a growing unhappiness in the early nineteenth century with the strictures of the Catholic Church on secular life in the province, the earliest known *sacre* being *sacrament*, which is said to have come into common use by the 1830s. But turning sacred words into swears is not confined to Québec: Italy, for example, has *ostia* ('host') and *sacramento* (and the related verb *sacramentare*, 'to swear'), along with *porco dio* ('pig-God') and *porca Madonna* ('pig-Madonna'). The greater an angel, the stronger a devil when he falls, according to C.S. Lewis's fictional demon Screwtape, while Sigmund Freud thought that the psychological mechanism of ambivalence was behind the diametrically opposite meanings of Latin *sacer* as 'holy' and 'execrable' (and was also manifest in the two senses of English *cleave*). Whatever the reason, the present-day Roman hierarchy in Québec, understandably unhappy about the widespread casual use of *sacres*, undertook a billboard campaign to raise public consciousness about the literal meaning of swearwords of this sort in an effort to persuade the Québécois to watch their mouths.

The process by which the literal meaning of a word or phrase evanesces is called *semantic bleaching* and was first elucidated in an influential book by the German linguist Georg von der Gabelentz in 1891. Invoking the metaphor of "the civil servant [who] is hired, promoted, has his hours cut back, and finally gets pensioned off completely," Gabelentz says that when new words get created from old, "fresher new colors cover the bleached old ones.... In all of this there are two possibilities: either the old word is made to vanish without a trace by the new, or it carries on but in a more or less vestigial existence—retires from public life." Essentially, what has happened with *sacres* and other such epithets is that the words have undergone semantic bleaching.

But that's only part of the story. Writing under the pseudonym Quang Phuc Dong, James D. McCawley, argued in a 1968 samizdat essay entitled "English Sentences without Overt Grammatical Subject" that swearwords might actually be doppelgangers of existing words with which they were homophonous and orthographically identical. This ingenious paper demonstrated the point by showing that such doubles had different syntactic properties from the originals. Refuting traditional explanations of such sentences as "Damn you" as being either straightforward imperatives or else hortatory subjunctives with an understood subject such as "God," McCawley showed that one can say, for example, "Lock the door after midnight," but not *"Damn you after midnight," and ruled out "God" as a possible subject by proposing the elegant absurdity *"Damn Himself."

McCawley called such words "quasi-verbs" and distinguished them orthographically from their look-alikes with subscripts; thus, Alexander Pope meant $damn_1$ in his "Damn with faint praise, assent with civil leer," while Marshall Dodge unequivocally intended $damn_2$ in his punch line "Damn you, Enoch; you *know* I got two hogs!" The same also applies, interestingly enough, to "bless," for while we do indeed say "God bless you," a straightforward subjunctive, *"Bless Himself" is likewise a non-starter, evidence for a quasi-verb $bless_2$ as well as the ordinary verb $bless_1$. *Curse* can be likewise dichotomized: "I curse the day I first bought this miserable car" versus "Curse this miserable car!"

BLESSINGS AND CURSES

Blessings and curses go hand in hand (as J. Wellington Wells, the eponymous sorcerer of the Gilbert and Sullivan operetta, tells us in the third line of his self-introductory patter song). Both can be fixed in content, as in the graces said before meals by the pious (e.g., "Bless, o Lord, this food to our use, and us to Thy loving service" to which may be compared the less pious "Good food, good meat, good God, let's eat") or the Execration Texts of the ancient Egyptians against those "who may rebel, who may plot, who may fight, who may think of fighting, or who may think of rebelling," which William James Hamblin describes as "standardized, with a type of fill-in-the-blank format for the name of the enemy." In the latter case, however, the formula is supposed to be followed to the letter in order for the supernatural intervention to occur at all (the common response to a nonworking spell being that one has not said it properly); conversely, one sign of a witch or sorcerer was supposed to be an inability to repeat the Lord's Prayer without a mistake, which almost (but, alas, not quite) saved Salem Village's former pastor George Burroughs, when he recited it flawlessly just before he was to be hanged for a warlock.

While the efficacy of prayer is not necessarily contingent on saying the right words and only those, and in the right order, many prayers are indeed standardized, providing the eloquent and inarticulate faithful alike with a common language of devotion. The Anglican Book of Common Prayer, originally compiled under Henry VIII's Archbishop of Canterbury, Thomas Cranmer, came at a propitious moment: Printed books were just turning into a commodity affordable to more than a wealthy few. (It has been argued that the entire Protestant Reformation would not have been possible but for the invention of printing, and there is no doubt in any case that printing accelerated it.)

An easy rule-of-thumb taxonomy of prayer is the acronym ACTS, a mnemonic for "adoration, contrition, thanksgiving, and supplication." The Sanctus of the mass is of the first sort, the words of praise Isaiah said that the cherubim were singing unceasingly when he visited Heaven in the year that King Uzziah died. "We are heartily sorry, and we humbly repent" (in the Book of Common Prayer's General Confession) is of the second sort, and the Magnificat ("My soul doth magnify the Lord... for he hath regarded the lowliness of his handmaiden, and behold, all generations shall call me blessed") is of the third. Any prayer that begins "We humbly beseech thee, o Lord..." immediately marks it as supplication (the riskiest of the four types, for as the proverb says, "Be careful of what you pray for, as it will surely be yours.")

But in form, prayers come in all shapes and sizes and points along the public-private continuum. There is the mealtime family grace (at least at Thanksgiving, in all but the most secular of households). There are invocations spoken by ministers at the opening of legislative sessions, and blessings said for new buildings and for animals (the Feast of St. Francis being particularly favored for the latter). In the Episcopal Church there are "Prayers of the People," recited every Sunday by a lay reader and the congregation antiphonally, as well as litanies and collects for particular holy days. There are bidding prayers, which straddle the line between prayer and homily in serving notice of an upcoming Eucharist and admonishing the faithful to participate in a right spirit, lest in taking the host they merely "press visibly with their teeth" but not actually receive the Body of Christ (or not in any way that counts spiritually). There are prayers for the newly baptized and prayers of committal at the graveside. And there are battlefield prayers, which tend to be very short (e.g., Sir Jacob Astley's at Edgehill during the English Civil War, "O Lord, thou knowest how busy I must be this day; if I forget thee, do not thou forget me.")

In short, if it moves and has its being, chances are someone has already composed a prayer for it, and while we Westerners think of prayer as primarily an oral phenomenon, halfway around the world there are prayer flags and prayer wheels as well, whose text is considered to be conveyed to the divine realm each time the devotee spins the wheel or whenever a passing breeze stirs the banner.

Pray comes from Latin *precor* ('I beseech/entreat'), which says something about its purpose; the other usual Latin term, *orāre,* is related to *oratory, oration,* and *oral,* emphasizing the mode of delivery. *Bless* comes from Old English *blētsian,* originally meaning 'to mark with blood [*blōd*] as holy,' and may have acquired its heavenly connotations by association with *bliss* (Old English *bliss* or *blīps;* compare *blithe*). *Curse* is from Old English too; though its earlier provenance is obscure, some have suggested that it is related to the Old Irish verb *cūrsagim* ('I censure/chastise').

It is of course quite possible to curse someone and to be praying at the same time, a form of supplication in which a deity is being asked to carry out the punitive action, as when Elijah says "As the God of Israel liveth, there shall be no rain...but according to my word," or Moses calls down the plagues upon the entire land of Egypt. ("What are all these *frogs* doing here? *Eeeuw!*") Nevertheless, we generally think of curses as being brought to bear by an agency that is far from heavenly and often quite the reverse.

This is partly due to the Church having given magic per se a bad name. By the Middle Ages, a clear distinction was drawn between the miraculous (*miraculosus*) and the magical (*magicus*); the former was the doing of God, often working through the saints, while the latter was condemned as trickery at best and sorcery at worst. (Both appealed to the medieval appetite for the marvelous or wonderful [*mirābilis*], marvels being the stock in trade of travel writers from Sir John Mandeville to Marco Polo.

But clergy and laity alike believed that demons existed, and that spells invoking their aid were not only possible but could be efficacious. It followed that witches and practitioners of magic must be rooted out, an activity given a substantial boost at the very end of the Middle Ages with the promulgation of a papal bull against sorcery, *Summis desiderantes,* by Pope Innocent VIII in 1484, followed three years later by the publication of a treatise called the *Malleus Maleficarum* ('hammer for female evildoers') by two Dominican priests in Germany, which codified and legitimized the theoretical basis for witch-huntings and the executions of tens of thousands of accused witches and warlocks in consequence.

Yet folk traditions of petty incantations and other holdovers from Europe's pagan past were not so easily to be stamped out. Ordinary folk got away with some of them because they called on saints rather than demons. "Matthew, Mark, Luke, and John / Bless the bed that I lie on" is arguably of this sort; the Church might deplore such charms as silly, but practice tolerated them (as would most certainly *not* have been the case for, say, a bedtime rhyme that went "Abraxas, Mephisto, Belpeor, Azezel: / Who vexes my bed, hex him into a weasel!") More open signs of magic and magical thinking could be displayed by the laity once there was a New World for religious dissenters to emigrate to; in religiously tolerant Pennsylvania, one can still see barns in the Penn Dutch country protected with brightly painted six-leaf medallions called *hex signs, hexen* being German for "work magic, conjure up" and *Hexe* meaning "witch."

Spells have a way of hanging on long past the time people take them seriously or even know what they meant once upon a time. Folklorists have suggested that at least some of the now nonsensical refrains of songs were originally incantations for example, the *Skowan earl grey...For yetter kangra norla* of the English katabasis ballad "King Orfeo," sung by John Stickle of the island of Unst and recorded by field ethnomusicologist Patrick Shuldham-Shaw in the 1950s, may in fact have come, according to Francis James Child, from Scandinavian *Skoven årle grön...Hvor hjorten han går årlig,* which he translates as "Early green's the wood...Where the hart goes yearly," though if it is a spell, its usefulness is anyone's guess today.

Nonsense refrains, of course, abound; some may be mere "mouth music" in imitation of instruments. (Such is the "Tinkatank, tinkatank, tinkatank" in Edwin's solo, "When First My Old, Old Love I Knew" in the Gilbert and Sullivan operetta *Trial By Jury,* a quite credible attempt to reproduce the sound of a stringed instrument played with a plectrum, such as a mandolin or banjo-ukulele.) Other refrains seem to be there primarily for their rhythm (*fol diggy die doh, fol diggy dee; rightful, rightful, titty fie day; ring, ding, dum-a-ding die oh; whack fol the diddle fol the die doh day; knickety, knockety, hey mow mow; twankydillo, twankydillo, twankydillo, dillo, dillo, dillo*). The pragmatic advantage of an easily remembered nonsense refrain is that it buys a performer some time to remember the next line or verse, but for most folksingers it would be an inconvenient side effect indeed if a demon were suddenly to appear in a ring of fire on the coffeehouse stage in front of them. ("Let's see—your share of the gate, $93; sanding and revarnishing the scorch mark, about a hundred. Let's call it even.")

The ancient Romans were not above using spells; Cato the Censor's treatise on agriculture includes the following formula, the recitation of which was supposed to help speed the healing of bone fractures: *Huat, hanat, huat; (h)ista, pista, sista; domiabo, damnaustro, et luxato.* (Or, to burlesque Petronius, "He mumbled some gobbledygook that he later attempted to pass off as Etruscan.") Nowadays, magic words are mostly confined to fairy tale and fantasy, and story-specific besides, though a few have attained paradigm status— notably the phrase *sim sala bim* in Germany (the last in no small part for its use in a pop song by the band Tool entitled "Die Eier von Satan" ['Satan's Balls']), in America *abracadabra,* and in France its cousin *abracadabrantesque,* a term coined by the nineteenth-century poet Arthur Rimbaud in his triolet "Le coeur volé" and the subject of a recent blog posting entitled "Mots ribonds: Une présidence abracadabrantesque," concerning words on the way to extinction that are brought back to life when, as the author puts it, "an important person comes along and breathes on the embers, and forgotten words can be reborn from their ashes," *mots ribonds* being the author's clever neologism playing on the words *moribond* 'moribund,' *mot* 'word,' and the verb *rebondir* 'to rebound.'

WHEN WORDS FAIL US

Of course, there are words which really *are* meaningless, those fillers such as *ah, er, oh,* and *um* with which we pad our speech instead of simply saying nothing when we are fishing for the next things to say. (Persian aptly calls such words *takya-kalām,* 'speech pillow.') These should be distinguished from interjections; compare the *oh* in "Oh, the turtle set out an hour ago" with that of "Oh! the turtle is still at the door of the cave!" Interjections without any real semantic content can nevertheless serve as what sociologist Erving Goffman called *response cries,* telegraphing our mental states. (Goffman also pointed out that such nonwords often do not have a fixed spelling; a case in point is the exclamation of disgust rendered above as *eeeuw*—the three-*e* string marking it as "not really English"—but also transcribed *ew*, *eeuw*, and *ewe*, this last a source of confusion, since it is a homograph of an actual noun designating a real animal.) In this same basket go what are sometimes called "discourse markers:" *like, you know, I mean,* and so on.

Then there are indeterminates, those words we use when we can't think of the actual word for something. These often resemble both nonsense refrains and ad hoc magic words in their sound texture: *whatchamacallit, thingamabob, doohinkus, frammis, whatsisname, doomyflotchit, oojah,* and so on. Such words can also be invented as euphemisms, as in the use of *hey nonny nonny* for the obvious rhyme in the round "He that would an ale-house keep / Must have three things in store: / A chamber and a feather-bed, / a chimney and a...." (Four things, actually. But who's counting?) *Ring dang doo* performs a similar function in the ballad so titled, avoiding a far less delicate anatomical term elsewhere euphemized as *mother of all saints, Holy Ground, map of Tassie* (i.e., Tasmania, which is triangular and just beneath the belly of Australia), and *the Lord knows where.* As with blasphemous oaths, euphemism in referring to sexual or excretory organs and functions gets them past the censor, while leaving most of one's audience in little or no doubt as to what one really means, thanks to the robust oral tradition that tends to preserve naughty words with surprising fidelity down through the years.

Of course, oral tradition has a habit of dropping a stitch between listener and hearer, as anyone who has ever played the party game "Telephone" knows. Indeed, there is a whole class of mishearings collectively called *mondegreens,* so named by Sylvia White from her childhood mishearing of the ballad line "and they laid him on the green" as "and the Lady Mondegreen." Common examples abound, such as the tutelary beings *Harold* (*be thy name*) from the Lord's Prayer, *Round John Virgin* from the Christmas carol "Silent Night," and *Good Mrs. Murphy* from the Twenty-Third Psalm; and most of us have our personal favorites as well, "Lead On, O Kinky Turtle [Lead On, O King Eternal]" being high on the authors' list.

Mondegreens arguably involve the same sort of misparsing as "knock knock" jokes, except that the latter entail a deliberate setup on the part of the initiator:

> Knock, knock.
> —Who's there?
> Sam and Janet.
> —Sam and Janet who?
> (sings): "*Sam and Janet Evening...*"

Interactive jokes of this sort are interesting on a number of sociolinguistic levels. On the formal level, of course, there's the setup for grammatical misparsing, typically involving some phonetic funny business (punning), but it is the social interaction required to make the joke work that distinguishes it from jokes involving a teller and a passive hearer, which may be likened, as a form of discourse, to oaths of both the solemn and epithet varieties in which there is a single speaker (the swearer of the oath) and a hearer who may be physically present (as Charles and Louis's soldiers or the hammer with which you whacked your thumb) or not (as the spiritual recipient of one's prayers).

In interactive jokes, which generally involve the initiator setting up the other party for an ostensibly nonhostile tweaking, the conversational turn-taking is set, and the initiator gets the last word. By contrast, in normal conversation in which the playing field is assumed to be reasonably level, each party is presumed to have a shot at having the last word (or, in the case of "he who laughs last laughs best," the last laugh, though it has been suggested that he who laughs last simply didn't get the joke). When the conversation is fundamentally adversarial (however friendly), the last word can go by any of several names—*punch line* if the conversation is an interactive joke, *comeback, riposte,* and *repartee* being among the ringleaders (with *retort* and *rejoinder* ready in the wings) otherwise.

Comeback (or *come-back*), often qualified by the adjective *snappy,* is an American coinage dating from the end of the nineteenth century. (*Snappy* dates from somewhat earlier in the century.) The snappy comeback typically involves quick terminal humor at the other guy's expense, whether in response to a feeble pickup line ("What's your sign?"—"Stop.") or something more in-your-face, as when (as legend has it) Dorothy Parker and Clare Booth Luce, wife of the publisher of *Time,* arrived at a door simultaneously, Luce waved her on with the line "Age before beauty," and Parker, sailing through, is said to have retorted, "Pearls before swine."

The ritual exchange of insults among young African-American men (called "the dozens") is well documented, such contests often involving slurs on the opponent's mother (e.g., "Yo' mama so old, she sat behind Jesus Christ in third grade!"). An analogue may be found in the trope of courtship-as-contest in songs such as "I Gave My Love a Cherry" and "Captain Wedderburn's Courtship," where the woman poses riddles which the man must answer to win her, which he successfully does, or the related flight-and-capture of such songs as the Provençal "Magali," in which the woman says she will metamorphose into various things (fish, bird, fog, flower…) to escape her suitor, who replies that if she does, he will become the corresponding thing (fisherman, bird catcher, wind, butterfly) and so catch her.

(This theme, said to be as old as Ovid, has been charmingly recycled as a dialogue between mother and child in Margaret Wise Brown's classic children's book *The Runaway Bunny*.)

Not all comebacks are snappy, of course. Indeed, some aren't funny or clever at all, like vice president Dick Cheney's widely (if sometimes euphemistically) reported reaction to a reproach from Senator Patrick Leahy about his ties to the Halliburton company. An obscenity, whether spoken (as in Mr. Cheney's case) or unspoken (as when one ends an interchange by giving one's opponent the Bronx cheer—the raspberry—or the finger), is generally considered to be a pretty lame conversational finale and can be taken as an admission of defeat, like "Yeah, right," "OK, you got me," or "Touché."

Originally a term from the gentleman's sport of fencing, *Touché* is a classy conversation ender borrowed from French, as are the winning *riposte* (also a fencing term, denoting a quick return thrust after parrying a lunge), *rejoinder* (originally a legal term referring to the defendant's response to the plaintiff's charge), and *repartee*. The *Grand dictionnaire Larousse encyclopédique* defines *repartie* as "(1) A lively, witty answer; reply: a vigorous repartee. (2) An instinct for the apt: to have an instinct for the apt." Undoubtedly fully aware of the true meaning of the word in English (which dates from at least the middle of the seventeenth century), Mark Twain offered the following tongue-in-cheek definition: "Repartee is something we think of twenty-four hours too late."

This is essentially the definition of *l'esprit de l'escalier*, the snappy comeback that occurs to you only after the conversation in which you might have used it is over. Like its cousin, the now archaic *after-wit*, which denotes the knowledge that, if you'd only had it sooner, might have kept you from doing or saying something that now you wish you hadn't, *l'esprit de l'escalier* as a sociolinguistic phenomenon is surely as old as human interaction. Unlike *after-wit,* which is attested in the 1600s, the expression, at least in English, is relatively recent. Its French pedigree is a matter of some debate, though the main contenders for the honor of originator pretty much boil down to the following:

- Pierre Nicole (1625–1695), philosopher of the Jansenist movement at Port Royal, is reported to have said in recounting an argument he had had with his friend de Tréville, "He beat me in my studio, but he hadn't reached the foot of the stairs before I confounded him."
- Jean de La Bruyère (1645–1696), member of the Académie française noted for his *Les Caractères,* a collection of meditations on the social mores of the time, is up next. The 1922 edition of *Hoyt's New Cyclopedia of Practical Quotations* has among its citations under the category of "Wit" the following: "Je n'ai jamais d'esprit qu'au bas de l'escalier. I never have wit until I am below stairs. LA BRUYÈRE, according to J.-J. Rousseau. Esprit de l'escalier, backstairs wit, is credited to M. DE TREVILLE by PIERRE NICOLE. For use of this phrase see *The King's English,* p. 32, Note," which sends the curious reader to a wonderful pronouncement by that arbiter of linguistic taste, H. W. Fowler: "The French have had the wit to pack into the words *esprit d'escalier* the common experience that one's happiest retorts occur to one only when the chance of uttering them is gone, the door is closed, and one's feet are on the staircase. That is well worth introducing to an English audience; the only question is whether it is of any use to translate it without

explanation. No one will know what *spirit of the stair-case* is who is not already familiar with *esprit d'escalier*, and even he who is may not recognize it in disguise, seeing that *esprit* does not mean spirit (which suggests a goblin lurking in the hall clock), but wit."

- Denis Diderot (1713–1784), philosopher and man of letters, in his 1773 dialogue concerning the actor's display of emotion and our own (genuine) emotions, *Paradoxe sur le comédien,* says, "Cette apostrophe me déconcerte et me réduit au silence, parce que l'homme sensible, comme moi, tout entier à ce qu'on lui objecte, perd la tête, et ne se retrouve qu'au bas de l'escalier." Walter Herries Pollock's 1883 translation of *Le Paradoxe sur le comédien—The Paradox of Acting—* renders this as "This apostrophe put me out, and reduced me to silence, because the man of sensibility, like me, is wrapped up in the objection to his argument, loses his head, and does not find his answer until he is leaving the house."

None of these cases involves the actual expression "l'esprit de l'escalier" as such. For that, we apparently have to wait until the second half of the nineteenth century, when the expression begins to sprout like daisies, as in the often cited 1886 letter in which the poet Paul Verlaine refers to "my characteristic *esprit de l'escalier*" in remembering to ask after some money owed him.

Why, asks the author of an essay posted on the French language blog *expressio* in June 2006, is it the staircase rather than, say, the corridor (*couloir*) or the front gate (*portail*)? Possibly, the author suggests, the repetition of the words' initial sounds was involved. While responses to the initial posting do not propose the escalator (*escalier roulant*) as an alternative to the staircase, its close cousin, the elevator (*ascenseur*), puts in an appearance, both vehicles of up-and-down personal conveyence dating from the 1800s. Actually, the first known people-moving elevator of record (in France, at least) seems to have been the *chaise volante* ('flying chair') that Louis XV had installed at Versailles in 1743 to enable discreet assignations with his then mistress, the Duchesse de Châteauroux, their boudoirs having been on separate floors of the château. Just how discreet these meetings could have been, given that the elevator was external to the building and operated by means of windlasses and levers worked by the servants, is open to question, to say nothing of the comfort of the ride itself. The statesman Georges Clemenceau may or may not have had this in mind when he remarked, a century and a half later, that love's most beautiful moment is when one ascends the stairs, though one wag has offered the rejoinder that the same set of stairs can just as well lead to Hell.

The Congolese master of soukous, Koffi Olomide, tells us that lying takes the elevator while truth takes the stairs. However, no matter which route brings you to the end of the conversation, you need never find yourself truly at a loss for words; as Captain Jean-Christophe Pitard-Bouet suggests at the conclusion of his essay "Avoir l'esprit d'escalier," "When you're at a loss for a come-back [*quand le manque de répartie vous gagne*], instead of bolting out the door, or admitting your lack of ready wit, simply say that you've been overcome by *l'esprit de l'escalier* [*l'esprit de l'escalier vous a gagné*]."

4

ON OR ABOUT YOUR PERSON

The Talk of the Territories of the Self

SECOND ONLY TO "WHAT'S FOR DINNER?" IN THE hierarchy of Big Questions we ask ourselves, "Who are you?" can be answered in several different ways—by our words, by our physical appearance, and by a wide variety of text-bearing adornments with which we accessorize our physical selves.

IN YOUR OWN WORDS

One of the first things we learn as children is to say our names (and shortly thereafter, our address and phone number, so that if we are lost, as a public-safety song instructed New York schoolchildren during the 1950s, we can go to the nearest police officer and "Give him your name and address/And your telephone number too"). At a certain point, we come to realize that we had no say in the name we were given and may not care for it, particularly if it provides a handle for ridicule by our schoolfellows. (One wonders what on earth possessed the anthropologist Ernest Hooton to name his son Newton, or the Cains to name their daughter

Candace.) It may be small comfort to us to learn that the choice of our name may not have been altogether an act of free will on our parents' part either; often the grandparents have a strong voice in the matter, and in Jewish families there is a very strong tradition of naming a newborn after the most recently deceased relative of the same sex.

In any case, and for whatever reason, you may wish to be known by some other name than the one on your birth certificate. This is where middle names come in handy; Eustace William Brown can style himself Bill Brown or even E. William Brown without having to go before a magistrate and plead for an official name change. A more extreme option may be to change your name entirely, as in the following example, reported in the Portland (Maine) *Press Herald:*

> **Geto Boy gets new name**
> Rapper **Bushwick Bill** has chosen a new name for himself: **Dr. Wolfgang Von Bushwickin the Barbarian Mother Funky Stay High Dollar Billstir.** The member of The Geto Boys said in a news release Thursday that since he is releasing a solo album, the name Bushwick no longer does him justice. He was born Richard Shaw.

Nicknames are another way out: Born Lowell Cabot Chickering, our hero embraces the name "Chick" in prep school and clings onto it for the rest of his days. On the other hand, one may not like one's nickname, either; James Bulger, fugitive brother of former Bay State politico Billy Bulger, is said to loathe the familiar "Whitey," prominently printed on his wanted poster, but there's little he can do about it; nor, if apprehended and convicted, would he likely to make much headway if he petitioned the warden at Cedar Junction to give him a different prisoner number he could remember more easily. Some things about your identity you're just plain stuck with.

It is in youth that we learn the nuances of how to let other people know who we are, from the schoolyard to the classroom. That mainstay of elocution lessons, "Show and Tell," is as much an exercise in presentation of self as it is a sharing of something that will edify our peers. The caption beneath the picture in our high school yearbook is perhaps the first of what may be many occasions on which we are obliged to give a compact presentation of self ("Antonia Bernardette Schiavi: 'Toni-Bee'—Field Hockey 1, 2, 3, 4; Girls' Basketball 2, 3; Chess Club 1, Debate 3, 4; Cheerleaders 2, 3, 4—'We having fun yet?'—always hanging with T.K. and F.X.McG.—'Kansas in August.' St. Dymphna College").

Others include the personal ad ("Professional WM 35, LA area, seeks WF 25–30 serious about marriage and family; must play mah-jongg…"), the job application ("résumé attached") and the interviewer's describe-yourself-in-one-word test question (to which our quondam colleague Joseph Maguire once answered: "Terse"), the Facebook entry ("Ayn Jostin. Feb. 27, 1949. My friends:…"), the memoir-in-six-words parlor game (Jane Goodall's: "Forest peace, sharing vision, always optimistic;" Deepak Chopra's: "Danced in Fields of Infinite Possibilities"), and the dust jacket blurb ("Frank Buncombe got the idea for a penguin forensic psychiatrist while stationed on Guam for two long years in the Marines. *Dr. Peterquin on Ice* is his third novel. An avid spelunker, he divides his time between Perth Amboy and the island of Mauritius"). While there is always the possibility that someone will check up on us and catch us fibbing, it is generally assumed that our self-representation in these forms is essentially truthful, allowing for the fact that we are putting our best foot forward (as who would not?), and the less said about certain unflattering episodes along the way the better.

IN THE FLESH

As far as the physical presentation of self is concerned, each of us is born with certain physical attributes, but some change as we age, and we can—and, indeed, society often urges us to—customize a lot of these, from nose jobs to face-lifts to liposuction to a range of medical procedures ending in -*plasty* too long to enumerate here. Erving Goffman's *Stigma: Notes on the Management of Spoiled Identity* is a good exposition of what one can and cannot disguise about one's identity (or what it might have been thought desirable to disguise in the early 1960s, when he wrote the book).

Of course, there is a continuum from such innocent personal enhancements as eye shadow, mascara, and foundation makeup (cosmetics with a pedigree of respectability stretching back at least three millennia) through tinted contacts, hair dye, and studio tan (considered venial if easily detected, as suggested by President Obama's jesting reference to House minority leader John Boehner as "a person of color, just not a color that is found in nature") to deliberately "passing" for a member of a dominant social group (white, gentile, rich, straight, male…) in place of one considered to be of lower social status (black, Jewish, impecunious, gay, female…)—the subject of many ballads and stage comedies and surely not a few tragedies offstage—all the way to the bewildering variety of disguises (false beards, Porky Pig masks) that are all but obligatory for master criminals and intrepid sleuths in detective fiction, not to mention spy stories. Perhaps the extreme real-world instance of the last is the now famous "Man Who Never Was," a fresh cadaver dumped into the ocean by Allied counterintelligence agents so as to wash ashore shortly before

D-Day with identification and other papers lending credibility
to his possessing the secret documents he carried misdirect-
ing the Germans' attention to a landing site far from Omaha
Beach and on some other day than June 6, 1944. This strategy
worked because we expect personal effects to *be* personal, i.e.,
pertaining to the bearer's identity and nobody else's.

BY DESIGN

For the most part, we assume that who we see is who we get.
The amateur sociologist inside most of us tends to make
judgments based on the material cues we offer in the way
we present ourselves in ordinary life: "Such-and-such says a
lot about you," where "such-and-such" can be your clothes,
your jewelry and other accessories, the contents of your wallet (bag, fanny pack), the photos and text on your Facebook
page, your car (and the bumper sticker or magnetic ribbon
attached to it), the political placard on your front lawn or in
your window, and so on.

One of the earliest surviving medical treatises, the Smith
Surgical Papyrus (ca. 1800 B.C.E., but showing evidence of
being a copy of a much earlier work), discusses physical
trauma starting with the crown of the head and working
downs toward the feet. This seems a sensible organizing
principle for our own discussion of those forms of writing
and their associated symbols which we carry on our persons
or within arm's reach. (It is again to Erving Goffman that
we owe the term "territories of the self," which he usefully
employs in parsing the various physical and conceptual
boundaries we recognize when distinguishing between our
selves and the world outside us.) For the most part, the bits
of writing and signing we carry about with us are succinct so
as to be portable, and project meaning even as they achieve
a heightened degree of semantic efficiency.

In Your Hat

In the United States, the tag showing your hat size will bear a number that is the quotient of the circumference in inches at the hatband divided by pi (a 22-inch hatband yielding a size 7); Europeans, being on the metric system, size their hats by circumference in centimeters (to convert, divide metric size by 8; thus 57 cm = U.S. size 7 1/8). Usually a hat will bear a manufacturer's trademark as well, though not always, especially when the wearer has been at pains to remove it. (As one of Dorothy Sayers's characters remarks, why be a walking advertisement for one's hatter?)

The hat itself as signifier should be noted here as well. From a considerable distance one can tell a bishop's miter from a firefighter's helmet, and both from a duke's coronet, a freshman's beanie, or a letter carrier's summer sola topee (pith helmets having been a standard U.S. Postal Service seasonal option since 1949). Vestments and uniforms aside, social convention and fashion limit the variations possible within situationally appropriate forms of headwear: In most parts of the United States at least, one does not expect to see a John Deere cap among the hats reverently removed by the mourning relatives at a graveside service for a deceased bank president.

Ironically, such "gimme caps" with company advertising on them may be worn precisely because their wearers wish to express their individuality by way of a conspicuous, literally in-your-face display of brand loyalty. That myriads of others may have the same brand preference merely widens this populist gesture into a working-class fashion statement. Similar caps with clever sayings instead of ads on them burlesque this sartorial phenomenon; mostly worn by middle-class youth, they are cerebral analogues to the T-shirt, protest button, or bumper sticker. A cap is also a suitable alternative place to attach a lapel pin, about which more below.

Around Your Neck

That our crania are much larger than the cervical verte-
brae and musculature that support them, which in turn are
much smaller than our shoulders, makes possible a variety
of message-bearing tokens hung from our necks by chains,
cords, or ribbons. A common way of combining a style statement with religious expression is the crucifix (sometimes
incorporating or accompanied by a Saint Benedict's medal)
worn by many self-identified Christians—optional for laity,
mandatory for at least some members of the clergy. But as
far as wearing, as a fashion accessory, the crucifix attached
to a string of beads that serves as a mnemonic for a set cycle
of prayers (both the necklace and the litany being called
"the rosary"), one of our informants said: "Never, never,
never. Every kid wanted to do it, and we were told it was a
sin. You carry it in your pocket."

Other sorts of group-identification symbols go here as
well: the peace symbol, originally a superimposition of the
semaphore postures of the N and D of "nuclear disarma-
ment" but now generalized to mean "I'm against (this)
war;" the six-pointed Star of David ("I'm Jewish"); the wavy
horn ("I'm Italian"); the Egyptian ankh ("I either like life or
bought this in the mistaken impression it was the alchemy
sign for 'woman'"); lambda ("I'm gay/lesbian"); the zodiac
sign of Pisces ("I'm whatever people born at that twelfth of
the year are supposed to be [including wishy-washy about
whether astrology itself is claptrap]"); the labrys or double-
headed axe of the Minoans ("I'm a fem-separatist"); an ele-
phant ("I'm a proud Republican"); a Phi Beta Kappa key
("I'm smart"); and so on. (Note that all of these could be
worn in pairs as earrings as well, and, the pachyderm perhaps excepted, often are.)

The neck is also a useful repository for person-specific
identification, from the civilian's "MedicAlert" (also worn as

a bracelet, and signifying particular conditions such as the wearer's being at risk for diabetic shock) to the pair of identical military dog tags bearing (in the U.S. Army version) the soldier's name, serial number (nowadays, Social Security number), immunization code, blood type, and religious affiliation. The "dog tag" metaphor—in German, *Hundemarken,* the term used for the registration tags required for the dogs of Berlin at the end of the 1860s—came to be used for the ID medallions issued to the soldiers of Prussia in 1870 during the Franco-Prussian War.

The United States would not adopt a uniform military tag till 1906; before that, soldiers concerned about misidentification in the event of serious injury or death would improvise by pinning slips of paper with their name into their uniforms, or buy commercially available tags designed for this purpose. The reason why they now come in pairs is so that in the event of a death under circumstances where the body can't be recovered immediately, one's comrades can remove one tag to take to the authorities, the other remaining with the deceased. Civilian knockoffs have been common at least since the 1950s.

Most European military tags come in two parts with duplicate information on both halves, perforated so that one part can be broken off and taken away, leaving the other on the body. A precursor of this may be the folk custom of lovers breaking a coin of which each party then wears half, which survives in a conventionalized broken-token-with-love-message pendant that is standard in the jewelry trade to this day, such as the heart in two pieces, each with a ring for a chain, offered by one Southwest jewelers' supplier bearing the legend "Best Friends" on the obverse and "Friend Forever Apart or Together" on the back. The object of one's affection may also be directly represented (and shared with others) in a miniature photo, sometimes, but not necessarily, in a locket—it was easy to pick out the followers of the silent guru, Meher Baba, from any crowd of hippies in the early '70s because they always wore his beatifically smiling picture on a cord around their neck. (A Civil War–era precursor was the lock of hair of a departed loved one in a glass-framed pendant like a miniature monstrance.)

Neckties, of course, can be a semiotic vehicle, as the expression "the old school tie" suggests, the weave showing affiliation of clan, church, college, and so on. Another type of neckwear with a message is the event lanyard, a printed strap with a ring on the end to which one can attach one's room key or temporary ID card during footraces, college reunions, and so forth. The lanyard legend ("Midsummer 5K Run Like Hell—Tucson, 8/9/09," "40th Anniversary Convocation, Hop Bitters University Class of '65," etc.) will often designate the event, thus creating an easily stored souvenir after it's over. Then there is the clerical collar, standard day-to-day wear for the clergy of some persuasions (Roman Catholic, Presbyterian, Anglican, A.M.E.) though not others (Baptist, Unitarian, Assembly of God), this sign of ministry serving to set the wearer conspicuously apart from the laity. Conversely, one of the authors knew a Jesuit who said he planned not to wear his collar while assigned to the province of Québec in the late 1960s, a time and place in which being perceived from the outset as a man of the cloth was not, he felt, the way to win friends and influence people.

On Your Body

The neck is by no means the only bodily site available for the wearing of ornament. We have mentioned topical earrings above; bracelets are also a vehicle for messages, including the metal POW bracelets of the 1970s, each inscribed with the name of a soldier who did not return from Vietnam and whose whereabouts remained unknown, and the more recent "awareness bracelet," generally made of flexible plastic and sold as a fund-raiser for the cause named in the text, not to mention those bracelets inscribed "WWJD" (short for "What Would Jesus Do?"), worn by evangelical youth as a reminder to seek godly solutions to everyday ethical dilemmas. Charm bracelets are expressly made for attaching multiple symbols (with or without text) of who we are and what we care about: miniature tennis racquets, dolphins, dancing shoes, dog/cat heads, mah jongg tiles, penguins, and so on; engraved silhouettes with names and birthdates of (grand) children or disks bearing the dates of marathons and how long it took the wearer to run them; little tags with common text-message abbreviations ("lol," "omg," "btw," "cul8r"). On the fingers, signet rings can indicate one's high school or college, often with a graduation year, while wedding rings are frequently engraved inside with the name of the wearer and spouse plus the date of the ceremony.

Such signifying ornaments can, of course, be removed at will; not so tattoos, which like body piercings (with which they share conventions and fairs) bespeak a more serious commitment to their message than does a removable fashionable accessory, and require a deliberate yielding of the self-other boundary of the skin to a presumably permanent (and at least momentarily painful) alteration. Tattoos on inner-city youth are so often signifiers of particular gang membership and drug use that Irwin Nebron, a juvenile court judge in California, recruited a plastic surgeon, Dr. Karl Stein, willing to help kids who wanted to turn their lives around by removing their tattoos pro bono.

Not everyone *chooses* to be tattooed in the first place: Under the Third Reich, serial numbers of concentration camp inmates were tattooed onto their wrists, at once a means of totalitarian control and an egregious flouting of Jewish prohibitions on body alteration. On the other hand, soldiers in today's American armed forces will sometimes deliberately have the information from their dog tags tattooed on some part of their body as a gesture of bravado whose ostensible utility (giving rise to the nickname "meat tag") is to provide a form of identification in the event that one's body is so badly deconstructed that the ordinary metal dog tags are gone.

On a less grim note, combat ribbons and other military insignia worn on one's uniform indicate rank and theaters of operation, along with decorations won for exemplary behavior such as getting wounded. Rank symbols—metal insignia for commissioned officers (whence the synecdochic "brass" for the wearers), stripes for enlisted personnel and noncoms—are worn on sleeves or shoulders as well as on helmets or hats. Civilians generally attach pins with a recognizable logo to lapels instead, to indicate group affiliation: the Rotary gear, the choir lyre, Christianity's cross, the vasectomy veteran's interrupted circle-and-arrow, the Stars and Bars, and so on. (The same sort of emblems can be found on tie tacks or tie bars.) Because of their small size, however, these provide interaction cues only to people who have already approached within close conversational range (or at least fight-or-flight distance).

"Protest" buttons, though an offshoot of the giveaway political campaign pins that go back well over a century, proliferated explosively during the 1960s and have been a robust discursive form ever since, allowing their wearers a vast range of slogans beyond actual protest ("Picket HUAC," "Free the Chicago Seven," "No Nukes," "How Many Vietnamese Fought in OUR Civil War?") and the quest for broader awareness of marginalized groups ("Black Power," "Save the Whales," "Legalize Pot," "How DARE You Presume I'm

Heterosexual!") to pop culture ("Frodo Lives," "AC/DC," "Shit Happens," "What, Me Worry?") and smart sayings ("If It Moves, Fondle It," "Nietzsche Is Pietzsche," "Visualize Whirled Peas," "Your Inner Child Needs a Spanking").

On Your Clothing

Brand-name clothing labels facilitate a kind of discreet snobbery. The golden-fleece symbol on the Brooks Brothers label is taken from Philip the Good's Order of the Golden Fleece in fifteenth-century Burgundy, itself a revival of an already archaic courtly culture well versed in medieval romances re-creating the exploits of the ancient Trojan War heroes and Jason's Argonauts. More conspicuously, the alligator shirt or the whale-motif wrapskirt (not to mention the '50s poodle skirt of fond memory) are fashion statements intended to display socioeconomic class, not merely something to wear to keep from being naked.

T-shirts and sweatshirts are a very common vehicle for graphics and text, like the protest buttons above and the bumper stickers below. For nonprofit organizations they make an attractive fund-raising item or appreciation premium (as do imprinted tote bags) not only because they can be relatively cheap to produce in bulk but also because their user then becomes a willing walking billboard (as with the brand-name gimme caps above) promoting the issuer's product, service, or identity. Again like totes, but unlike buttons and bumper stickers, tees can be printed front and back, which allows the possibility of two-liners with a pause in between. (Front: "I'd Like to Help You Out." Back: "Which Way Did You Come In?") And given their viewing distance—midway between button and bumper sticker—Ts and sweatshirts allow reference beyond the wearer's body as well (sideways arrow with legend "I'm With Stupid").

In Japan, where uniforms remain compulsory for youth in school, T-shirts are a favorite vehicle for casual wear and often bear slogans in "atmosphere English," such as "Feel Coke." China saw a flash-in-the-pan explosion of snarky T-shirts on teenagers in June 1991, including such slogans as "Cleanse the World of All Evil Beasts," "I don't fear suffering, I don't fear death, and I don't fear you," and "Mama taught me a little song: 'Without the Communist Party, we wouldn't have this new China.'" (By the end of the month, unsurprisingly enough, such shirts were confiscated from the free-market makers and their wearing was banned.)

Maine Public Radio commentator Charlotte Renner says that the T-shirt, "the uniform of our time," is "our way of being undressed," by wearing openly "something we think of as underwear, only it isn't underwear any more because it has words on it, and if you put words on underwear, who would read them?" But underwear itself can incorporate text and symbols too, albeit for a far more restricted audience: Day-of-the-week briefs supposedly indicative of one's ephemeral mind-set ("Sunday" is generally chaste white script on white fabric, while "Saturday" is often lurid scarlet embroidery on a black field); leopard print bra-and-panty sets (subtext: "You Tarzan, me Jane"); youth themes and slogans ("Superman," "Cinderella," "Hottie," the bunny with the caption "I'm cute. Let's put me in charge"); seasonal motifs (Santa, Valentine, Halloween).

While the "innerwear as outerwear" fad of the '80s seems to have mercifully been consigned to the Goodwill donation box of history, it facilitated the migration of fetishware into the mainstream (e.g., leathermen and -women wannabes) and a blurring of boundaries between outer and intimate apparel—sag pants exposing the top three inches of men's boxers, low-cut jeans on women wearing high-riding thongs. Novelty socks feature a less controversially public show, with computerized weaving able to display patterns of stars, pigs, even skeleton feet.

In Your Pocket

Pouches—whether pockets that are sewn into our clothing or the separate purses, wallets, handbags, or fanny packs we carry on our persons—contain a rich array of texts and signifiers of who we are as well as the social sphere in which we move and have our being. The following is a partial inventory, and each item undoubtedly can be studied in more detail than we can possibly hope to do here, the rest (as our teachers would say) being left as an exercise for the student. Note that the wallet per se is a pouch within a pouch, or put another way a personal space within a personal space (pockets for men, handbags for women—for it is still considered by most Americans a serious territorial violation to rummage through a woman's purse without her express consent, though not as serious as rummaging through someone else's pants pockets while that person is wearing those pants).

Currency Spare change? Money talks, with an eloquence belied or indeed enhanced by the terseness of its text. While the first coins were little more than more or less equal slabs of metal hacked off a billet, a modern coin at a minimum needs to bear some indicator of the issuing authority, traditionally that of the head of state, whose image on the obverse is framed by a legend with name and title. Canadian coins bear a portrait bust of Queen Elizabeth II, the third such depiction in her long reign, and she is identified as "D·G·Regina" (short for *dei gratia regina*, 'Queen by the grace of God') but not as *defensor fidei* ('defender of the Faith') as she is on the coinage of Britain in her capacity as head of the Church of England.

Because coins by their nature tend to stay in circulation once a government releases them, a coin may long outlive its regime, despite the concerted efforts of subsequent administrations to call it in (whether through a shift in valuation or the desire to remove circulating images of a head of state the current regime just ousted). The coinage of Haiti is a case in point: The 50-centime coin issued in 1907 and 1908 under President Pierre Nord Alexis (familiarly known as Tonton Nò, i.e., "Uncle Nord"), remained current until the 1990s, when inflation rendered it worth less than its metal value and almost all of the issue was taken out of circulation. This coin showed the head of Tonton Nò on the obverse and a palm tree on the back; hence the Haitian for "heads or tails" remains *tonton nò osnon palmis* ('Uncle Nò or palm tree') to this day. (By a similar process, "two bits" is still a slang term applied to the U.S. quarter, though the days when a dollar was considered equal in value to the Spanish eight-*real* piece in wide circulation in the former colonies are well over two centuries behind us.)

Folding money has two strikes against it: Nowadays, increasingly sophisticated printing technology must be employed to make it counterfeit-proof, and then it wears out in a couple of years anyway. It is for this reason that Canada has already dispensed with one- and two-dollar bills, though a drive to dump the fiver was derailed by popular opposition. (The current five-dollar bill features a portrait of Sir Wilfrid Laurier, prime minister from 1896 to 1911, whose face looks remarkably like that of Mr. Spock from *Star Trek* when augmented by *détournement* with bushy eyebrows and pointy ears, a practice known as "Spocking." The bilingual bill also has an illustrated quotation from a short story by Roch Carrier ("Une abominable feuille d'érable sur la glace," translated as "The Hockey Sweater") to provide a bit of reading material while you wait in line to make your purchase.)

Credit/Debit Cards America's economy thrives on credit, insofar as it thrives at all. In the 1950s, individual stores would open revolving charge accounts for qualified customers, issuing them metal "charge-a-plates" on which one's name and account number were embossed in the manner of military dog tags; these would be run through a slide press to imprint store receipts in duplicate on carbon paper sets. The problem, however, was that one needed a plate for every store. Four investors started Diners Club in 1950 as a way of facilitating transactions with multiple merchants; American Express, already in the travel-services business (begun as a shipping company, it had introduced the first Travelers' Cheques in 1891), launched its own travel and entertainment card in 1957, with Carte Blanche entering the field around the same time.

Strictly speaking, these "T&E" cards were charge cards rather than credit cards: The customer was obliged to pay off the entire balance at the end of the month. Bank of America introduced the first true credit card in 1958 in a bold dumping of 60,000 unsolicited cards on households in Fresno, California (where it had a 45 percent market share); expecting a 4 percent default rate, the company was stunned when the first year's deadbeat percentage was 22 percent, and its initial losses were officially stated to be almost nine million dollars. Nevertheless, the die had been cast, and with the formation of the Interbank Card Association in 1966 and the issuing of the first MasterCard (originally named Master Charge), America was launched on what credit card historian Lloyd Klein has called "the important transition from actualizing the inner self to marching toward conspicuous consumption." Meanwhile, Bank of America would spin off its credit card operations and the new company would rename the product VISA, the name it retains to this day.

Driver's License   Most people in America aged sixteen and over have one, issued by a state authority. (There are also federal driver's licenses, including military ones.) Whatever the state, your license will bear a photograph and serial number, and should have your current address (and certain other information, such as whether you need to wear corrective lenses to drive). This has led to its widespread use as the touchstone identity-verification document in other contexts.

From a semiotic perspective, a driver's license is not just a license to drive: The mere fact that one has one in one's wallet (assuming it is indeed one's own) is itself a prima facie sign that the person in the picture is old enough to drive and has no neurological or perceptual problem that would impede this (or at least didn't the last time he or she was road-tested, one reason some jurisdictions make you take the test again periodically once you're past a certain age). The government-vetted information it bears makes it handy in other contexts than a roadside chat with the constabulary: The age shown on it allows the bartender or liquor-store clerk to make a lawful sale; the election-day poll worker uses it to verify that one is indeed legally entitled to vote in that precinct; the bank uses it to verify, as by law it must, that one is who one claims to be in order to accept the new depositor's money. With a completely bogus ID, of course, one can be anybody one's fancy desires; as the proprietor of a bar in 1960s Amherst, Mass., used to say, "C'mon, show me your IDs, the fake ones too—they're more interesting!" Of course, not everyone has a driver's license, and a lack of uniformity from state to state makes even the existing ones something short of the national ID cards of other nations (e.g., Israel), although as this book goes to press Congress is under pressure to enact some version of "Real" ID, to the horror of civil libertarians and others who feel with some justification that it is the slippery slope for various other types of registration and tracking of citizens (culminating, as some think, in the inscribing of the Number of the Beast on each of us, without which nobody will be able to buy anything in the impending End Times).

Meanwhile, it is still possible to manage without a license at all (one of the authors has done this for the last forty-four years), providing one has a passport and some corroborating document such as a utility bill or the label off one's IRS packet to show residence. Never mind that one has grown a beard and a head of gray hair, not to mention gaining thirty pounds, since that last passport picture was taken (up to ten years ago): It's a government photo ID and will do the trick.

Identity theft, on the other hand, relies on the perpetrator's being taken for someone else, at least long enough to wipe out that person's bank balance and rack up a huge credit card debt. This is a lot easier than it used to be, thanks to the technology of personal data management having exploded into an epistemic and moral vacuum: Despite warnings from privacy advocates for several decades, by no means all data handlers have yet figured out why it isn't such a smart idea to make promiscuous use of Social Security numbers for frivolous nongovernment purposes, so there is still plenty of sensitive data lying around for the taking in inadequately safeguarded commercial databases.

And even among those who are well aware of the danger, there can be hideous accidents, such as the theft of a laptop containing the Social Security numbers of 65,000 Ohio citizens from a feckless aide's automobile one fine weekend, or the massive security breach at a major national credit card processing center that forced many banks to issue new cards to all their depositors. You and I may be, as Carol King's record album famously asserted, "free to be you and me," but when push comes to shove, I'm not *really* free to be you, or vice versa.

School ID   Sometime called a bursar's card because it is keyed to the university's accounting department, the identification card carried by students, faculty, and staff allows both a ready triage of those on campus and the summary exclusion of those who don't belong there. It is a surprisingly effective means of social control: One may be asked to show it as a prerequisite of taking books out from the library or being fed in the dining hall, and in the event of a disturbance (such as the taking of Harvard's University Hall by Students for a Democratic Society in the spring of 1969), campus police may be empowered to confiscate such cards from anyone seen to be misbehaving, requiring offenders to present themselves to a university authority if they want to recover it. In the 1960s, a plastic card embossed with name and bursar's number, which could be run through a manual charge-plate machine, was considered sufficient; nowadays they come with photos and magnetic strips. (In recent years, public secondary schools have begun to adopt student photo IDs as well, but these are usually worn as exposed clip-on tags like workplace ID badges instead.)

Draft Card   For a centralized state to raise an army, it must have a way of knowing who and where its citizens actually are; when most of them were serfs and the answer was "on the estate," it goes without saying that none of them had to carry a draft card. Although conscription was briefly resorted to in Massachusetts and Virginia during the War of Independence, the United States as such waited fourscore and seven years from the Declaration of Independence to institute a military draft (in July 1863), perhaps partly due to our national indignation at such practices as the press-ganging of seamen into the British navy off American ships, one of the causes of the War of 1812.

Although the draft was briefly brought back by President Wilson in the First World War, it was the Second World War that made conscription an everyday reality in America, when no fewer than ten million American men were under arms. With the exception of a fifteen-month hiatus starting with the expiration of the 1940 Selective Service and Training Act in 1947, the draft persisted through much of the Cold War (and the two Asian hot wars)—remarkably, under the same director, General Lewis B. Hershey, appointed by President Roosevelt in 1941.

Universal registration of young men for the draft meant that for the first time ever, the carrying of a national identification card was mandated by law for the male population. Actually, there were two cards: the Registration Certificate and the Notice of Classification. The specific information recorded on the Registration Certificate has changed over the years, reflecting changes in the society. Thus, in 1917, when the Selective Service System began to issue the cards, in addition to your name and address and year of birth, the registration card noted your citizenship, country of birth, your present trade or occupation, your employer and place of employment, your marital status and whether you had any dependents among your relatives, previous military service (and for which nation or state), and whether you claimed exemption from the draft (and, if so, on what grounds). At the bottom of the card was a space for "signature or mark." The bottom left corner of the card contained the text "If person is of African descent, tear off this corner." Today's card assumes that you can sign your name and ignores your ethnic history.

The Notice of Classification card, which came along later, served to indicate one's current draft status, from I-A (signifying that you were liable to be called up at any time) to 4-F (signifying that you were considered, for one reason or another, "unfit for military service"). This card, like the Registration Certificate, contains on its verso instructions to keep the card in your personal possession at all times, to notify the authorities of any change of address or "any other fact that might change your classification," and to refrain from mutilating or otherwise misusing the card. It was public disregard of this last provision that brought the case of David O'Brien, who burned his Selective Service Registration Certificate on the steps of a Boston courthouse in 1966, to a two-year journey through the courts before the U.S. Supreme Court upheld his original sentence for violating the 1965 amendment to the 1948 draft law by which Congress explicitly forbade the knowing destruction or mutilation of draft cards. While the decision allowed the Court to skirt the larger question of symbolic freedom of expression and the First Amendment (at least for the moment), the publicity surrounding the case certainly served to fuel the debate over the war in Southeast Asia and the inequities of the draft. The role of the case in ending the war and the draft (for which young American men are still required by law to register) is perhaps best left moot.

Social Security Card/Medicare Card   Since the government explicitly states on one's Social Security registration card that it is not to be used for identification, many people do not bother to carry it, having memorized their Social Security numbers early in their working days. (Social Security was signed into law in 1935.) However, the payoff when one attains a certain age is the related program of Medicare, the ID for which a patient shows whenever obtaining medical services to be reimbursed by it. (The same is true for the newly instituted Medicare Part D, the hodgepodge of mandated private-sector prescription drug plans.)

Business Cards Although most of us tend to carry a few of our own business cards in our wallets, where at least temporarily we stash those proffered to us as well, some of us have separate little folders for this express purpose. In Japan the art of presenting and receiving the *meishi* (business card) has been refined to a ceremony freighted with significations of status and protocol: If yours is printed in Japanese on one side and English on the other, present it to your Japanese receiver with the Japanese side up; bow when taking or receiving it; take and give it with both hands and examine it closely as sign of respect; NEVER write on it or put it in your pocket or wallet, as this dishonors it; check the pronunciation of the giver's name, if necessary, on receiving the card, as it would be impolite to do so after the fact; distribute to multiple recipients in order of status—and do NOT begin the business meeting until the *meishi* have all been given and received. An American company once, in a fit of creativity, printed up cards for each of its representatives in a variety of hues, bewildering the Japanese to whom the U.S. businessmen gave them because they couldn't figure out what status messages were intended by the different colors.

Business cards of sex workers in England are used as advertising and left in phone booths, whence the term "phone cards." Meanwhile, several companies have experimented with "mini-cards" smaller than the usual business card and containing just name, website URL, and e-mail, the idea being that these are handier than regular-sized cards and get an edge on attention by being easier to stuff in your wallet. (We have known job applicants to use a similar strategy in submitting résumés on other than 8½ × 11 paper. Sometimes it works. Sometimes it doesn't.)

While not strictly business cards per se, in the same slot in one's wallet are apt to be discount cards, including the "punch this ten times and get a freebie" variety. Here too go the pictures of your spouse, your kids, your pet. And since wallets tend to have several card-sized compartments, here too may be found your library card, your HMO card, the card reminding you of your upcoming appointment with the dentist, your exercise club ID, your Kinko's copy card, that scapular your godmother gave you (but not the holy card from her funeral, which gets stuck in your shirt pocket instead until you can go home and stuff it with all the others in your family Bible), the card from the lingerie shop with your wife's undergarment sizes on it, and that little giveaway year-at-a-glance calendar from your bank that handily doubles as a celluloid strip in case you get inadvertently locked out of your apartment. Scarcely any room left over for your folding money, in fact—but that's one of life's little ironies, isn't it?

Address Book The proverbial Little Black Book, its space for names and addresses can vary: Three lines per entry is tight, especially now that so many households have a cell phone or two in addition to their land lines, but a five-line box with preprinted categories makes for a lot of dead space and either fewer people or a bulkier address book. Moreover, cheap memory has made it possible to store a great deal of that sort of information on one's Palm Pilot or BlackBerry instead, relegating the dead-tree address book to one's desk at home. But it seems unlikely that this item will simply disappear, any more than the printed book will; for one thing, it is still the hard-copy backup in case your electronic address book crashes irretrievably.

On/Under Your Feet

As fans of the TV show *Forensic Files* know, evidence from shoe prints, thanks to distinctive tread patterns, has led to the apprehension and conviction of suspects in several recent American murder cases. (So have the unique whorl marks left by bare feet, no less individual than our finger-prints.) And footwear can be designed expressly to convey text: Sandals are now available at seaside-resort boutiques that print "Love" in the sand with every footstep. One may also use one's footwear to stash a text: The second part of a set of Israeli army dog tags is conventionally tucked away in the soldier's boot, this being considered a more reliable place to assure postmortem identification than around one's neck, particularly when the opposition has a penchant for using explosives.

OUT OF BODY

Two common extensions of the person deserve passing mention here: one's car and one's home.

Your Car

We are what we drive. Cars trumpet our self-identification loud and clear, from luxurious Cadillacs and BMWs to SUVs to modest compacts to vans to top-of-the-line sports cars. We may fine-tune the automotive presentation of self with such add-ons as bumper stickers, awareness ribbons, and vanity license plates.

Bumper stickers are slogan buttons writ large, the idea being that the driver of the car behind you should be able to read yours without having to tailgate. Early bumper stickers in America were mostly either political affirma-tions ("In Your Heart, You Know He's Right") or souvenir advertising ("South of the Border"), but nowadays they run the gamut from the hortatory ("Practice Random Acts of Kindness") to the erudite and surreal ("Colorless Green Ideas Sleep Furiously"), not to mention the oval (also called a Euro-sticker) enclosing real or spurious country-code letters: MV ('Martha's Vineyard'), KW ('Key West'), LAX ('lacrosse'—inviting a double take rooted in another short form, since LAX is also the luggage-tag terminal code for the Los Angeles airport.)

By contrast, Israeli bumper stickers are primarily a vehicle for political expression, and their ubiquity and aggressiveness has been said to be symptomatic of an aggressive style of driving in Israel generally. Thus, shortly after the 1995 assassination of Yitzhak Rabin, a phrase from his final speech that called for a reduction in violence ("Dai la'alimut") was widely reproduced as a bumper sticker on many cars (*alimut* means 'violence'); there was a reduction in road casualties in subsequent weeks, while it was reported that many people peeled stickers with more provocative messages off their cars. (This was not a trivial act: One ethnographer noted that removing a sticker with a religious assertion, e.g., about the link between God and the land, was thought by some to be followed by bad luck.)

Magnetic awareness ribbons are an analogy twice removed, displacing to your car the awareness-ribbon pin you might wear on your lapel, which is in turn a more permanent form of the temporary cloth ribbon associated with the cause of your choice (yellow to show solidarity with the armed forces overseas, pink for breast cancer, rainbow for sexual-orientation inclusiveness, and so on). These allude to the military hat-cockade, in turn descended from the practice of troops attaching a sprig of whatever was growing in the field in which they happened to encamp to their helmets, so that in the heat of battle they would be able to tell friend from foe (whose tents were presumably pitched far enough away that the plant they stuck to *their* helmets wouldn't be the same as your side's). In a recent fusion of the POW bracelet and awareness ribbon, one now sees magnetic ribbons bearing the names and birth and death dates of fallen soldiers.

A car's glove compartment is likely to contain, at a minimum, your car registration, as well as an owner's manual and some maps, though the latter are rapidly being made obsolete by electronic global-positioning hookups with onboard display screens. This technology, of course, also makes it possible for someone else, for instance, law enforcement, to locate your car, at least as long as its computer is running; when the car is disabled, however, the helpfulness of any onboard system is apt to be compromised, which is why we predict that glove compartments will continue to contain owner's manuals in hard copy for some time to come.

The state's Department of Motor Vehicles allows us to further express who we are (and distinguish our teal Kia from all the other teal compacts in the grocery store parking lot) by selling us the vanity plate of our choice (TIAMAT, AGRAV8R, VIOLINS, SOX RULE)—that is, assuming our choice is not on the list of plates that will not be issued under any circumstances owing to their being obscene, blasphemous, or otherwise patently offensive. Hence there is a constant race between wise-guy motorists trying to get naughty plates and DMV watchdogs trying to spot them. One of our friends reported seeing, in the 1960s, an apparent victory on the part of the former, the California license plate QQQQ. Nor is the race always to the slow. Sharper eyes prevailed at the Massachusetts Registry of Motor Vehicles in 2000 when veteran special plate department manager Pat Wormstead realized that a variant spelling of boxer Mike Tyson's last name, on a plate already printed up and ready to go out, read "No Shyt" backwards. (Win some, lose some.)

Your Home

To an even greater degree than one's car, the size and location of one's home likewise announces one's identity, here embedded in a complex web of signifiers with various trimmings, from the doormat to the Keep Off Grass sign at the edge of the lawn.

Since, up until recently, the standard formula for financing a home purchase entails a substantial down payment (20–25 percent) and a long-term mortgage (thirty years is not uncommon), the house down the street with the new neighbors may reflect not so much their net worth as their present cash flow from earnings based on a double wage income, in serious peril if either of them gets laid off or even put on reduced hours, and almost certain to go on the market, often at a deep must-sell discount, if the couple divorces. Economic uncertainty among newlyweds may militate in favor of a "starter house" with a rental unit attached, which can always be used to house an elderly relative later on if the expected raises come through on schedule. (Not for nothing are such apartments often referred to as "mother-in-law" units.) But wherever we choose to live tells our friends and neighbors who we are and to what level we currently aspire. And in all likelihood, our neighbors will be at about the same place, unless we are rash enough to purchase the most expensive house on the block.

A mat in front of the front door is ostensibly a utilitarian item for cleaning/drying one's shoes, but it often bears a message, the default being "Welcome." Parodies include "Inscape" and "Go Away," but a common variant is simply the name of the family, often with a superfluous apostrophe ("The Jones'," "The Smith's"). Family names can also be affixed to mailboxes in places where the mail delivery is made from a postal service truck rather than by a carrier going door to door on foot, and the mailboxes themselves, within fairly broad U.S.P.S. guidelines, can vary from the stock arch-top with flag to such novelties as miniature barns, oversized golf balls, or plastic open-mouthed game fish, again designed to advertise the personality of the owner.

As a text vehicle, the mailbox provides one kind of sign (if only the bare minimum street number); actual signs on the property are another, often bearing messages intended to prescribe and regulate the behavior of callers vis-à-vis the boundaries of your extended personal space: "No Trespassing," "No Soliciting," or the more sinister "Beware of Dog," or, in Mexico, *Respete mi cochera y respeto tu auto. ¡Gracias!* ('Respect my garage and I'll respect your car. Thanks!'): Keep off my property or I'll sic my dog on you, and don't block my driveway, or I'll trash your car. Temporary signage in the window or on the lawn can be plugs for one or more political candidates; it can also include advertising by contractors at work on the house ("Roofing by Bidwell," "Rutgers Painting") or the realtor's "For Sale" sign with its Plexiglas box for leaflets touting the property. The presumption is that such signs will be removed once the election is over, the contract is up, or you have sold the house and moved away.

5

ON THE LAM

The World of Word Crime

WE WARN YOU FOR MAKING ANYDING PUBLIC OR
for notify the Polise the child is in gut care. (Ransom
note ascribed to Bruno Hauptmann)

that money I ask for is nothing to u (Prostitute's text
message)

CON EDISON CROOKS, THIS IS FOR YOU. (Mad
Bomber's note)

Bulger is an avid reader with an interest in history.
He is known to frequent libraries and historic sites.
(FBI wanted poster)

The preceding quotations exemplify the stock-in-trade of
the forensic linguist—a practitioner in the field of formal
analysis of the language used in the commission, investigation, and prosecution of crime. As varied as its subject matter, the forensic linguist's investigative tools have included
methods ranging from graphology (the procedure, now
often dismissed as pseudoscience though still in use, of
determining personality traits from handwriting samples)

to sophisticated word-frequency analysis, which can be used to establish a statistical likelihood of the authorship of a given document, based on the patterns in which words and phrases appear, and can also be used to make an educated guess as to the likelihood that a suspect under interrogation is telling the truth. Increasingly, forensic linguists have also turned their attention and analytic skills to the language used by the members of the legal system with whom the suspect becomes involved—the police, lawyers, and the judge.

THE SUSPECT SPEAKS

Language, spoken or written, is a key element in a wide variety of crimes—perjury and certain forms of solicitation, for example, typically involve speaking (as with Lewis "Scooter" Libby's "And I said, no, I didn't know that" to a grand jury, or the john's "Are you working?" to a streetwalker) while forgery and plagiarism (which may only get you an F on your term paper but may land you in court if your book has quietly borrowed material under copyright too freely) are typically done in silence. Kidnapping, blackmail, and bank robbery may involve both oral and written communication, as may threats of illegal activity or after-the-fact commentary by the perpetrator of that activity.

Kidnapping

The fatherless child is snatched from the breast; the infant of the poor is seized for a debt. (Job 24:9)

Kidnapping as a crime is as old as history, though the abduction of an individual solely for the purpose of extorting a ransom has only relatively recently come to prominence as a particularly heinous and alarming crime. (While *kidnapping* and *abduction* are often used interchangeably, like *murder* and *homicide,* there are some technical differences in meaning between the older Germanic form and its newer, more highfalutin Latinate stand-in, the differences between Anglo-Norman *ransom* and its Latinate cognate *redemption* being somewhat more wide-ranging.) Indeed, kidnapping had been considered a misdemeanor in the United States up until the sensational Lindbergh case in the 1930s.

For centuries, unlucky souls who were captured in warfare were typically kept as slaves or as bargaining chips. From the seventeenth through the nineteenth centuries, British warships were at least partially staffed by "pressed" men in what was essentially a legally authorized kidnapping. (Ironically, the verb *press,* from earlier *prest*—cognate with French *prêter* and Spanish *prestar* 'to lend'—originally referred to paying a man part of his wages in advance as an inducement to enlist for military service and only later took on the sense of forced employment.) The American version of this practice—*shanghaiing*—filled merchant ships with dazed new recruits until it was finally outlawed in 1915. In these cases, "crimps" (agents for labor-hungry ships' captains) would somehow render their mark unconscious (the mind reels) and then forge his signature on the ship's articles, so that legally he would have to remain on the ship until the voyage's end.

Women and young children, while exempt from involuntary naval service, ran other risks. Early New World anxieties, in addition to the fear of food shortages, disease, weather, and animal attacks, included the constant fear of Indian attack and abduction. In Mary Beth Norton's account of seventeenth-century Salem, *In the Devil's Snare,* this life of constant fear of abduction is given as one of the major sources of the community hysteria that led to the witchcraft panic and subsequent Salem witch trials. The fact that those who had been abducted didn't always wish to return home when subsequently given the opportunity (as described by John Demos in *The Unredeemed Captive*) was another matter of societal concern.

The fear of female and, especially, child abduction remained as an element of the social fabric well into the nineteenth century, receiving a sensational boost with the 1874 abduction of four-year-old "Little Charley Ross." Having lured the child with the promise of fireworks into a waiting horse-drawn wagon, the kidnappers sent the following handwritten note to the presumably wealthy boy's father:

July 3

Mr. Ross—be not uneasy you son charly bruster he al writ we as got him and no powers on earth can deliver out of our hand. You wil hav two pay us befor you git him from us. an pay us a big cent to. if you put the cops hunting for him yu is only defeeting yu own end. we is got him fitt so no living power can gits him from us a live. if any aproch is maid to his hidin place that is the signil for his instant anihilation. if yu regard his lif puts no one to search for him you money can fech him out alive an no other existin powers don't deceve yuself and think the detectives can git him from us for that is one imposebel yu here from us in few day

Over the next days, several other notes arrived requesting $20,000, a sum worth at least $400,000 in today's money. The patterns in the original note, and subsequent notes, reflect a structure still in use today:

- Announcement of abduction
- Assurance of safety of the abductee

- Threat that the abductee will come to danger or death if instructions are not complied with
- Admonishment not to involve the police or other authorities
- Demand that the control of all communications will rest with the kidnapper
- Demand for money or other object of value
- Elaborately detailed instructions (usually appearing in subsequent notes) for the delivery of the ransom
- Deliberate obfuscation of kidnappers' identity within the note itself (optional)

Christian Ross never saw his son again, spending an estimated $60,000 over several years and triggering a nationwide, frenzied, media-driven manhunt; only one man, thought to be only peripherally connected with the case, was brought to trial. In addition to being the first sensationalized kidnapping for cash, several other firsts (or at least firsts on a national scale) are notable in this groundbreaking case:

- National media coverage of nearly every detail and speculation, including editorial speculation on the meaning of the case
- Distribution of millions of flyers with images of the victim at the time of the kidnapping, followed by periodic "age progression" renderings of the victim as he might have appeared at the time of the current flyer
- View of the parents as victims in the crime, becoming characters in the ongoing media narrative
- Publication of a best-selling book by one of the parents about the experience, together with the concern that the child, if alive and recovered, might be changed to the point of nonrecognition—"not my son"

- Claims by various adult men over the years to be the abducted child now grown up.

A rash of what would today be called "copycat" kidnappings followed "little Charley's" abduction, but it wasn't until 1924 that the nation witnessed a kidnapping that would be termed the "Crime of the Century." Two wealthy teenagers, Nathan Freudenthal Leopold, Jr., and Richard A. Loeb, planned a kidnapping as "the perfect crime," which they, with their superior intellect, could successfully bring off where so many others had failed. However, despite their bulging intellects, the crime became a cock-up almost from the start, with Leopold dropping his custom eyeglasses at the scene of the crime, the rapid discovery of the child's body before the family could even respond to the ransom note, and a quick confession following a short interrogation. The role of forensics was significant in the apprehension and conviction of the two perpetrators, specifically regarding the analysis of the ransom note, which was typed (rather than handwritten, though the typing was identified as that of a hunt-and-peck typist) and whose language betokened an educated writer (though parallels in structure and content with a ransom note in a recent short story in the pulp magazine *Detective Story Magazine* suggested a reader with questionable tastes in literature). Locating the typewriter on which the note had been written helped seal the prosecution's case.

The next "Crime of the Century" would come just eight years later in what H. L. Mencken would call "the biggest story since the Resurrection," the kidnapping of the Lindbergh baby. Like the note in the Charley Ross case, the initial Lindbergh ransom note was rife with errors:

Dear Sir,

Have 50,000$ redy 25000$ in 20$ bills 15000$ in
10$ bills and 10000$ in 5$ bills. After 2–4 days will
inform you were to deliver the Mony.

We warn you for making anyding public or for
notify the Polise the child is in gut care.

Indication for all letters are signature and 3
holds.

Forensic analysis of this and the kidnapper's subsequent
notes was undertaken in an effort to discover the kidnapper's identity. The numerous consistencies in spelling in the
notes led the investigators to conclude that they had been
written by the same person. Once they had their suspect,
Bruno Richard Hauptmann, in custody, an analysis by several handwriting experts of his orthographic and spelling
skills found that there were numerous differences between
Hauptmann's writing and the ransom notes. However,
despite a lack of adherence to the state's own handwriting analysis protocol, a series of other handwriting experts
convinced the jury that Hauptmann had written the notes
(despite his testimony that he had been beaten by the police
and forced to change his handwriting so that it matched the
ransom note).

The jury was apparently also unskeptical when Lindbergh himself testified that he could positively identify as
Hauptmann's the stranger's voice he had heard utter the
six words "Hey Doctor, over here, over here." at a distance
of 100 feet in the dark several years before the suspect's
capture. Today, as Solan and Tiersma point out, a forensic
linguist would be required to testify as to the statistical likelihood that a given document could be identified as having been written by "John" when compared to documents

created by two other suspects, "Bill" and "Rudy," and Lindberg's claimed ability to identify a stranger's voice, briefly heard—once, several years in the past—would surely be dismissed as a near impossibility.

It's hard to imagine today the social and popular impact the Lindbergh case held in the public mind. Concern over a possible epidemic of kidnapping and reports of the involvement of organized crime even brought Al Capone into the act: From his prison cell, he offered a large reward and his own services to solve the case. In a time before twenty-four-hour news networks, news of the case of the "first baby of the land" dramatically increased sales of newspapers that often went into multiple editions during that trial. The first baby monitor, the "Radio Nurse," and its matching transmitter, the "Guardian Ear," were commercially introduced in the wake of the hysteria, not only to monitor the child's health but also to listen for baby-snatching in the next room.

Blackmail

Originally, *blackmail* referred to tribute paid to Highland chiefs for protection against plunderers (possibly in the chiefs' employ), and it has usually included the physical threat of violence. As we know it today, blackmail comes in three basic flavors:

- False entrapment confidence game. A good example would be the "badger" game. This is basically an extortion scheme, usually a one-time con with a married man as the "mark" who is tricked into a compromising position to make him vulnerable to blackmail. In a common scenario, a man brings a woman back to his hotel room, and a couple of minutes later her "husband" bursts into the room, threatening violence but settling for cash. As with a "Stick-'em-up" street mugging, the transaction is strictly oral.

- Blackmail from coconspirator. Here, the victim has committed a criminal act with another but has more to lose than his compatriot if the crime is exposed. A couple of classic examples: A married man visits a prostitute and is threatened with exposure; a wealthy gentleman in Victorian England has a chance, possibly sexual, encounter with a man in a lower social class and is threatened with exposure. In the first case, the man could risk his marriage and his social position. In the second case, depending on the year, exposure could mean the gallows on the mere testimony of the second man. Blackmail in both cases could continue for years. In theory, both blackmailers face risk, since they have taken part in a crime as well. But in the first case, the petty prosecution can be considered the acceptable risk of the prostitution racket, and in the second case, the younger man of a lower social class could argue that the gentleman, who should know better (having a superior education and birth), had corrupted an innocent.

- Blackmail from third party, the most familiar scenario, in which an uninvolved person has knowledge of a criminal or embarrassing activity in which the victim has engaged. For example, an accountant discovers embezzlement by a coworker or superior and threatens exposure. In this case, the blackmailer's exposure of the case might result in acclaim or even promotion. The blackmail threat in such cases may be written or oral.

In all blackmail cases involving notes, the notes passed may not (if the blackmailer is smart) spell out the crime, but instead rely on implication, veiled threats, and indications of serious demands:

that money I ask for is nothing to u

The foregoing note was a cell phone text message: The recipient was a successful Boston businessman and the blackmailer a prostitute threatening exposure with increasingly higher demands for cash. In this contemporary case, the prosecution allowed the businessman to retain his anonymity in exchange for cooperation on the case, essentially turning the blackmailer's game on its head: The risk of complete public exposure had been removed.

Legally, the crime of extortion is distinguished from blackmail. In blackmail, the blackmailer threatens to do something that would be legal or normally allowed, for example, exposing a crime to the police. In extortion, the threat is essentially illegal, for example, physical violence or a threat to a person's property. Extortion is also technically different from robbery: With extortion the threat is promised, whereas with robbery it is realized. With extortion the threat can be in a written message, which, if the mode of transfer could potentially be considered "interstate commerce" (mail, e-mail, telephone, etc.), would make the crime a federal offense. Interestingly, the message need only be sent to be considered a crime, since the receipt of the threat is not actually legally required, a moot point in the case of the bank robber, whose note to the teller is always hand-delivered.

BANK ROBBERY

Regardless of what we've seen in the movies or on television, the vast majority of bank robberies do not involve crazed

gangs of masked gunmen, cool tuxedo-wearing international con men, precision tunneling teams dressed in black
turtlenecks and matching watch caps, or even passionate
revolutionaries striving for a new world order. Such things
do exist, but these days upwards of 90 percent of bank jobs,
as they are called, are committed, often on the spur of the
moment, using what the FBI calls "demand notes." Most
demand notes are written on the spot, in the bank, usually
with intentionally startling brevity:

give me the money or die

This note was the handiwork of the aptly titled "money or
die bandit" who committed a string of robberies in Los
Angeles, netting anywhere from $40 to $9,000 each time.
He never showed a gun, his note being considered as good
as his word.

Outside of murder, bank robbery is the crime with the
highest percentage of successful prosecutions, not because
of fancy electronic surveillance or dedicated police work
(although those certainly contribute), but because "note
jobs" are so easy and so lucrative, and, as with potato chips,
thieves can't stop at just one: If it worked once, why change
anything? Most thieves are totally monogamous with what
works—the same note, outfit, time of day, etc.

Since the average take is relatively small—these "one-on-
one" robberies, as the pros call them, bring in an average
of five thousand dollars—most banks shrug them off as a
minor cost of doing business, along with lousy free coffee
and rain bonnets. If a bank guard costs $30,000 a year, it
would take a lot of note jobs to justify the expense.

Since most notes are hastily written, there can be confu-
sion. Like the "I have a gub" scene in Woody Allen's classic
Take the Money and Run, cases of misunderstanding abound.
One bandit, whose first language was clearly not English,

had so much trouble making both his note and himself understood that he gave up, only to try another bank later on the same day; this time he evidently took his time crafting the demand note and was at last successful.

There are occasions in which demand notes take on the relative length and complexity of a Russian novel. Typewritten multipage notes with stories of hard luck and remorse must leave the teller wishing for the "money or die" bandit. Some robbers even write follow-up letters to the local paper extending an apology.

Most notes threaten violence:

> This is a robbery, don't make it a murder
> ...@least $1,000...My guns are very real, keep it str8. Business as usual, Right...?
> $2500.00 dollars in cash, $20 dollar bills only or someone behind me dies...and no dye packs.
> Give me all the money now and no (one) will get hurt! Love me

In this fast food of crime, nervous crooks need the entire event to be over in less than two minutes (the average response time after the teller has pressed the silent alarm for the police), hoping the robbery appears to be a normal transaction. Haste can lead to less striking notes:

> give me the mony, bicth
> 10's and 20's only

Since the note is often the only physical evidence left at the scene, other than surveillance footage, some learned crooks have taken to enclosing the notes in a clear zippered bank bag or a pencil case with a clear plastic window, or demanding the note's return:

> $20,000 cash or someone dies and return the note.

Sometimes the haste of the crime results in a quick apprehension, as in the case of a robber in Englewood, Colorado,
who wrote the demand note on his own check, or the one
who failed to notice the policeman behind him in line. One
reason for this inattention in a large number of note jobs
is that they are committed repeatedly by addicts, which is
also why Friday is the busiest day in the bank for robbers as
well as regular patrons. If one is feeding a habit, it can be a
long time until Monday morning, the other red-letter day
for robbery.

The dramatic rise of the note job, of which there are
thousands every year in cities such as Los Angeles and
Atlanta, means that such a robbery is pulled every few minutes. Social scientists, economists, and law enforcement
experts have their own theories to explain this increase. It
is said that the spread of branch locations and expanded
hours has, ironically, made banking more convenient for
crooks and customers alike. In addition, the increased use
of credit cards has meant that stores and potential mugging victims are less and less likely to have wads of cash on
hand. And, as one might guess, there is a direct correlation
between the unemployment rate and the rise or fall of the
note job.

Since most banks consider bank guards a poor investment
and since other surveillance methods such as high-definition
cameras, while they can help to catch the crooks, don't often
recover the cash (the recovery rate is less than 20 percent),
a new approach has been developed to meet the impulse-
shopper nature of the typical note job. A new counter-crim-
inal strategy, developed by the Seattle FBI office, is called
"Safecatch" and relies on the "neutral confrontation" of
"customer service on steroids." If a customer walks into your
bank on a hot summer day with a heavy overcoat, hooded
sweatshirt, and sunglasses, a customer service representative

would offer to help him with his banking needs and escort him to the first open teller window. Our casual thief finds this attention a little too unsettling and decides to get four quarters for a dollar instead of walking out of the bank with a quick four grand. Initial results of this approach in Seattle have indicated a 70 percent drop in note jobs.

MAD BOMBERS

A kidnapping, blackmail, or bank robbery typically involves a rather small cast of characters. Acts of terrorism, whatever their motivation, tend to involve larger numbers of participants, especially among the victims, actual or intended, and often involve communication before or after the fact by the perpetrator(s). Such communication can prove critically useful in the identification and apprehension of a terrorist.

George Metesky, known as the Mad Bomber, was a case in point. Metesky was a factory worker who was injured in an explosion at a New York Consolidated Edison generating plant in 1931. After twenty-six weeks on sick leave recovering from pneumonia exacerbated by tuberculosis, he filed for workers' compensation but was denied it because he waited too long to file the claim. He appealed his case for the next five years without success, developing a burning resentment against the Consolidated Edison company. For the next sixteen years he built and detonated crude gunpowder pipe bombs that he made in his garage workshop, the first at a Consolidated Edison power plant with an attached note (handwritten in block letters):

CON EDISON CROOKS, THIS IS FOR YOU.

This device may have been an intentional dud, since the note was attached to the bomb itself. (As Ewing and

McCann put it, "Investigators found it curious that the bomber would have attached a note to his device since, had the bomb gone off, the note most likely would have been destroyed.") What unfolded over the next sixteen years was a correspondence of sorts between Metesky and the society that had wronged him. He wrote to the police and to newspapers, even making telephone calls to the buildings where he had planted bombs. By the time he was apprehended, he had planted at least thirty-three bombs, twenty-two of which exploded, injuring a total of fifteen people.

The patriotic Metesky did take a break during the war:

I WILL MAKE NO MORE BOMB UNITS FOR THE DURATION OF THE WAR—MY PATRIOTIC FEEL-INGS HAVE MADE ME DECIDE THIS—LATER I WILL BRING THE CON EDISON TO JUSTICE—THEY WILL PAY FOR THEIR DASTARDLY DEEDS...F.P.

This note, incidentally, was not, like most of his other written communications, handwritten in block capitals, but rather consisted of letters cut from a newspaper and pasted together to form the message, a tried-and-true (if labor-intensive) format for anonymous threats whose demise might have been assured with the steady rise of the cost of newsprint and the migration of the news to the Internet were it not for the wealth of Web applications that have sprung up to allow you to generate such notes at the keyboard (figure 5.1). While he didn't blow up anything between 1941 and 1951, Metesky faithfully kept up a crank letter-writing campaign, mostly handwritten in his characteristic block printing.

Police knew they were dealing with someone who had a grudge against Con Edison, had machinist's skills (evidenced by the sophistication of the unexploded bombs, not to mention the fine motor skills he had to employ in

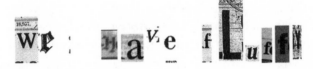

Figure 5.1

cutting out and gluing all those newspaper letters), and was of possible European origin (evidenced by features of his handwriting). Most bombs were placed, enclosed in a woolen sock, in public locations such as movie theaters and train stations. Police formed a special new group, the Bomb Investigation Unit, and sent photographs of the bomber's notes to anyone who might recognize the script. They also began to develop a portrait of the bomber, going outside the force to work with Dr. James Brussel, a criminologist and psychiatrist from the New York State Commission for Mental Hygiene. After an analysis of crime scenes and the bomber's letters, Brussel and the police put together what would now be called a "profile" and even predicted that when the bomber would be arrested, he would be wearing a double-breasted suit.

Brussel urged the police, against their better judgment, to publicize the profile by passing it to New York newspapers, hoping to provoke a response from the bomber:

Single man, between 40 and 50 years old, introvert. Unsocial but not anti-social. Skilled mechanic. Cunning. Neat with tools. Egotistical of mechanical skill. Contemptuous of other people. Resentful of criticism of his work but probably conceals resentment. Moral. Honest. Not interested in women. High school graduate. Expert in civil or military ordnance. Religious. Might flare up violently at work when criticized. Possible motive: discharge or reprimand. Feels superior

to critics. Resentment keeps growing. Present or former Consolidated Edison worker. Probably case of
progressive paranoia.

While this led to an epidemic of false bomb scares and false
confessions, shortly after the profile appeared in the news
Metesky rose to the bait, sending a series of letters to the
New York Journal-American, to which the paper responded by
asking the bomber to provide more details so that a fair
hearing of his grievances could be held. Amazingly, Metesky
complied, providing details of his failed workman's compensation claim, even including the date of his accident,
September 5, 1931: "My medical bills and care have cost
thousands—I did not get a single penny for a lifetime of
misery and suffering." Alice Kelly, a clerk at Con Edison,
sifted through old files of worker's compensation cases
and found a file describing an employee who had worked
at Edison from 1929 to 1931 before being injured in an
industrial accident on September 5, 1931. Crank letters
in the old file used language similar to the letters in the
Journal-American, including the unusual phrase "dastardly
deeds." Kelly contacted the police with her research, and
Metesky was arrested shortly before midnight the next day
after being asked to write a capital "G." Changing out of
his pajamas into a double-breasted suit, he was taken to
the police station. He was subsequently determined by the
court to be a paranoid schizophrenic and was committed
to the Matteawan Hospital for the Criminally Insane, from
which he was finally released in 1973. While considered by
his doctors to be harmless, Metesky still held his grudge
against Con Edison:

> I wrote 900 letters to the Mayor, to the Police Com-
> missioner, to the newspapers, and I never even got a
> penny postcard back. Then I went to the newspapers

to try to buy advertising space, but all of them turned me down. I was compelled to bring my story to the public.

He returned to his home in Waterbury, Connecticut, and died twenty years later at the age of 90, not quite two years before the arrest of the so-called Unabomber, who had carried the torch, so to speak, from 1978 to 1995 as the country's reigning Mad Bomber, a story too long to tell here aside from noting that it was largely on the basis of the language of the Unabomber's "Manifesto" that he was finally identified and apprehended.

POLICE LANGUAGE

On the other side of the law, police have historically tried to apply scientific methods and hard-won experience in their use of language to bring about a uniform system of clear, accurate, and standardized communication. Police need to be able to communicate clearly and be careful when listening when taking evidence and to retain that information in a standardized format so that other police can work on the same crime without confusion; to communicate information to the general public by, for example, creating "wanted" descriptions that a layman could find helpful; and ultimately to be clear, precise, and effective in the courtroom. And it is from police reports that local newspapers write their "Off the Blotter" columns, possibly the equal in popularity of their "Speak Out" and obituary sections.

The goal of clarity can be elusive, as suggested by some of the translations of Police Talk to Standard English proposed by Val Van Brocklin in her article, "Cops Talk Funny and It's Hurting Their Credibility in Court":

- I ascertained the location of the residence…I found the house
- I observed the subject fleeing on foot from the location…I saw him running away
- I apprehended the perpetrator…I arrested the man

Nevertheless, the quest for clarity in the language of law enforcement reflects a history in which police investigation has struggled to approach scientific rigor. At the dawn of the professional police force, investigation and prosecution relied largely on eyewitness testimony for the description of the suspect, which could be wildly unreliable. Enter Alphonse Bertillon (1853–1914), a French police officer and researcher who created "anthropometry," a system by which an individual could be uniquely described by precisely measured body features (with particular attention to those of the head and face)—a sort of nineteenth-century DNA test—supplemented by a verbal description and photographs (prototypical "mug shots," though Bertillon himself was skeptical about the reliability of photographic documentation, in part because a photograph does not account for aging, which is not a consideration in, say, the dimensions of an adult's cranium). He termed the resulting description a *portrait parlé* ('spoken portrait').

Bertillon's intention was to promulgate a universal standard language that could be used by law enforcement personnel to identify criminals (specifically, recidivists, who were thought to be especially dangerous), putting the criminal's description on file, indexed by feature. That every person arrested should be photographed and systematically identified for a database that could be referenced later, and that a classification system would create easy index searching, are principles still in practice in every modern police system.

Wanted Posters

When you need to involve police in other areas or engage the general public to locate a fugitive, you'll want to make the best use of your space and to employ a language of description that ordinary people can understand. With luck, there exists a set of standardized mug shots and a recent description of the subject, or if no photo exists, a facial composite, an artist's rendering of eyewitness descriptions from memory. In this age of constant surveillance, digital images of reasonable quality, and even movies, are available for release to other law enforcement personnel or the general public, often via television news.

Nostalgia has resurrected the American Wild West poster, but these were often the product of private companies offering rewards, such as the Pinkerton National Detective Agency, usually shortened to "Pinkertons." During the rapid expansion of the country, agencies like the Pinkertons were hired by banks, railroads, and other wronged corporate entities to provide protection at a time when little could be guaranteed by the national, state, or local government. The Pinkertons staff at one point was larger than the standing army of the United States of America, and as a result, the state of Ohio outlawed the agency in the fear it could serve as a private army or militia. Typically, an agency's wanted posters (called "circulars" by Pinkerton) would list first and prominently the reward value, with a photo or drawing of the criminal, details of the crime or crimes, a detailed standard description (age, height, build, hair color, facial features, eye color, and any distinguishing characteristics like scars, tattoos, prominent limp, typical modes of dress, etc.), country of origin, and local contact information.

The first case of a "composite" image used in a wanted poster appeared in England in 1881. Percy Lefroy Mapleton, who became known as the "railway murderer," was identified and captured as the result of the dissemination in the *Daily Telegraph* and on wanted posters of an image created on the basis of eyewitness testimony (someone who knew Mapleton personally). Artist's composites are still in use on wanted posters when a photographic image of the person sought is not available.

Nowadays, the hard-copy wanted poster, once a fixture in American post offices, is being supplanted by its online variant. In a trip to a local post office in the Boston area, we were told that wanted posters were kept in the back because they "cluttered up" the customer area. Currently cluttering up the Internet are large numbers of sites dedicated to the dissemination of endless categories of posters. Like most things on the Internet, there's something for every taste. The kings of online wanted posters have a long history of the traditional variety. These are the FBI and the U.S. Marshals Service, and both offer almost endless variety of sorting (Ten Most Wanted, Most Wanted Terrorists, Crime Alerts, Featured Fugitives, Kidnappings and Missing Persons, Parental Kidnappings, Unknown Bank Robbers, etc.). The FBI's famous "Ten Most Wanted" list compilation starts with a list of suspects provided by local field offices. To make the big list, one must be considered both particularly dangerous and a person whose chances of apprehension would be increased by the publicity attendant on list membership. Once on the top ten list, you'll stay there until you are caught, have the charges against you dropped, or become somehow determined no longer to be a public menace. The FBI claims a high capture rate of those on the list, although six of the ten on the current list have been on the top ten since the '80s and '90s.

Many smaller agencies have gotten into the act, offering their own wanted lists, which may feature descriptions not only of fugitives but of the missing, especially children, who receive wider attention through television clips, milk cartons, supermarkets, billboards, and now the multichannel AMBER (America's Missing: Broadcasting Emergency Response) alert system, which uses an existing weather alert system to transmit a unified message quickly over commercial and satellite radio, television, e-mail, electronic traffic-condition signs, and billboards with electronic functions. The messages are short and standardized: the name and description of the abductee and, if possible, a description of the suspect, plus a description and license plate number of the suspect's vehicle. This system has been widely praised for its timeliness in situations such as stranger abduction (which, when they involve a murder, do so within three hours 75 percent of the time), though the system is not without its critics who claim that most of the recoveries are from estranged parents rather than the child-killing strangers from whom the system was set up to save the children.

Perhaps the most successful attempt to publicize and capture criminals is one of the longest-running television programs, *America's Most Wanted,* whose "Watch Television, Catch Criminals" premise claims to have captured more than 1,000 criminals. Its low-budget approach with fuzzy reenactments of the crimes and the "dirty dozen" top fugitives have given the show respectable ratings since its premiere in 1988. While its initial focus of tracking missing children has expanded to include all criminal activity, the structure of the show, with a narrative of the case, a reenactment of the crime, and a profile of the suspect, has remained a staple. The show has also spawned many local versions (*Wisconsin's Most Wanted,* for example) and offshore versions such as *India's Most Wanted.*

A local DYI variant of the wanted or missing person poster is the notice of the lost pet. Seen on many an urban or suburban street corner, these posters are handmade, often hand-drawn (though personal computing has raised the form to an art), offering an attention-grabbing headline ("Lost Cat," "Reward!"), a brief narrative describing the time and place of the disappearance, often a photo, a description of the pet ("answers to 'here kitty, kitty, kitty'"), an indication of the heartsick nature of the family at their loss (optional), contact information, and often a promise of a cash reward. Sometimes these posters survive the elements and last for several years, but inclement weather often takes its toll.

You can also seek your lost pet (or wallet, or car keys) through other media. For example, the classified version of the lost and found has existed since the advent of the newspaper. The history of the lost and found reflects the social history of the time—items lost in battle, runaway slaves, items lost in overland travel, lost relatives separated during a family's emigration, lost or strayed cattle, lost children, young women abducted and feared sold into white slavery (though, as often as not, such women proved to have simply eloped, to Dad's displeasure).

The newspaper's classified ad has been seeing hard times recently, from both recessionary conditions and the popularity of online modes of classified advertising, primarily craigslist.org. At one time, classified ad revenue contributed anywhere from 20 to 40 percent of total newspaper revenues. The contemporary online version offers free listings for most postings, and your missing long-haired calico can be online in a matter of minutes.

Who's Who

Part of the problem with finding people is in finding the right person. Misidentification has been shown to be the leading cause of wrongful imprisonment cases subsequently overturned by DNA evidence. Eyewitness identification remains a problematic central part of determining whom to arrest and whom to convict: Pressure on witnesses for a positive ID of someone briefly seen at a distance under less than ideal conditions can be strong, and widespread dissemination of a description, however accurate, has resulted in many mistaken identifications, some well meaning and others nefarious. Fingerprinting has been in practice for well over a hundred years, first in India and the United States, as a means of uniquely identifying individuals, often to sort out immigrants as well as criminals. Widely considered an unimpeachable form of identification, its success rate has many variables in the human side: the taking of the prints, the recovering of prints at a crime scene, and the manual comparison of the prints, all of which can introduce error and uncertainty. Errors in identification and clerical errors have resulted in the overturning of a number of convictions that were based at least partially on fingerprint evidence.

Still, fingerprinting remains an inexpensive and popular method of identification, leading many parents to have their child fingerprinted preemptively in local community-sponsored events (Print-A-Thon, Thumbbuddy) where your children's safety can be guarded in a "high energy child safety event." Criticism of the construction and maintenance of a large database of information on ordinary citizens has been largely nullified by the desire for safety. DNA databases such as the Combined DNA Index System (CODIS) have followed the structure of the automated fingerprint identification mechanisms commonly used since the 1980s.

Indeed, it was a fingerprint that proved key in establishing the true identity of the focus of a recent case of parental kidnapping. The man who gave his name as "Clark Rockefeller" on his arrest for kidnapping his daughter during a parental visit turned out to have used so many assumed

identities during his life that it took authorities some time
to determine his actual identity with complete certainty.
Prior to that time, the *Boston Globe*, in "1 Man, 3,629 Lies,"
offered a summary:

> Yale at 14. Friendships with Britney and Helmut Kohl.
> Aristocratic bloodlines. The man who called him-
> self Clark Rockefeller—expected to stand trial this
> spring—concocted incredible stories and displayed a
> stunning ability to keep a ruse going. Here, we lay out
> the best of his tall tales.
>
> . . .
>
> My Names
>   –Christian Gerhart Reiter
>   –Chris Kenneth Gerhart
>   –Christopher Chichester
>   –Christopher Crowe
>   –Christopher Mountbatten Crowe
>   –Clark Mill Rockefeller
>   –James Frederick
>   –Michael Brown
>   –Charles "Chip" Smith
>
> My Family Ties
>   –I am Christopher Chichester XIII, that is, 13th
> baronet.
>   –I'm a descendant of Sir Francis Chichester, who
> sailed around the world in his ketch Gipsy Moth IV
> in the 1960s.
>   –I'm a descendant of Lord Mountbatten, the Brit-
> ish naval officer.
>   –My mother is the child star Ann Carter, known for
> her starring role opposite Humphrey Bogart in *The
> Two Mrs. Carrolls*.

Eventually, a fingerprint on an application for a stockbroker's license in the name of Chris Chichester matched those of the man the print media had taken to referring to as "'Clark Rockefeller'" or "'Rockefeller'" (as in "'Rockefeller' Print Linked to Stockbroker Application") and a German national named Christian Gerhart Streiter. Mystery solved.

6

IN THE NEWS

All That's Fit to Print, and Then Some

"NEWS! NEWS!" SINGS AMERICA'S THIRTY-SEVENTH president in John Adams's opera *Nixon in China*—as well he might, given the spectacular media opportunity enjoyed by the real Nixon in his unprecedented meeting with Mao Zedong in Beijing in 1971. The speeches, the theatrical performances, the banquets, the toasts, the mutual pledges of friendship were all pounced upon and covered in exhaustive detail by the press corps and reported to an eager public on the airwaves and in print.

The news can make or break a public figure's career, as amply demonstrated with the downfall and resignation of that same president just a few years later when the Watergate scandal broke. A major factor in his administration's implosion was the gavel-to-gavel broadcasts, on public television stations, of the Senate Select Committee's hearings into criminal acts by Nixon's henchmen (incidentally propelling into national fame a hitherto relatively obscure good-ole-boyish Southern senator named Sam Ervin).

But this was a notable exception to a general rule: News as reported is almost always a highly concentrated condensation of reality, for air time and column inches are expensive, even when amortized over a large audience. A 125-word public service announcement for radio broadcast, for example, takes just about a full minute to read over the air—roughly the amount that will fit on a 3-by-5-inch index card—while a newspaper story 12 column inches long runs to about 500 words, the approximate equivalent of a page of single-spaced typescript, the limit of what most of us can read before our minds start to wander unless we are really concentrating. As the features editor of a New England daily once told us, "Space is real estate."

"But *is* it news?" the same editor would often ask. That is, is the narrative a reasonably accurate description, from a trustworthy source, of a recent development, or at least of one that has only recently come to light? Technologies of travel and communications are the handmaidens of getting the word out. In 500 B.C.E., a good road and a system of way stations with relays of fast horses enabled the Persian kings to send dispatches in just nine days from their imperial capital, Susa, to Sardis, on the Aegean coast of Asia Minor—a distance of more than 1,600 miles at an average speed ten times that of a marching army.

This speed of long-distance communication would be occasionally imitated but never surpassed for over two thousand years (it was matched only by the Pony Express in the early 1860s) until the Industrial Revolution fostered the creation of networks first of railroads and then of telegraphy, including the first viable transatlantic cable in 1866. (The original cable completed in 1857 repeatedly snapped; it took another nine years of trial and error to get one that worked reliably.) Before then, news from across the Atlantic could take as much as a month to arrive by boat. The War of 1812 had officially ended in the Treaty of Ghent on December 24, 1814, but since nobody in Louisiana knew yet, British and American troops went ahead and slugged it out at the battle of New Orleans on January 8, 1815, more than two weeks later. Even the news of Lincoln's assassination took twelve days from the shots at Ford's Theater to the eyes of newspaper readers in Europe.

But already the telegraph was changing all that—news of Lincoln's death reached California in minutes through this medium. Because business firms generally try to take advantage of knowing about distant events before their competitors do, Paul Julius Reuter had already pounced on a golden opportunity in 1849 by bridging a gap between the end of one telegraph line and the beginning of another with a flock of carrier pigeons; when the gap was finally wired through, he relocated his firm to England and began using the new Calais-to-Dover cable to coordinate information from the stock markets in Paris and London, soon expanding his coverage to general news as well. To this day Reuters retains a generous share of the world wire-service market.

So does Associated Press, founded in 1848 by a consortium of ten newspaper editors who pooled reporting as a more cost-effective alternative to having ten reporters lined up at the telegraph office, each waiting to file essentially the same story to their respective papers. Wire services would play a vital role in disseminating reports on such events as the explosion of Mt. Krakatoa in 1883, the news of which was received by the underwriting house of Lloyd's in London just three hours after the catastrophe itself. The swap for speed was terseness, and sometimes stories fleshed out from fragmentary first reports would have to be revised in later editions, such as the initial cables about the sinking of the *Titanic,* when it was still believed that most of the passengers had survived.

Even today, with all-but-instant communications through e-mail, satellite networks, and cell phones, the tradeoff remains: If it is to be truly news it must cover current events that really are current, yet reporting in haste guarantees at least a risk of error. Former owner of the *Washington Post* Philip Graham was not far off the mark in calling newspaper reporting "the first rough draft of history." News reports have the cachet of being fresh from the scene, in a way that a professional historian's carefully weighed and multisourced account may not, but they are also manifestly *positioned* knowledge reflecting a particular time, place, and individual perspective, which is why newspaper editors are forever cautioning reporters to triangulate a story (i.e., talk to at least three sources, or two others if an eyewitness oneself, whenever humanly possible). It has been said that news is to short-term memory as history to long-term memory; the analogy is by no means far-fetched.

Is the news true? One difference between news—the reporting of events in real time—and history—the reporting of events viewed in retrospect—is that we tend to expect the latter to be scrupulously accurate as a matter of course—making allowance for the writer's bias, to be sure: A Southerner's *History of the War Between the States* and a Yankee's *Memoirs of the Civil War* might reasonably be expected to embody different perspectives even on identical incidents. But we are less likely to ask "Did these events actually take place?" By contrast, we expect our news only to be *substantially* true, possibly needing details to be tweaked after the fact (whence the corrections box usually found on page 2 of the front section); that is the bargain we're willing to make for having the news be current and thus satisfy "the thursty desyer that all our kynde hath to knowe," as William Patten nicely put it.

Even the names of newspapers often allude to traditional means of satisfying this appetite: *Miami Herald, New York Observer, San Francisco Oracle, Exchange Intelligencer, Hartford*

Courant, Daily Mail, Washington Post, Philadelphia Bulletin, Telegraph and Texas Register, Maine Sunday Telegram, Boston Transcript. Newspapers will be the primary focus of the rest of this chapter, despite the fact that they are considered by many people in and out of the news industry to be an endangered species: They are a familiar genre, and each issue of one offers a rich variety of short forms worthy of analysis.

WHAT'S IN THE NEWS (AND WHO CARES)?

We take it for granted that we know what news is: It's what's on the front page of our daily paper, and for some pages beyond. National and international stories usually carry a wire-service dateline saying where and when the story was filed, and sometimes a writer's byline as well (though this is much commoner, however, for state and local stories). Many news stories follow a set pyramidal pattern that goes into increasing detail as one gets farther down the page or past the *jump* ("Continued on page A5"), which allows editors to cut from the bottom as space constraints may dictate. (There are other patterns as well, however, such as the "hourglass.") Generally, national and global stories run in the first section of a daily paper and local news in the second. Weekly newspapers tend to cover local news almost to the exclusion of statewide stories, let alone national and international ones, the assumption being that one will get that sort of news somewhere else (radio, TV, or the nearest city's daily).

Closely related to news as such are feature stories; these are nearly always bylined (as are news analysis stories, something of a hybrid between straight news reporting and features). Here too there is a set pattern, most such stories starting with a catchy *lede* (the first paragraph, so spelled to disambiguate from the *lead* used to cast type in a linotype machine) to grab the reader's attention, the actual topic statement coming two or three paragraphs down in what is called the *nut graf.* Some features conclude with a *shirtsleeve,* a tag sentence saying something about the writer. ("Weaver-in-Residence Ælfreda Tidd writes her weekly column from the East Presumpscot Sheep Park.")

The news/features dichotomy owes much to the introduction in the early twentieth century of what were then called the "women's pages," newspaper publishers having discovered that women wanted to read newspapers too and could be expressly targeted for advertising in a section devoted to their concerns. Food columns, society columns, bridge columns, and other specialty content flourished, with comics for the small fry for good measure. (There had, to be sure, been comics for several decades before, such as Windsor McKay's *Yellow Kid,* and political cartoons for more than a century before that.)

Whether news or features, every newspaper story runs under a headline; indeed *in the headlines* is another way of saying that an event is newsworthy and getting the press exposure it deserves. Headlines are a highly compressed form of communication, particularly for a tabloid given to very large type for the headline of its front-page top story. Perhaps the extreme was reached when an exclusive if slightly blurred photo of a woman's execution in Sing Sing's electric chair, taken on the sly by a reporter with a miniature camera strapped to his sock, ran in a Manhattan daily under the immense single-word headline *DEAD!* While most headlines are not as terse as that, the ambiguous syntax imposed by space constraints mean that ludicrous gaffes can and do occur: "Squad Helps Dog Bite Victim," "Truck Leads Police to Molest Suspect" (there wasn't enough room to print "molestation"), "Panda Lectures This Week at National Zoo," "Police Stop Slaying Suspect Look-Alikes." Indeed, such howlers are so plentiful that the *Columbia Journalism*

Review has a regular department devoted to them, called "The Lower Case," on the inside back cover of each issue.

So what else is in the newspaper, besides "news" per se?

Editorial Pages

Here will be found the house editorials giving the paper's unsigned official position on issues of the day, as well as signed opinion pieces, often by syndicated columnists and not infrequently in pairs, one liberal and one not, on the "op-ed" page facing the in-house editorials. Here also will run letters to the editor (usually limited to a couple of hundred words and edited at the newspaper's discretion), and at least one editorial cartoon (also usually syndicated; few dailies nowadays have the luxury of keeping a staff artist). Rarely do the editorial and op-ed pages exceed a double-page spread.

Speak Out/Gripe Columns

A quick-and-dirty analogue of letters to the editor. You call the newspaper's Gripe Line answering machine and record your gripe. The editors cherry-pick the best and publish them, usually without much tweaking beyond tidying up the grammar and eliminating the ums and ahs and the dirty words. Depending on the paper, sometimes these are included in the online version and sometimes not. Some papers encourage and print readers' responses to others' gripes as well. Firing short bursts of passionate intensity, this column is often the readers' favorite.

Sports

Gotta have sports. Gotta have tables with game scores and league standings, and lotsa pix. (Robert Ripley drew his first "Believe It or Not!" for the sports page of the daily he worked for.) Reporting style real down-to-earth and even a little hard-boiled. A gag now and then doesn't hurt. (Think Damon Runyon. Lousy outfielder, but boy could he write.)

Stock Pages

Like sports, a form of news with a lot of tables, enlivened with a business feature story or two thrown in. For the ordinary stockholder, yesterday's open, high, low, and close are recent enough news, but serious speculators can follow not just Wall Street but all the world's stock exchanges on the Internet instead. At the same time most newspapers have cut back on the space allotted to tabulations and now cover fewer markets. (As might be expected, *The Wall Street Journal* has bucked this trend.)

Art/Entertainment Previews and Reviews

News in the sense that the performance or exhibition being covered is or will be a current event in real time, and even books and recordings qualify on the grounds of being of recent issue, though the time scale is more generous than, say, for a concert. "Roundups" are common: omnibus theater or music columns previewing the coming week's events, usually compiled by distillation from the presenters' press releases. TV listings and columns (e.g., Tom Shales) go here as well, along with daily, weekly, and seasonal calendars of events (in effect, bare-bones roundups in tabular form).

Travel

Pago Pago. Mahi-mahi. Holoholo. Imagine a week somewhere, say in the vast Pacific, with a lot of empty beach, great rolling breakers, exotic reduplicative nouns, and cheap motorbike rental. Never mind that the next sand we're *actually* going to get between our toes is the Jersey Shore, renting that same ho-hum little bungalow as last time—reading the travel section and daydreaming over the luscious pictures of faraway places allows us to put ourselves, for a few blissfully escapist minutes at least, in the places of the lucky stiffs who can actually afford to go there. More modest offerings feature domestic destinations and even day trips (e.g., the Newark *Star-Ledger*'s "Trip on a Tankful" columns). Sidebars abound in this genre, giving nuts-and-bolts details about directions, reservations, price ranges, and so forth.

The Police Blotter

Although technically falling under local news, police blotter columns differ from ordinary news reporting in their eclecticism; they tend to be both terse and formulaic, just a little less so than the legal notices—though unlike deed transfer notices and probate or divorce court actions, the information is already old news to those most affected by it (defendants, plaintiffs, their attorneys, and people working for the justice system). Rather, such a column plays to our schadenfreude: The ordinary reader is pleased that it's happening to someone else, while indulging an appetite for vicarious drama (and reading yet more evidence that the world is going to the dogs, tsk tsk), tickled now and then by deadpan items such as the following, from the *Ellsworth* (Maine) *American*'s Bucksport police correspondent: "A suspected dead body in the Penobscot River June 27 turned out to be a blue bucket." Some papers (e.g., the *Watertown* [Mass.] *Tab & Press*) print a map above the police report, keyed by number to the items in it to show where in town each one happened.

Gossip Columns

Hedda Hopper's first column for the *Los Angeles Times* was published in February of 1938, and she would go on to have a radio version of it as well that was on the airwaves through 1951. Hopper, a former chorus girl and silent-film actress, wrote in a chatty style and along with her rival Louella Parsons, of the Hearst papers, was held in awe and even a degree of fear in Hollywood, whose goings-on, public and private, were her stock-in-trade. Readers loved such columns, which offered vicarious brushes with greatness on familiar terms; the studios were ready to give Hopper and Parsons inside information because the threat of either columnist telling *all* she had learned about actors' misbehavior furnished management with a big stick to keep the wayward ciné-thespians in line. (This method was used successfully to break up more than one on-the-set romance between actors and actresses one or each of whom was married to someone else.)

Gossip columns such as Hopper's and Parsons' in Hollywood, or Dorothy Kilgallen's "Voice of Broadway" (which eventually would be carried by 146 newspapers through King Features Syndicate), were close kin to the society columns that ran in most papers and chronicled the local social scene. In 2006, AP picked up a local story from Tennessee about 103-year-old Roxie McClendon, then in her twenty-eighth year of writing a society column for her town's weekly. Such columns, however, "appear to be dwindling, along with detailed wedding and birth announcements," according to the reporter, Elizabeth A. Davis, thanks to a "shift to a faster-paced, online news environment" and "the passing of a graying generation of society mavens." Nevertheless, celebrity gossip is alive and well in magazines such as *People* and Sunday-supplement columns such as "Walter

Scott's Personality Parade." In local weeklies, this genre sometimes merges with an editor's miscellany, often under a whimsical name (e.g., the *Lexington* [Mass.] *Minuteman*'s "Scene and Herd").

Advice

Like the police blotter, advice (or "agony") columns bring out the voyeur in us, but closer to home: the snoring spouse, the mooching sibling, the boorish in-laws, the demanding boss, and so on. One of the first and longest-running advice columns was started at the New Orleans *Daily Picayune* in 1896 by Dorothy Dix (real name Elizabeth Meriwether Gilmer); her "Dorothy Dix Talks," an articulate mix of insightful suggestions rooted in old-fashioned common sense, would be carried in 273 papers throughout the English-speaking world during its half-century run.

Dix was the model for many admiring imitators, including the twin Friedman sisters, Esther Pauline and Pauline Esther, who got their start as coauthors of a campus gossip column at Morningside College, their alma mater. Esther went on to compete successfully for the assignment of taking over the advice column in the Chicago *Sun-Times,* begun by Ruth Cowley in 1943 under the name "Ann Landers," after Cowley died suddenly in 1955. Esther would write the widely syndicated column for the next 47 years, up to her death in 2002.

Pauline Esther Friedman, not to be outdone by her sister, began writing *her* advice column for the *San Francisco Examiner* in 1956. After reading the paper's incumbent advice columnist, she went to the editors and convinced them she could do a far better job of it. Under the name Abigail Van Buren, she would write "Dear Abby" well into the 1990s. Her daughter, Jeanne Phillips, officially took over the name and the column in 2002 when it was announced that Pauline was suffering from Alzheimer's—Phillips had been writing much of the column since her mother became incapacitated.

Esther's daughter, Margo Howard, did not take over the Ann Landers column (subsequently renamed "Annie's Mailbox")—two other nonfamily writers did—but has continued the family tradition, much as the offspring of Emily Post have done, first with her column "Dear Prudence" and then its successor, "Dear Margo."

Etiquette columns such as Judith Martin's "Miss Manners"—heiress to the grand tradition of Emily Post and Amy Vanderbilt—are no less popular reading than the general advice mavens; upward mobility remains to this day the American dream, and with it, anxieties about socially correct conduct are legion. As with the police blotter, the reader gets to peek through a window at other people's embarrassments, but Miss Manners' terse critiques of such episodes are entertaining reading in their own right.

Thanks to concerns raised about "scientific" child rearing from the 1920s on, most newspaper women's pages would have been incomplete without a column about it, such as psychologist John Rosemond's back-to-basics "Living With Children," which he began publishing in the late 1970s in the *Charlotte* [N.C.] *Observer*. (The more liberal Dr. Benjamin Spock, author of the best-selling *Baby and Child Care* on which much of the postwar baby boom was raised, did not write for the newspapers, but was for years a columnist for both *Redbook* and *Ladies' Home Journal*.) With the boomers hitting their teens came advice columns such as the *Boston Globe*'s "Ask Beth," started in 1961 by Elizabeth Coolidge Winship (wife of the *Globe*'s publisher and sister of a Cambridge psychiatrist) and offering advice on coping with parents, school, boy-girl relationships, and sex. Sensible, frank, and compassionate without gush, "Ask Beth" came to enjoy wide syndication, and though Winship retired from the column in 1998, her daughter Peg carried it on under the same name until discontinuing it in 2007 to pursue the mitigation of global warming.

25/50/100 Years Ago

Journalism about journalism, the news of yesteryear recycled as today's feature. Such columns are a surefire nostalgia trip for older subscribers who well remember the good old days they evoke, and at least some of the personalities and events mentioned. But they also can engage subtexts provided by the editors' and readers' informed hindsight: The fanfare heralding the state's first nuclear power plant coming on line may take on an exquisite irony when reprinted a quarter century later, six months after the plant's permanent shutdown due to all those heat-cracked pipes. Who knew?

Miscellaneous Features (Food/Wine/Car/Pet/Games/Puzzles/Horoscope)

Like entertainment gossip, these specialty items are mainstays of feature sections, often nationally syndicated (such as Charles Goren's long-running bridge feature), but not always: The rural Maine weekly *Ellsworth American* has its own upbeat and droll wine-and-beer column (appropriately called "Cheers"), by the paper's managing editor, Stephen Fay, while Portland's *West End News* offers a wholly original take on the horoscope in its regular feature "Liz Looks at the Stars."

Syndicated features frequently begin as local ones, and as with Hedda Hopper's gossip column, there is often a crossover with radio. Thus *Car Talk* by Click and Clack, the Tappet Brothers (real names: Tom and Ray Magliozzi), began with a locally produced radio show at WBUR, the

Boston University radio station; they then got picked up by National Public Radio, with which WBUR was affiliated, and the syndicated newspaper column was a spin-off.

Some types of specialty features, of course, are not well suited to radio because of their graphic requirements, such as a bridge or chess column; puzzles such as crosswords, Sudoku, and word search are by their very nature a print form. These usually will be found on the same recreational pages that include the comics (another form not normally presented over the air, though Mayor Fiorello LaGuardia famously did just that for the kids of New York during the 1945 newspaper strike).

The weather map excepted, such items may be thought of as niche markets among the general readership that allow for divvying up the paper without domestic mayhem: The avid reader who wouldn't miss a week of the travel section may have little use for the chess or bird-sightings column, and vice versa. The important thing is that there be enough readers to constitute a following for any given feature of this sort. To find out how fiercely loyal to a given column the readers are, all an editor need do is propose to cut it, then see how many letters stream into the mailroom begging that it stay on.

Pictures

Up to the 1840s, newspapers had very few pictures. In England, one newspaper revolutionized that: the *Illustrated London News,* founded in 1842 by Herbert Ingram and run by his family for the next four generations. The first issue carried a breaking story of a great fire in Hamburg, with an archival picture of the city from the British Museum, reengraved to show smoke, flames, and spectators. The issue contained thirty-two illustrations altogether, cost sixpence, and sold 26,000 copies; circulation would reach 60,000 by the end of that year.

Ingram went to great pains to assemble a "dream team" for his new paper, including two artists best remembered today for their illustrations for Charles Dickens—George Cruikshank and Hablot Browne ("Phiz"). Artwork was transferred to the end-grain surface of boxwood blocks, from which everything but the lines to be printed was cut away. This very hard wood could take tens of thousands of impressions without significant wear; after the press run, the blocks were planed down and reused.

In America, this technique would feed an already burgeoning market in newspapers and magazines and add fuel to the "art labor" movement of the late nineteenth century. Winslow Homer had scarcely settled in New York when *Harper's Weekly* dispatched him to the Civil War front; the drawings he sent back were engraved, sometimes by different engravers on multiple blocks which were then pieced together on the bed for printing. Nearly 300 of Homer's drawings survive in this form. Newspapers also published engravings copied from collodion wet-plate negatives taken and developed in the field by such pioneering photographers as Mathew Brady.

Wood-block engraving would remain the primary method for newspaper illustration for most of the second half of the century, even as Ingram and other publishers searched for a less labor-intensive way to reproduce pictures. The introduction of photoengraving in the 1870s and of the halftone process in the 1880s put an end to the boxwood engraving boom—art historian Diana Korzenik reports that by the 1890s, fully 95 percent of the illustrations in *Harper's* were printed from photomechanical blocks. Meanwhile, thanks to George Eastman, dry plates became commercially available in 1880 and negative film in 1885; now it was possible for a newspaper to send a photographer to wherever local news was happening and shoot a picture that could be reproduced on a photosensitized printing plate in time for the next edition. The advent of AP wire photos, or "telepix," introduced in 1935, made it possible to receive pictures of faraway news events as well.

The standard equipment for everyday on-the-spot news photography at midcentury was the Speed Graphic, a folding camera with an extending bellows that took a 4" by 5" negative and weighed about five pounds; strapped to the hand, it made a useful ram for clearing one's way through a dense crowd as well. In order to produce an image that could be halftoned and make the next edition, 4×5 negatives were often processed in "hot soup"—that is, developer at a high concentration and well above the recommended temperature; though this exaggerated the graininess of the negative, the large format required little enlargement. (And if time was really short, the just-developed negative would sometimes be spindled on a pin stuck into the eraser end of a pencil, dipped in alcohol, set afire, and then twirled, the burning alcohol quickly drying the negative so that a print could be made immediately.) The 4×5 format gave way to 35 mm in the latter part of the twentieth century, thanks to the advent of faster and finer-grained films for no longer exotic single-lens reflex cameras that could shoot multiple frames quickly (at which the 4×5 was always at a disadvantage over any roll-film camera). This technology would in turn be displaced by digital photography, the gold standard by the turn of the millennium.

Given the dramatic increases in the number of images available, one might wonder why a paper such as the *Los Angeles Times* would continue to run only one or two photos on its front page. Partly this was due to a high-culture/pop-culture dichotomy with the tabloids (e.g., New York's

Daily News, with its signature front-page photo, generally the width of the page). Although the *L.A. Times* August 7, 1945, lead story was (not surprisingly) the dropping of the Hiroshima atom bomb, the only two pictures on the front page were for other news stories, the head-and-shoulders shots accompanying reports of the deaths of Sen. Hiram W. Johnson and Maj. William ("Bing") Bong the previous day. To be sure, there would sometimes be photo-spread pages inside the paper, but that sort of thing was not for the front page. Besides, weekly magazines such as Henry Luce's *Life* were already supplying the public with lots of news photos on better paper and at finer halftone resolution than any newspaper could hope for; for a newspaper with at least pretensions of high culture, it made more sense to stick to providing news stories in depth rather than to attempt to compete with the photograph-rich magazines on their own ground.

The tabloids, on the other hand, proceeded on the assumption that pictures sell papers, and the more titillating the better. The freelance paparazzo armed with a good tele-photo lens and egregious chutzpah has become a feature of early twenty-first-century journalism, snapping celebrity crotch shots and catfights for the sensation-hungry masses. Sometimes a picture really *is* worth a thousand words—and at ten cents a word for freelance stories, probably a good deal more.

A more modest use of the photograph may be found in two other sections of the paper: the cheerful pages devoted to the announcements of engagements and weddings (but never divorces), and the rather more somber pages devoted to obituaries and memorials to the departed. The photo-graphs of those just married or about to be married are of the moment (and typically the work of a professional photographer), while those accompanying an obituary or memorial, while typically upbeat, can come from virtually any period of the subject's life and, like the accompanying text, are often the work of a family member rather than a professional.

But whatever their source, what all forms of news have in common is that they position us at least at one remove from the events described: If we were there ourselves, we would have no need of an intermediary to tell us what happened. But in addition, news—whether print or broadcast or brought on horseback by someone fresh from spying two lanterns in a steeple across the Charles River—allows us as its consumers not only to be informed but to *feel* we are up-to-date (the point behind E.B. White's "Irtnog," a short-story fantasy about how the digests eventually themselves got condensed into one daily word of six letters, itself meaningless but satisfying the public need to be *au courant*). As telephone historian H. M. Boettinger nicely puts it, "reception of the message of the act is more important than the act itself."

ADS

If news is a newspaper's skeleton, sinews, and muscles, then surely advertising is its lifeblood. This does not mean (as a managing editor once said in our presence) that "the advertiser is the customer," for without circulation, there would be nobody to advertise *to*. Indeed, this is true whether the circulation is paid or not, as a number of "alternative" papers would discover from the 1960s on—the pioneering late-'60s arts weekly *Boston After Dark,* for example, subsisted entirely on its ad revenues, as have its successors and a host of other free urban tabloids throughout the country.

Advertising can be categorized in several different ways. One way is by function: creating product awareness ("Summer scorcher? Crack a Voozie, the refreshing umbrella in a bottle!") versus establishing company identity ("The Porcanid Corporation—keeping pigs fat, healthy, and happy since 1973!") versus reinforcing a purchase already made ("Saw the nation by wheel in my Brontomobile!"). Another is by target market: teens, young moms, new home buyers, graying baby boomers, SWFs 26–35 N/S no hangups.

Newspapers, of course, can and do capitalize on robust markets in genres of offerings from individual sellers by devoting one day a week to a special feature section on, say, automobiles, which will include not just classified ads from individual sellers but also display ads from car dealers, local reporting on car-related topics, Click and Clack's *Car Talk* column, and so on. Most common are entertainment inserts published in advance of the coming weekend, and so generously laced with ads for performances and restaurants that they are sometimes distributed free. But they also are often the locus for personal ads, perhaps on the theory that as long as you're thinking of going out somewhere this weekend, maybe you'd like to go there *with* somebody.

Moreover, a newspaper may get a reputation for carrying personal ads of a particular sort, the demand for which boosts circulation and in turn makes that paper more desirable for just that kind of advertising. Thus in turn-of-the-'60s New York City, the forthrightness of *Village Voice* personals branded that paper as an attractive venue for niche-desire mate-shopping at a time when editorial restrictions on content mandated the use of obscurantist euphemisms for such ads in more mainstream publications.

Of course, if the whole point is advertising, one can dispense with news altogether: There are publications such as the Los Angeles–based *Recycler,* consisting solely of classified ads and supported not by revenue from sellers—who with the exception of those placing personals pay no fee for their ads at all—but from the per-issue price paid by the buyer. Conversely, the first known newspaper ad was something of an afterthought, placed by the publisher of an otherwise all-news newsbook to mention the fact that he had back issues for sale. Since the early newspapers of the seventeenth century were largely read by the coffeehouse set, most of the ads in them were for luxury items such as periwigs and theater tickets. The breadth of commodities and volume of advertising we know today would only be made possible with the advent of the Industrial Revolution, and with it a much expanded reader base having both an appetite for conspicuous consumption and the purchasing power to satisfy it.

Unlike print display ads, which ask a large fee from the advertiser for what may be proportionally a very small amount of newsprint "real estate" in a modestly priced publication whose purchaser is getting a lot of other content as well, classified ads presuppose something like a level playing field between seller and buyer. Each party has a comparable interest in the transaction. Sellers pay a low per-word fee for a pithy description of the item offered (including themselves, as we shall see shortly when we come to the personals), and readers scan the page looking to acquire just that type of commodity, or at least fantasize about it. To achieve their purpose, such ads have to be specific enough to save both parties from wasting their time while being terse enough to be affordable, so every word (usually defined for such ads as a string of characters with no space in it) needs to tell.

In consequence, a form of English creole has come to dominate such ads, its bare-bones syntax (with, for example, its general absence of definite articles and limited use of verb inflections) readily intelligible to speakers of the standard language, but its abbreviatory conventions taking some getting used to. The personal ads (and the form you fill out to place one) sometimes offer a glossary of abbreviations for such standard categories as gay, white, black, bisexual, male, female, Jewish, Christian, and so on, though you are generally left to figure out the meanings of such stock abbreviations as LTR (long-term relationship) and N/S (nonsmoker). At one time, the Montréal arts and entertainment weekly freebie, *Voir,* allowed you to accompany your personal ad with an icon chosen from a labeled list at the bottom of the page, running the gamut from "Fétichisme" (high-heel shoe and a bit of mesh stocking) to "Aime enfants" (picture of a baby carriage).

In his 1996 sociolinguistics study, *The Discourse of Classified Advertising,* Paul Bruthiaux looked at a corpus of ads from two publications (one of them the Los Angeles all-ads *Recycler* mentioned above). Calling abbreviations "a defining characteristic" of classified ads, Bruthiaux points out that ads for secondhand cars and for apartments are laced with them: "81 MAZDA GLC, 4dr, 5spd, air, am-fm cass, gd int, 105M, $950 obo." Most readers, recognizing it as a car ad by the manufacturer's name, will have no trouble unpacking this as "1981 Mazda GLC four-door, five-speed transmission, air conditioning, AM-FM radio with cassette player, good interior, odometer reads 150,000; seller is looking to get $950 or, failing that, your best offer," which takes almost twice as many characters and more than twice the number of words.

While to be sure, Bruthiaux says, editorial policy rather than customer choice imposes these abbreviations, readers of the ads seem to have no problem with it. By contrast, job and personal ads tend much more to spell things out; Bruthiaux plotted his corpus of ads in four categories (job, housing, cars, and personals) and found significant differences in abbreviation-to-full-word counts: for autos

and apartments, respectively, abbreviations accounted for
27.3 percent and 29.2 percent, the latter approaching double the ratio for jobs (16.5 percent) and triple for personals
(10.2 percent).

A second feature Bruthiaux notes is the presence of lexical collocation—that is, "prefabricated segments [consist-
ing] of content words" such as *walking distance, lose weight,
no gimmicks, sparkling clean,* and of course *meaningful relationship.* (Compare the stock Spanish requirement *sin vicios*
'without bad habits' or the French self-description *bien dans
sa peau* 'comfortable in his/her skin.') Moreover, certain
nouns are qualified by a limited inventory of adjectives;
Bruthiaux found that in his corpus of eighty-three car ads
with the word *condition,* slightly more than half were modified by *excellent,* and of the rest, twelve were modified by
good and another eight by *mint.* Such "recycling of previously encountered segments," he suggests, is probably due
to "cognitive factors such as ease of encoding."

Other types of advertising have their own linguistic
particularities as well. A. H. Fatihi, in a 1991 study of pro-
motional language in India, stresses the importance of
adjectives such as *nayā* ('new, fresh'), *kifāytī* ('economical'),
tezasī ('splendid, lustrous'), and *lājawāb* ('matchless') "to
magnify the minuscule difference between the products, as
if the consumer is vitally curious about minute details." In
India there is the added wrinkle of the two largely overlapping vocabularies and grammars of Hindi and Urdu with two
quite different writing systems, as well as a large segment of
the population conversant in English (with its own writing
system different from both); this gives rise to such gestures
as dots added over Roman letters in display ads, in imitation
of *nuqta,* the diacritical marks used in Urdu script. (Compare the use of a backwards R—Cyrillic *ya*—when spelling
"Russia" in a display ad. That the actual Cyrillic equivalent

for English R looks like an uppercase P—as in CCCP—is quite beside the point for the advertiser, who wishes merely to evoke the *flavor* of Russian orthography.)

Moreover, the mixing of English words—such as the transliteration into Hindi or Urdu script of, for example, *jūsi flevar kristals* ['juicy flavor crystals'] embedded in an otherwise native-language ad goes beyond the sort of "atmosphere English" common among Japanese youth, for the English words are intended to pull their semantic weight, as well as adding their cachet of westernization and modernity. "Even the brand names have been remarkably influenced by English," writes Fatihi. "It is generally believed that the concept of modernization is not fully communicated in Hindi unless the advertising message is…literally or metaphorically transcreated through English."

Thanks to the pioneering work of 1950s Madison Avenue admen, informed by psychologists such as Freud's student Paul Bernays, today's advertisers understand very well that status, fashion, modernity, sex, security, and other deep-seated drives are powerful motivators, a great deal more so than desire for the actual commodities in whose marketing they may be enlisted. Gender relations in particular offer a wide range of opportunity: Most consumers wish to think themselves sexually attractive, and the manufacturer whose promotion can best turn that capacity into arousal for the product will make the sale.

This can be as blatant as the nude models draped over a new automobile at the car show (as actually happened at the Motor Show Earls Court in England in 1971) and the Fiat billboard ad whose copy read "If it were a lady, it would get its bottom pinched" (to which a spray can *détourneuse* nicely added, in letters of similar size, "If this lady was a car she'd run you down"). In a British display ad recruiting for the Royal Navy, traditional gender (and perhaps imperial) roles are evoked by British men rescuing women and children in a foreign land, headlined "She's still scared of the wind but loves our helicopters."

But there are also ads that manage to shake up such stereotypes even while subtly reinforcing them, such as the Wrigley's ad in which a young man on an intercity bus offers the young woman across the aisle his last stick of gum, which she breaks in two and gives him half back; he gets off at the next stop, and she interrupts her own trip to get off and be with him. Aside from its obvious product-awareness message (gum transcends mere mastication to become courtship token), the ad's long shot of the bus aisle is a deliberate allusion to a church wedding, but the woman's forwardness in leaving the bus to pursue the man is a reversal of the usual boy-meets-girl script. Such a mix is part of the overall ambiance in a British Gas ad showing a couple in the kitchen—she's wearing an apron, but he's the one grating the cheese—with the body copy telling us that "Margaret is a physicist....Vance is an historian of science." Advertising may be most effective when it nurtures our fond fantasies of having our cake and eating it too.

7

ON THE PHONE

Your Call Is Important 2 Us

WITH THE POSSIBLE EXCEPTION OF TELEVISION, FEW
objects of technology have changed the world's social patterns as radically as the telephone, which continues its evolution in fits and starts from its origins as an outgrowth of
the telegraph, itself a technological leap forward from the
semaphore and other long-distance signaling systems. Alexander Graham Bell, whose famous "Mr. Watson, come here.
I want to see you" has been enshrined as the world's first
telephone message, was in fact working on ways to improve
the telegraph when he accidentally discovered that sounds
could be transmitted "using electricity." (A similar accident
a century later led to the introduction of Brazil's first chat
line, Disque Amizade, apparently the result of crossing telephone lines in the implementation of Luiz Carlos Bravo's
dial-a-joke service, Disque-piada.) Bell was not alone in
claiming to have invented the device, however. The race to
make the telephone a commercial product resulted in years
of bitter legal battles that began when Bell and Elisha Gray
(remember him?) filed patents for the technology within
hours on the same day, February 14, 1876. The courts

decided in Bell's favor, although persistent tales of stolen ideas, bribery, and favoritism have left this controversy in the category of "we'll probably never know for sure."

In the beginning, it was hard to envision a practical use for this novelty. The sender and receiver needed to be in fairly close proximity, with each person taking turns shouting a message into a device; each person's telephone line was a distinct wire running from one's house or business to the local telephone exchange building; long-distance calls, say from Boston to San Francisco, were decades away, and when the technology and infrastructure eventually became available, they would have to be made via prearrangement at the local telephone switching office. But gradually the kinks were worked out of the system so that, if you had the money, you could be among the elite early adopters of the technology.

To make a call, you'd call an "operator" (all male at this point) and let him know the name of the "subscriber" with whom you'd like to connect. Small "directories" of subscribers were distributed, the first being that of the New Haven District Telephone Company in 1878, which was limited to a single page. These early exchange operators had to memorize quickly all the names of "subscribers" to the service to connect one to the other. This kind of familiarity required both training and, one might imagine, a concierge-like sensitivity to the comings and goings of one's clients. The notion of a telephone number representing an individual was at first vociferously rejected by customers as an indignity and a loss of personal identification. However, a measles epidemic forced the use of untrained operators, and by 1895 most operators were required to ask, "Number please."

Once the numbering scheme was established, the technology enabling individuals to dial a sequence of numbers and contact another caller without the direct intervention of an operator was introduced. In 1927, a silent film short appeared in theaters explaining this soon-to-be-implemented fancy innovation. "How to Use the Dial Phone" used cartoons and models explaining the newfangled dial feature and the innovation of a "dial tone," which audiences were told is a "steady humming sound indicating that the line is ready for you to dial." When the big switch was made, everyone's telephone number was changed, and new directories were delivered to every home or business with a phone.

The telephone's rapid expansion and increasing casual use had a substantial social impact: People now felt required both to answer a ringing phone and to make an immediate response to the person on the other end. It may be unfathomable to modern readers, but there was a time when the previous fastest communication, the telegram, still allowed for contemplation of the message, and one could spend one's leisure pondering and composing a reply:

CANNOT MARRY YOU MR. SMITH STOP MY HEART BELONGS TO ANOTHER STOP

Until the widespread use of home answering machines in the 1980s, when the phone rang, you answered it, ready or not. To this day, a ringing phone in the middle of the night can still bring fear and doubt, a fact played upon to great effect in a political advertisement aired during the 2008 Democratic primary race asking the voters whom they would prefer to answer the presidential hotline at 3:00 A.M.

In earlier times, the "party line" known to most people was apolitical. Also known as the "multiparty line" or "shared service line," this feature allowed several households to share a single telephone line. If the phone was in use when you picked up the receiver, you'd be obliged to try again later. Each household would have a selective ring (one long ring, followed by two short rings, for example) that would signal that the call was for you. You would quickly get to know the other members of your party, and social interactions and familiarity could be forged, especially in a small community where the party line could even be used to let others know quickly about local emergencies or gossip. One could also eavesdrop on others (inadvertently or otherwise), though this was clearly frowned upon as a breach of etiquette, much like reading a letter unbidden over somebody's shoulder. By the 1960s, the party line had become a thing of the past, except in some isolated rural settings, where the "single line service" had become the norm.

HELLO?

What do we say when we answer the phone? Among the more benign issues of debate at the birth of the telephone was the question of what one should say when picking up the receiver; Bell had proposed "Ahoy Ahoy" or "Ahoy hoy" as the appropriate response, while Thomas Edison favored "Hello." The *Oxford English Dictionary*. notes that *hoy* ("[A natural exclamation.]") had been in use since 1393 in the sense of "A cry used to call attention; also to incite or drive beasts, esp. hogs. In nautical language (also written *hoay*) used in hailing or calling aloft." (*Ahoy* is first attested in print in 1751.) *Hello* is a relative newcomer, at least in its present spelling, first appearing in print in 1827 as an interjection "[u]sed as a greeting" and in 1877 "[u]sed to answer a telephone call." Actually, *hello* is simply the latest in a series of spellings for the utterance we pronounce [həlóᵘ], earlier spellings having included *hullo, hollo,* and *hillo,* all traceable to the early sixteenth-century *holla,* a borrowing of French *holà,* itself first attested in the twelfth century and a compound of *ho* and *là*—'hey there!' (It is, incidentally, from our interjection *hey* that we get our familiar greeting *hi.*)

It is likely that French has borrowed our *hello*-qua-phone-greeting as their *allô* (though an alternative derivation—from *allons* 'let's go'—has also been proposed).

The origin of the British "Are you there?" has sometimes been attributed to the use of public telephones in which the caller deposited a coin, dialed a number, and waited for the recipient to pick up. At this point, the caller could hear the recipient but the recipient could not hear the caller. The caller could complete the connection by pressing the telephone's button A to let the coin drop, at which point the recipient could hear the caller. (Why the recipient was supposed to ask "Are you there?" instead of, say, "Why don't you press button A like a good fellow?" is not clear.) In the case of an apparent wrong number, a change of heart, or no answer on the other end, the caller could press Button B to cancel the operation and retrieve the coin. Not surprisingly, frustrated callers did not always remember to perform this last step, whence the down-and-out artist Gulley Jimson's rule of thumb in the classic film *The Horse's Mouth:* "Never miss an opportunity of pressing button 'B.'"

Other languages have opted to use meaningful words whose semantic content in the context of answering the phone has been "bleached," that is, reduced to a simple social signal, what sociolinguists call a turn-constructional unit—"I've spoken; now it's your turn"—as, for example, the various possibilities in different parts of the Spanish-speaking world: *oigo* ('I hear'), *bueno* ('good'), *dígame* ('tell me'), to mention only three.

A formalized etiquette developed as the telephone became ubiquitous, and what one said on the phone could suggest "good breeding." For example, as the telephone began to eliminate the more formal written dinner invitation, we are reminded in *Mrs. Oliver Harriman's Book of Etiquette* in 1942:

In telephoning an invitation, don't ask, "Shall you be busy Sunday evening?" The listener may think you are about to propose something she may not want to do. Make yourself known and say at once, "We are giving a little informal dinner Sunday night and should like so much to have you come."

A decade later, as "Jack" learns in the 1953 educational film *Mind Your Manners*, children were taught the following basic script for answering the phone:

Hello, this is the Merenti residence, Benny Merenti speaking.

May I speak to Fred?

Who may I say is calling?

A number of etiquette books from the '30s and '40s admonish youth and grown-ups alike not to play the "Guess who this is?" game when calling others, a gaucherie equal to the caller's asking "Who's this?" as a response to "Hello."

Adults, according to the 1937 *Pocket Book of Etiquette*, should announce their name as it would appear in a hotel register (Mr. John Smith). However, by 1958, etiquette books were beginning to drop the requirement of announcing which home you had reached, at least partially suggesting that the volume of calls a typical household received made such a formal response impracticable. In the contemporary United States, children, when they are allowed to answer the phone, are now told never to give out helpful information:

Hello?

Can I speak to your mother?

> My parents are here, but they are cleaning their guns and can't come to the phone.

Phone calls are typically ended with a polite "good-bye," though the convention is seldom followed in television or the movies, where the phone is unceremoniously hung up. What would otherwise be considered a serious breach of etiquette (even when the caller is a telemarketer calling as you're about to sit down to dinner or it's a wrong number at 3:00 A.M.) no doubt speeds the dramatic action, and may well go unnoticed by the audience, given that the sign-off is almost free of semantic content.

HEY, WHO *IS* THIS?

For new generations of teenagers in America, the telephone became a part of the fabric of their social structure. The images of the teenage girl gossiping for hours on the family phone and the teenage boy awkwardly asking a girl for a date became not only a stock image in burgeoning "social hygiene" educational films such as *Are You Popular?* (1947) and *Mind Your Manners* (1953), but also a social reality. These post-Depression youngsters with an increasing amount of leisure time on their hands became frequent users of the new technology. Teenagers became such frequent telephone users that it was not unusual to see their own line listed in the phone directory:

> Smith, Mr. Adam.....555–1234
> Children's line.....555–2345

Children also helped to usher in the age of the "prank" call, typically by pretending to be another person, a game that adults can, of course, play too, as when Canadian disk jockey Pierre Brassard, posing as then Canadian prime minister

Jean Chrétien, asked Queen Elizabeth II to record a speech in support of Canadian unity ahead of the 1995 Québec referendum. Most children's prank calls follow the pattern of the classic "Prince Albert" call to the local tobacco shop: "Do you have Prince Albert in a can?" When the unsuspecting clerk responds "Yes," the caller follows up with, "Well, you'd better let him out!"—which Prince Albert of Monaco, in an interview, stated that he found quite funny. Clerks who have heard this one a million times are less likely to be amused.

The prank call (like the more sinister obscene call) is intended to be anonymous, though nowadays caller ID has largely stripped the caller of his anonymity. In fact, even without caller ID, the concept of telephone anonymity is to some extent a matter of degree.

Salespeople have been closing deals since the telephone first came onto the scene, first as a way to expedite what is now called business-to-business communication, but when a telephone began to be in the home of every person with money to buy something, the "cold call," the equivalent of the door-to-door salesman, arrived on the scene. Cold calling has evolved into the science of "telemarketing" or "telesales," the latest wrinkle being the "Robo-Call," which can sequentially and tirelessly dial a series of numbers until a live person answers the phone, at which point an automated message can be delivered or the call can be switched over to a live operator who can personally deliver the sales pitch. In both cases, the caller is not likely to identify himself (herself, itself) with a full name or a number to call back, though will always be happy to tell you where to send your money.

On the flip side, anonymous calls that an adult might make in the private sector could be to a 900 number for paid phone sex, to a free dial-a-prayer (-weather forecast,

-joke, -song), or to one's local newspaper's "Speak Out" or "Gripe" line. Caller messages left on the "Speak Out" answering machine range from the unintentionally humorous "Why are there so many squirrels and why isn't the town doing something about it?" to the xenophobic "Why are there some many Russians (fill in the minority group of your choice here) in town and why isn't the town doing something about it?" These are typically anonymous, though some papers ask for at least rudimentary identification (so they can print the caller's initials or home town to attest to the caller's bona fides), and even when they don't, anonymity isn't necessarily guaranteed: A local Boston editor recognized the thinly disguised voice of a repeat caller to the "Speak Out" line from the same number in support of a town official (herself) and duly noted that fact in the column. Other papers may print the caller's initials, sometimes accompanied by the name of the caller's town.

ANSWERING MACHINES—WE STOP ANSWERING THE PHONE

One modern way to avoid the question of what to say when you answer the phone is to let technology do it for you. The idea of a device that could answer calls and take a message for you has been in the air for almost as long as the telephone itself. In 1898, the Danish telephone engineer and inventor Valdemar Poulsen patented a wire recording device called the Telegraphone. Fast-forward to 1949 and we find *Time* magazine describing a "Robot Secretary" that can magically "answer the telephone when no one is home:"

> When the phone rings, a mechanism lifts the receiver and turns on a phonograph record. The owner's own recorded voice announces that he is out, asks the

caller to leave his message at the sound of a chime. When the owner returns, a meter tells him how many calls have come in, and a wire recorder repeats the messages (up to 60 minutes of them). The wire can be erased and used over again. Retail price: $198.50.

That's $1,800 in today's money, suggesting that the "early adopter" of this technology (like the early adopter of the telephone) must have been fairly well-to-do.

The answering machine began to enter private homes in a major way with the introduction in 1971 of the Tron-Tech Phone-Mate 400. Weighing in at a hefty ten pounds, this wooden box was about the size of the Manhattan yellow pages and cost $300, but it could screen calls and hold up to twenty messages on a reel-to-reel tape, and later models could even retrieve messages remotely. It had one tape system for the outgoing message and the larger tape system to record the incoming messages, a configuration that would be copied using cassettes and microcassettes in later, much smaller models.

Crucial changes that this device brought to society were:

- You didn't have to be at home to get a message.
- You didn't have to answer the phone even if you were at home.
- As a corollary, kids didn't need to be trained to answer the phone for their parents.

Small changes perhaps, but for generations, "waiting by the phone" and the intrusion of always feeling forced to answer the phone "because it might be important" were part of the burden of telephone technology that the answering machine now alleviated.

For a time, novelty handmade outgoing messages that might reflect a young adult's personality (and puzzle the parents) were widely popular with that person's circle of friends, if annoying to others. Perhaps the most commonly referenced is the somewhat classic: "Hello?" (long pause for the caller to begin a conversation) "Ha ha ha! This is an answering machine, leave a message at the tone."

Users of these new devices were admonished not to record an outgoing message that announced:

> This is Mary Smith. I'm not at home right now. Please leave a message at the tone.

but, instead, to create something like:

> You've reached 555–1234. No one can come to the phone right now. Please leave a message at the tone.

where the message does not reveal your present where-abouts, your gender, that you live alone, or much of any-thing else.

After a legal ruling in 1988, phone companies could offer a host of services, including an integrated voice mail. The function was essentially the same, but the user would "call in" to retrieve the messages. This new technology ush-ered in a new era in the business world, as a 1988 *New York Times* article breathlessly declared: "[T]he interoffice memo has learned to talk." A world without secretaries scrawling something illegible on little pink "While You Were Out" pads appealed to the accountants, and it was argued that the new technology was more efficient:

> Real-time communication, Mr. Bender of Travelers explained, is quite inefficient. "Sixty percent of the telephone calls made among Travelers people did not require two-way communications," Mr. Bender said, explaining that many calls simply imparted or requested information that was not immediately needed.

Seventy-five percent of calls do not reach the intended recipient and 90 percent of the written phone messages contain at least one error, he added. Voice messages are also more succinct than conversations. "The innate need to socialize that you have on the phone is not there," he said.

While answering machines and voice mail have filled a communication void for decades, their use seems to be on the decline, especially among the younger generation, in part because of the number of steps it takes to retrieve voice mail, but largely because of the proliferation of competing modes of communication, such as text messaging, e-mail, Twitter, and Facebook. A 2009 *New York Times* article quotes a survey from a company that operates the voice messaging systems of several cell phone carriers and shows that "over 30 percent of voice messages linger unheard for three days or longer and that more than 20 percent of people with messages in their mailboxes 'rarely even dial in' to check them," whereas "91 percent of people under 30 respond to text messages within an hour, and they are four times more likely to respond to texts than to voice messages within minutes, according to a 2008 study for Sprint conducted by the Opinion Research Corporation." Voice mail has stayed more relevant thanks to its adding more visual displays, such as the iPhone voice-mail application that displays the origins of the callers in a format much more like e-mail, as well as by several software services such as Google Voice and PhoneTag that can transcribe your newly old-fashioned voice mail into neatly organized text messages, but all this may simply be a finger in the dike.

On the other hand, one phone system that seems only to grow in the business world is the nearly ubiquitous call center telephone support system, or lately, the interactive voice response system (IVR). By now everyone has had the experience of navigating through a phone menu system (press "1 for support, 2 for sales," etc.), and it is clear that while the stated goal is to connect you expeditiously to the correct person to handle your needs, most of us suspect that the main goal is to keep us from interacting with a live (and more expensive) human being. Many news articles and websites, such as Get2Human.com, have tried to give the inside code that will bring you to an actual human, for example:

Press 1, then *#,*#,*#

Even with such shortcuts, the road to a real person can seem as long and wearying as Dante's through the Inferno (and with a prerecorded sales pitch or Muzak instead of Virgil to keep you company into the bargain).

IVR systems take the push-button menu system to a new level with their ability to recognize your voice and interpret them as commands. Many of us perhaps heard this for the first time when buying air travel on the phone. The voice recognition system can serve to gather initial information (name, account number, dates, destination city, etc.) before turning you over to a live person, or even completing the transaction itself. The system can work well if you can speak slowly and clearly without an accent, but can be frustrating for those of non-U.S. extraction or with a speech impediment, or even a person with a cold. An article in *Speech Technology* notes that it is

> particularly difficult for the applications to recognize names that are short or have very "soft" sounding consonants. The speech systems' abilities to recognize words, phrases and sentences are often complicated with thick or foreign accents. Outside factors such as speakerphones and some cell phone transmissions have also skewed the recognition.

The software also needs to filter out words that do not contribute to completing the request, such as *um, ah, er,* and other "speech pillows." While the technology continues to improve, some common phrase combinations can be difficult to interpret. One is reminded of the famous T-shirt worn by Apple developers:

> I helped Apple wreck a nice beach
> ("I helped Apple recognize speech.")

Current systems break down the customer request into small bits: "OK. Now tell me which city you'd like to fly to," and may, like Amtrak's "Julie," repeat what the software *thought* it recognized ("I think you said 'chuck you tharlie.' Is that correct?"), but are a long way from being able to parse a full sentence.

GOING WIRELESS

Ever since Dick Tracy enjoyed the convenience of instant portable communication, people have dreamed of making this fantasy a reality. Like the comic-strip detective's "2-way wrist radio," early mobile communication involved a radio transmitter on one end and an ordinary telephone on the other. An example of this technology is the "ship-to-shore" radio telephone: A radio operator would call on a fixed radio frequency and connect to a telephone operator on shore, who would then connect the transmission via telephone line to a specific caller. The number of calls were limited by the number of radio frequencies (channels) available in the local area, and since it was transmitting on a well-known frequency, anyone with a multiband radio could listen in on the whole call. This technology was also the basis of early "car phones," essentially radio transmitters that could automatically connect (if a channel was available) to a telephone number.

Completely wireless telephone communication involving a transmitter/receiver at one end (say, in your car), plus a network of relatively low-powered "radio cell" sites (typically, towers mounted with a microwave antenna) to receive and transmit messages over the airwaves to their ultimate recipient, was a long time in reaching the public (development and deployment having apparently been stalled by the desire to protect existing telephone company monopolies). The first such service available to the public appeared in Japan in 1978. The first cellular phone available to the public in the United States (the Motorola DynaTAC 8000X) was authorized by the FCC in 1984. The device cost $3,995 ($8,000 in today's money), weighed two pounds, and allowed you to talk for only thirty minutes per battery charge.

However, within five years almost a million cell phones were in use in the United States, and agreements among cell phone carriers had made possible a dramatic expansion of the usable area in which your phone (now costing a mere $2,000) could operate. The linkage between two or more carriers' networks introduced the concept of the "roaming" charge, typically fifty cents per minute, for both incoming and outgoing calls, leaving callers in the late '80s with a monthly phone bill of between $100 and $150.

Yet the convenience of not having to look for a pay phone, plus rapidly declining prices, led to the speedy expansion of cell phone usage by ordinary people, not just tycoons and drug dealers. Eventually, in the classic "razors and blades" economic model, carriers would either steeply discount phones or even give them away as loss leaders for the contract governing customer use.

Again, the changes in telephone technology brought changes in social behavior. In an age in which "everyone" has a cell phone, we have seen the slow death of the pay phone, the home phone (or "landline"), and the expectation of quiet. Parents give their children cell phones so they can keep in constant contact, and businesses enjoy the ability to stay in touch with salespeople and customers. Husbands call their wives from the supermarket, and when watching older films, it's easy for us to say, "This movie would have been over in fifteen minutes if everybody had a cell phone."

On the one hand, social bonds with family and friends can be tightened because we can call each other at any time and place. In fact, according to James Katz, a professor at Rutgers University who studies the social impact of cell phones, about half of all cell phone calls we make are to just three or four numbers in our personal repertory. But informal connections can be altered. For example, Eric Weiner, longtime correspondent for National Public Radio, notes that

> ...cell phones loosen the bonds with those outside our inner circle. Standing at a bus stop, for instance, we're less likely to strike up a conversation with a stranger. Instead, we reach for our cell phone and call a friend or colleague.

On the other hand, a concern about the ability to be connected to someone at nearly all times, according to University of Colorado professor Leysia Palen, is that

> ...we have a generation of people coming up who are not well practiced at being alone. They don't know how to be alone, and that is really important. That's why some have labeled cell phones "pacifiers for adults" or "electronic tethers."

All this bad behavior has been a boon to writers in the etiquette business, favoring us with such titles as *Teen Manners: From Malls to Meals to Messaging and Beyond* and online quizzes promising, with mysterious cataphora, "They're annoying.

They're loathsome. And you could be one of them! How good is your cell phone etiquette? Take our quiz and find out!" It's telling, however, that most etiquette books in the beginning of the twentieth century were directed to showing you how to act like a person of good breeding, while today's guides seem to exist largely to make an example of the egregious behavior of others that you should avoid. An article discussing a recent Harris poll on cell phone behavior, aptly titled "Everyone but You Is Being Rude with Their Mobile Gadgets," noted that most of those polled had witnessed horrible behavior (82 percent said they'd seen bad public mobile use, with 56 percent noting poor etiquette in restaurants, 47 percent at concerts and movies, and 26 percent in restrooms), but only 28 percent admitted to "discussing private matters in public" in public via their phone.

Often identified as the most annoying cell phone behavioral offense is talking at the top of one's voice. Early cell phones lacked an appropriate feedback mechanism—that is, a means of putting a little of your voice back in your earpiece—which resulted in people's automatically talking a little loudly, behavior that early etiquette books were quick to caution against. (Indeed, much attention was given to proper "telephone voice.") But advances in technology have removed the lack of auditory feedback as an excuse for a lack of volume control in public telephone conversation. Another social no-no often breached is the broadcasting of the cell phone user's half of a conversation with subject matter better kept private—your fellow commuter really doesn't want to hear about your gallbladder or how drunk you got last weekend.

For better or for worse (depending on your perspective), it is also considered impolite to become in any way involved in the conversation—eavesdropping has always been considered bad form (unless it's part of your job as a professional spy), and interrupting a cell phone conversation to tell the speaker to shut up might well be considered the act of a sociopath. The concept of "civil inattention" comes into play here—the notion that individuals in close proximity, such as on a bus, on the sidewalk of a large city, or in a confined office space of cubicles, are aware of each other, yet maintain a fiction, a theatrical role really, that they do not see or hear each other. Socially, this construct keeps us from running the risk of becoming involved and overwhelmed by all the personal trivia and trauma that surround us, but also increases the risk that our cool indifference likewise reduces any thought of ethical responsibility. In other words, we survive living in a city surrounded by a mass of others' personal stories, positive and negative, without going crazy, but may become callous to real individual suffering. The same norms apply to cell phone use in public close proximity—we pretend not to be appalled at the personal discussions occurring feet away, and the corollary is true: Callers can pretend they are shrouded in a magic dome of anonymity. Even the current queen of etiquette, Peggy Post, acquiesces to the need to talk on one's cell phone in public:

> If you must take the call, speak softly and briefly, or walk to a less congested area. And steer clear of conversations involving medical or business problems; they create an awkward situation for those listening—and you never know who that might be! As more people go cellular, the situation will only get worse. So, the next time you're getting ready to dial and chat, think about how you'd feel if you were the person in the next seat over.

We also don't like cell phones to interrupt our social interactions, say, when we're in direct conversation with someone only to be interrupted when that person accepts a call on his or her cell phone. As Olivier Tchouaffe of Southwestern University warns, primacy of cell phone use over personal contact signals a greater societal breakdown:

> The first casualty of the cell phone is the disintegration of 'noble' civic practices. First, cell phone usage normalizes the "failure to listen and reflect;" it institutionalizes rudeness, driving social relationships on the basis of power, rather than solidarity. Within these conditions, the uses of cell phones are, de facto, changing the meaning of public space and accordingly what it means to be informed. Cell phones introduce a culture of immediacy, often bridging the gap between the public and the private to challenge a culture of verification and gatekeeping. This mode of communication is *horizontal* not *vertical*. Thus, it often orients the discursive flow with a unidirectional influence that seems to empower the *sender*, rather than the *receiver*, to install a repressive culture of marketing and peer pressure.

Judith Martin, in her *Miss Manners' Guide to Excruciatingly Correct Behavior*, does not view the cellular assault on our social fabric as a new problem requiring a new solution:

> Why do you people keep asking for new rules when you haven't yet used the old ones?
>
> Oh dear, please forgive Miss Manners, who didn't mean to turn testy. It's just that when the telephone was invented, we kept it tethered with a cord for nearly a century in the hope that during that time, people would get the idea that it shouldn't be taken everywhere. Even before that we had rules against shouting in public, making noise in theaters, ignoring the people

that one is with, spoiling the atmosphere of a quiet and dignified place and appearing to do business under social circumstances. These are still in effect.

YOU RANG?

To announce incoming calls, early telephones included a "ringing" mechanism consisting of two miniature gongs separated by a magnetized clapper that vibrated when activated by an alternating electric current (originally generated through the operation of a hand-cranked magneto—remember magnetos?). The use of bells as an alert was familiar enough and easily took its place beside the doorbell and its pre-electric forebears, the church or town clock announcing the hour (sometimes a person's final hour), the current location of one's cow, and so on. In the 1950s, AT&T introduced a ringer with two sets of bells so that one could tell which phone was ringing when several were present. Eventually, in the 1980s, the magneto, clapper, and gongs finally gave way to the oscillator and piezoelectric transducer.

One of the early features offered by the cell phone was to allow the owner to change the sound that the phone made when "ringing." Once limited to a handful of monophonic tones (a small range of single notes played in a loop), sometimes crudely making out the basis of a melody, "ring tones" have become much more sophisticated and are now a multi-billion-dollar business. Not only do modern cell phones allow you to download polyphonic ring tones—snippets of your favorite songs, say—or bits of digitized speech, but you can assign a different ring tone to each different caller, with Mom's ring as a police siren and your boyfriend's as the melody to "Hot Stuff."

Ring tones can also provide moments of embarrassment as when you begin an important business presentation only to have "Hot Stuff" blare from your briefcase. Ring tones have also taken on an international political flavor, as when King Juan Carlos I of Spain told Hugo Chávez, president of Venezuela, "¿Por qué no te callas?" ("Why don't you [just] shut up?") at the 2007 Ibero-American Summit in Santiago, Chile, when Chávez was interrupting Spanish prime minister José Luis Rodríguez Zapatero's speech. The phrase became an overnight sensation, soon offered for sale in digital form as a must-have for your phone.

These annoying tones have also created a backlash, with the profusion of "Please turn off your cell phone" and "No cell phone zone" admonishments appearing at theaters and concert halls, and at least one case of a frustrated performer storming off the stage after being repeatedly interrupted by ringing. Those individuals who legitimately cannot be separated from their phones (e.g., doctors) can have an usher hold their phone and then, if necessary, discreetly whisper the nature of the emergency in the callee's ear. In some countries, proprietors of theatres and concert venues have taken to "jamming" or blocking incoming calls, a practice not yet legal for the disgruntled masses.

While public talking over a cell phone seems to be a cultural universal, within certain age ranges "texting," or sending text messages using a SMS (short message service), is increasingly popular. At some level, the text message is little more than a passed note in a classroom, yet there are important differences. Text messages can be sent anywhere, to virtually anyone with a modern cell phone, and at any time. Text messages can be very brief ("wassup?"), since there is a cultural anticipation that a reply is imminent. The possible length of a text message is determined by a standard digital size set by an international protocol, but since different languages store their characters in different ways, languages can have different maximum message lengths.

In what is called the seven-bit system for Latin-alphabet languages like English, French, and Spanish, a text message can be up to 160 characters, while sixteen-bit or "double-byte" (since the characters are encoded in pairs of eight bytes) languages like Japanese and Chinese are limited to seventy total characters.

On a basic cell phone with the standard cell phone keyboard (called the E.161 keypad), there are twelve keys, with the numbers 2 through 9 each representing three (or, on the 7 and the 9, four) possible characters (take a quick look at your phone now if you don't "text"). These letters were first added to help telephone operators and callers with a mnemonic device to remember common exchanges (as in KLondike 5-3247). You can type out messages on this keyboard by either the "ABC" method, where you would press the 7 (PQRS) key four times quickly to type an "s," or by using a "predictive text" software application found on most cell phones, such as the T9 system, where you would type a number sequence and stop, and the system would predict, using a dictionary of common words, the most likely word for the typed sequence—for example, if you had pressed 8, 4, and 3, the system would "guess" you probably wanted the word "the." If the guess is right, you'd press the 0 key to accept the choice and move on to your next word, or if the guess was wrong, you'd press the *key to cycle through other options until you found the correct word. There can be a steep learning curve for either method, but one can get quite speedy, as demonstrated by seventeen-year-old Elliot Nicholls, who, blindfolded, texted this 160-character message (including spaces) in forty-five seconds:

The razor toothed piranhas of the genera Serrasalmus and Pygocentrus are the most ferocious freshwater fish in the world. In reality they rarely attack a human.

Another method of speeding up the text entry process is to use commonly understood abbreviations. Most are actually fairly intuitive, such as this response to a message that wasn't understood:

?

whose meaning, depending on the context and the people involved, could be "Huh?" or "Are you crazy?" whereas

ttyl

will be understood as "talk to you later."

It is these abbreviated messages that have caused such a stir—charges that the youth of today are speaking in a secret code, or that a kind of pidgin language is developing that will eventually destroy our language and culture, as in the following from an article entitled "I h8 txt msgs: How Texting Is Wrecking Our Language":

> It is the relentless onward march of the texters, the SMS (Short Message Service) vandals who are doing to our language what Genghis Khan did to his neighbours eight hundred years ago.

The linguist David Crystal argues in a number of articles and a fine book, *Txtng: the Gr8 Db8,* that we should come off the ledge. First, he says, it's important to note that studies have shown that the shorthand words that the Genghis Khan texters are using make up only 10 to 20 percent of the total content of the messages. Since the goal of any communication is to be understood, no one would deliberately use an obscure substitution when there was a chance that the texter's message could be misconstrued.

Second, the overall syntax of the message does not differ dramatically from standard language construction, since most text terms are substitutions or abbreviations. For example, letters or digits can replace word or symbols: *are* becomes "r" and *ate* becomes "8" to make "gr8" (*great*).

Third, the abbreviations used are not often novel, and those that are are merely an extension of accepted practice. People have, after all, used abbreviations for centuries; consider that Romans began a friendly letter with the abbreviation *SVBE* [*Si vales, bene est* 'If you're well, that's good'], and in English, IOU can be traced to the year 1618, while SWALK [sealed with a loving kiss] had started to appear in valentine greetings by 1648.

Finally, the case can be made that "text speak" is not the result of poor spelling skills, since the texter must have some understanding of the word that he or she is truncating either through abbreviation or substitution.

The level of language awareness required by texters in double-byte languages like Japanese, Chinese, or Korean is even more impressive. Here, the native character sets are used almost entirely, except in the cases of common English abbreviations of phrases, such as, in Japanese, *AM* for *atode mata* (後でまた)—or 'see you later!' Similar mixing and matching of character sets occurs in Chinese texting, where Arabic numerals (which take fewer bits to encode than regular Chinese characters) can be used as stand-ins for their homophones (or at least phonetically similar cousins) to create such messages as "520" [*wu erh ling* 'five, two, zero'] for 'I love you' [*wo ai nin*].

8

IN THE MAIL

From SVBE to SWAK

WRITING WAS INVENTED INDEPENDENTLY IN AT LEAST three different locales—China, Mesopotamia, and Meso-america—and there is some evidence to support a claim for two more, India and Egypt, the oldest writing systems being those of the Sumerians and the Egyptians, both dated to the fourth millennium B.C.E. Since then, people have been sending written messages to each other when direct oral communication was not an option. From the military com-muniqué written on a lead tablet two and a half millennia ago to the picture postcard from your vacation in the Rock-ies last summer to the suspicious e-mail from Nigeria this morning offering to make you rich, written messages have gone back and forth in a variety of media and modes of conveyance, some to be saved for posterity and others to be consigned to the trash bin.

WHAT'S IN THE MAIL?

In Book 6 of the *Iliad,* probably composed in the eighth century B.C.E., Homer recounts the story of the upstand-ing demigod Bellerophon who spurned the attentions

of the wife of Proetus, King of Tiryns, who then told her
husband—hell hath no fury—that Bellerophon had made
improper advances to her. Angered but reluctant to murder
the fellow himself,

> he sent [Bellerophon] to Lycia with many miserable
> life-destroying symbols [*sémata lugrá*] scratched on a
> folded tablet [*grápsas en pínaki ptuktôi*] and told him
> to show it to his [Proetus's] father-in-law [Lycias] that
> he [Bellerophon] might be killed.

There is some question as to what sort of writing was meant
by *sémata* (literally, 'signs, marks,' and, as Liddell and Scott
say in their *Greek-English Lexicon,* "*written characters,* first in Il.
6, 168, 176 of the σήματα λυγρά carried by Bellerophon,
which however were *pictorial,* not *written*"). The usual term
in Greek for "letter" in the sense of "a written message from
one person to another" would have been *grámma* or its plural form *grámmata* (from the same verb, *gráphein* 'to scratch,
engrave, write,' as *grápsas* above), which Liddell and Scott
gloss as "*that which is graven or written, a written character, letter,*
Lat. *litera,* and so in plural, *letters, the alphabet…* usu. in plur.
like Lat. *literae, a letter.*" (English gets its word "letter" in
both senses through French from the Latin, whose origin is
obscure though its meanings seem to have been influenced
by Greek.) The other standard Greek term for "letter" is
epistolé, which Liddell and Scott gloss as "*anything sent by a
messenger, a message, command, commission…* but most usu.
a letter, Lat. *epistola…,*" the noun being derived ultimately
from a verb whose basic meaning is "to send, dispatch."

In any case, the gist of the message that Bellerophon carried with him and the medium on which it was
"scratched"—a folded wooden tablet—were clear enough.
Waxed wooden tablets and tablets made of lead were the
standard media for letters in the earliest days of letter-

writing in the West before the introduction of papyrus, on which numerous communications, both official and personal, survive from the third century B.C.E. onward. (Surviving letters written on lead and wooden tablets can be dated to two centuries earlier, and there is evidence that much Akkadian state correspondence was exchanged in these media long before that.) With these media, the Greeks evolved a standard format for letter-writing that the Romans borrowed and that we continue to use pretty much unchanged to this day:

1. Identification of the sender and recipient
2. Greeting
3. Body of the message
4. Parting salutation

Typically, the Greeks and Romans combined the first two of these components. For example, Mnesiergos writes in Greek to the folks back home in the fourth century B.C.E.: "Mnesiergos mails his greetings and good health to the household" (*Mnēsíergos epésteile toîs oíkoi chaíren kaì hugiaínen*), and seven centuries later, Apollonios writes to his brother, "Apollonios sends his greetings to his brother Artemas (*Apollṓnios Artemâ tô adelphôi chaírein*). The verb *chaírein* (whose basic meaning was 'rejoice, be happy') shows up in various forms as an opening salutation and sometimes as a farewell. Essentially, the wish is for the addressee's well-being, which is sometimes followed by assurances that the sender is in good health as well.

Both conventions are also, perhaps not surprisingly, typical of Roman letters. Cicero begins a letter to his friend the Proconsul Lentulus: "M. Tullius Cicero wishes the proconsul Lentulus the best of health" (*M. Tullius Cicero salutem dat plurimam Lentulo proconsuli,* which he abbreviates elsewhere to *M.T.C.S.D.P. Lentulo procos.*). The openers *S.D.* (for *salutem dat* or *salutem dicit*), *S.P.D.* (where the *P.* for *pluri-mam* is basically an intensifier), and the popular *SVBE* (for *si vales, bene est* ['If you're well, that's good']) were all common (the last attaining the status in the spoken language of an acronym, pronounced "soobay"), suggesting that such conventional openers are essentially phatic, that is, formulas with minimal lexical content whose function is simply to grease the social wheels and provide an open bracket around that which is to follow.

Nowadays, our snail mail has the information necessary to identify the addressee on the outside of the envelope, where a return address may identify the sender. This information may also appear (often with the date) at the beginning of the letter proper, followed by the opening salutation ("Dear John," "Dear Ms. Jones," "To Whom It May Concern," etc.). With e-mail, the sender is identified in the list of your messages, typically with an indication of the missive's subject and the date and time it was received. This information is repeated in the header of the e-mail itself, along with the e-mail addresses of the recipient or recipients and the subject of the e-mail. (Some senders, cutting to the chase, use the subject line to begin the message, including a salutation or skipping the salutation altogether.) E-mail salutations, when one is included in the message, vary in their formality with the intended audience, as do their hard-copy next of kin. Tweets, for a variety of reasons, both practical and social, omit the address and, often, the salutation.

Skipping over the body of a letter for the moment, we come to the close bracket, the sign-off that marks the end of the message (unless there is a postscript—literally, something written after the writing). Just as the beginning and end of a spoken conversation are usually marked by something like "Hello" and "Good-bye," the same goes for a letter. For the Greeks, the formulaic closer was usually some variation on "I pray for your strength, that is, your good health" (*errôsthai se eúchomai*). Romans tended to use the pithier *Vale* (literally, 'Be strong'). We have continued the tradition of the sign-off, which typically includes the sender's name, either by itself or preceded by a closing salutation—"Sincerely," "Yours," "Love," "SWAK [sealed with a kiss]," "XOXO," or, more formally (if vaguely), "Best." (The *X* of *XOXO* is generally held to be an onomatopoeic kiss, and the *O* is probably not short for "osculation" but rather a glyph for a mouth.) E-mail endings may include, in addition to the standard snail-mail inventory, emoticons (character-based or clip-art) and such abbreviations as *bfn* ("bye for now") and *cul8r* or simply *cul* ("see you later"). Again, Twitter tends to eschew farewells.

But the real meat of a letter is, of course, the text between the opener and closer. The contents of a letter can fall into any of a number of subgenres of the form. The story of Bellerophon suggests that the poison-pen letter has been with us for millennia, and actual letters from the world of the Greeks that have been preserved from the fifth century B.C.E. onward have included the military or political dispatch, the letter of recommendation (or safe passage), business correspondence (bills of lading being among the earliest), and the personal. Subsequent years with a growing world population and increasingly sophisticated means of transmitting messages have seen the expansion of the genre (or genres, if we draw a fuzzy line between the epistle and the letter) to include the legal notice, the mass mailing (in both paper and electronic form) asking you to buy something or contribute to some worthy cause, or bringing you up to date on the family's news of the past year; the job application, offer, acceptance, and rejection letter, and letter of resignation; the *billet doux* and the Dear John letter; the crank letter and its electronic sibling, the e-mail flame; the Facebook wall posting and the tweet—to mention only a few.

The earliest personal correspondence that has come down to us was largely the product of the wealthy, the high-placed, or church or state staff, and, above all, the literate: Letters presuppose a person on either end of the correspondence who can read and write (and sometimes act as translator, as when the sender and recipient speak different languages). One can quickly call to mind the letters of Cicero or the epistles of Paul to his fledgling Christian communities. (Of Paul's letters to the Corinthians, a wag once asked, "Did they ever write back?" playing on the technical distinction between the *epistle* as a monologist's polished think piece and the *letter* as a speaker's contribution to what is essentially a conversation.) Personal letters from ordinary people to each other do survive from early times, and are often touching in their ageless concerns, as in the following admonition from two Greek sisters to their younger siblings:

> Apollonia and Eupous to their sisters Rasion and Demarion, greetings.
>
> If you are in good health, that is well. We ourselves are in good health too. You would do us a favour by lighting the lamp in the shrine and shaking out the cushions. Keep studying and do not worry about Mother. For she already is enjoying good health. Expect our arrival.
>
> Farewell.
>
> And don't play in the courtyard but behave yourselves inside.
>
> Take care of Titoas and Sphairos.

DELIVERY

Leaving aside those letters that you write in anger and have the sense to refrain from sending, a letter is meant to be sent and received. The means of conveying a written message from one place to another have evolved over time with the variety and number of correspondents and the technologies available to them. Xenophon describes the Persian postal system in the early fourth century B.C.E. in his biography of Cyrus the Great, the *Cyropaedia,* as a complex system of post-horses and day and night messengers, claiming that "this is the fastest overland traveling on earth." This system was most probably just for Cyrus's benefit (it's good to be king), and scholars will continue to argue about who was first, since establishing this type of permanent infrastructure to move messages around is going to be repeated for millennia.

The Roman emperor Augustus set up a mail system along the Persian model, with staged couriers who could cover fifty Roman miles (*mille passuum*—a thousand paces), or about forty-six of our miles, in a single day. Known as the *cursus publicus* ('public road'), it was meant to be the official state link between Roman provinces. The Byzantine historian Procopius notes that the system consisted of

> eight stages in some places, in others less, but hardly ever less than five. Forty horses were kept for each stage, and grooms in proportion to the number of horses. By frequent relays of the best mounts, couriers were thus able to ride as long a distance in one day as would ordinarily require ten, and bring with them the news required.

The roads that they traveled on were the result of highly regulated construction of engineered roads, covering at one point 250,000 miles, all leading into Rome from all corners of their far-flung empire. This mail system continued in deteriorating form into the sixth century. To be clear, the purpose of this system was to transport state messages and tax revenue, not the ordinary person's postcard from their holiday by the sea. A system this elaborate was bound to be an expensive drain on the state, and this cost was surely one of the factors in its decline, the disintegration of the Roman Empire with its centralized and wide-reaching government being, of course, the crucial blow. The Roman Empire split in two at the end of the fourth century C.E., the western part eventually splintering into individual states and the eastern part, with its capital in Constantinople (formerly Byzantium), falling to the Ottoman Turks in the middle of the fifteenth century at approximately the time that Gutenberg's printing press made its appearance.

During this time, before the invention of the printing press and the concomitant increase in the numbers of the literate, the delivery of the mail was in large part handled by the private sector: The written affairs of the Church, the guilds, and well-to-do individuals were carried on such roads as there were, largely catch-as-catch-can, opening an opportunity for local entrepreneurs to go into the business of carrying the mail. Eventually, with the stabilization of nations, the development of international trade, and the improvement of the highway system to facilitate that trade, the state reentered the game, initiating a battle for a monopoly on the business of delivering the mail that simmers to this day.

One would think that the combination of greater literacy and the relative ease with which mail could now be delivered would have produced a dramatic growth in written correspondence. A nagging impediment to this growth, however, was the cost of postage. In early America, for example, mailing a single letter could cost as much as a day's wage, and delivery was slow and haphazard. David H. Henkin, in *The Postal Age*, states that "receiving a letter was, for most Americans, an event rather than a feature of ordinary experience." For starters, the price of postage was based on a calculation of weight and distance traveled and was paid on the receiving end at the nearest city post office, meaning that once you found out that a letter was waiting for you, you had to travel to the city to pick it up. If you couldn't pay, the letter remained in a back room of the post office's ever-growing "dead letter" office. The entire process, from start to finish, could take months, and you often took a chance that the letter you had to pay to redeem might be, if not junk mail, something for which you would have preferred not to pay.

An oddity of the early American system was that for a fraction of the cost of a letter, you could send a newspaper through the mail, and for a time the newspaper was a popular form of correspondence allowing you to share local news along with your current location and the information that you were in relative good health (at least well enough to get to the post office). Patrons tried sending more personal messages along by marking words in the paper, but this practice was quickly outlawed. Postal rates were dramatically dropped, first in England, and then in America, with the idea that the increased volume would pay for the increased business. Mail also became more user-friendly, first with standard postage stamps prepaying the mailing at a fixed rate by weight, then the slow development of local delivery of mail, even to rural addresses.

As with many rapid technological changes in communication, some new anxieties came as part of the mix. Like someone who is not computer-literate in our age, a person with poor handwriting and letter composition skills could feel like a yokel who was "not with it." An explosion of hand-writing guides and letter-writing manuals, complete with sample letters, such as *Frost's Original Letter Writer* (1867) or *Martine's Sensible Letter-Writer* (1866), helped assure the novice "that we may improve in our writing." In addition to spelling and common grammatical tips, a staple of such guides that persists to this day is the sample letter for almost every conceivable occasion. These samples might include "A letter from a serving Man to his Master," or "From a young lady at school, to a former companion," or "From a Father to a Tradesman, to take his son on trial," or "To a friend with a barrel of apples," addressing all ages, classes, and both social and business applications. Also handy, and still a fixture in letter guides and student dictionaries, is instruction as to how to address, say, the pope, in a letter. We are also admonished to avoid using poor-quality paper, sloppy handwriting, and any sort of underlining (which can "greatly deface a letter"), for writing a letter is not only an art, but serious business:

> ...remember, that whatever you write is written evidence of your good sense or your folly, your industry or carelessness, your self-control or your impatience. What you have once put into the letter-box may cost you lasting regret, or be equally important to your whole future welfare. And, for such grave reasons, *think before you write, and think while you are writing.*

Words to live by, to which may be added the more recent injunction (Bohr's Rule): Never write more clearly than you can think.

Another source of social anxiety centered on the idea that a woman could now send and receive her own mail. That a woman could enjoy such freedom of communication was accompanied by the concern that she might encroach on a male space, the post office, a bastion of commerce and testosterone. By using mail, a woman could maintain a secretive relationship outside the purview of her husband. A woman entering a post office might be thought to be posting adulterous love letters, regardless of her actual business. A woman might enter a post office and be confronted by the crudities of the male gender. A woman might enter a post office, open a letter containing bad news, and swoon in emotion. Such issues actually shaped postal policy and even the architecture of the post offices themselves: Among the solutions proposed were separate entrances for men and women and home delivery of the mail (to avoid all that potential public swooning).

PICK A CARD

During the epistolary explosion of the Victorian age, new forms of correspondence began to appear. Cheap postage and modern manufacturing methods saw mass-produced versions of greeting cards, Christmas cards, postcards, and valentines all arriving in America and England between 1843 (Christmas cards) and 1861 (postcards) with great popularity. The precursor to all these printed cards was the visiting or calling card, which came with a complex set of rules and rituals surrounding who could leave a card with whom, and when. The design of the card varied by sex and class. An 1882 etiquette book, *Our Deportment,* sums up attitudes about the card's usage and social importance:

> To the unrefined and underbred, the visiting card is but a trifling bit of paper; but to the cultured disciple of social law, it conveys a subtle and unmistakable intelligence. Its texture, style of engraving, and even the hour of leaving it combine to place the stranger, whose name it bears, in a pleasant or a disagreeable attitude, even before his manners, conversation and face have been able to explain his social position.

Calling cards were standardized in size, typically a little larger than today's business card, but varied by the age in which they were used (the cards got larger in the Victorian period), men's being slightly smaller than women's and typically a little more staid and plain. When "calling" socially and you missed the party, you would leave your card, possibly with a short personal note on the reverse, on a silver tray (a *salver*) along with any other callers' cards, which, as etiquette allowed, you could riffle through to see who else had been visiting. In a nineteenth-century hybrid of the answering machine and Facebook, we can easily imagine callers enjoying the social aspect of an inner circle of friends. Calling card etiquette also had a social function for the grieving, allowing well-wishers to leave cards without disturbing the mourners. The social sharing went both ways: You might leave the card a prominent person had deposited on your own salver as a way of letting subsequent callers know that you were "in with the in crowd," as many of us can recall from Jane Austen's *Persuasion,* where we see our heroine Anne Elliot's shame at her family's reaction to this practice:

> They visited in Laura Place, they had the cards of Dowager Viscountess Dalrymple, and the Honourable Miss Carteret, to be arranged wherever they might be most visible: and "Our cousins in Laura Place,"— "Our cousins, Lady Dalrymple and Miss Carteret," were talked of to everybody.

There were elaborate rules governing the exchange of cards between the sexes, though almost none between men. And like the proliferation of take-out menus stuck in any urban mailbox today, large colorful "trades" cards could be dropped at any address as a kind of Victorian spam. Indeed, the Polaroid of the day—the daguerreotype, a single image

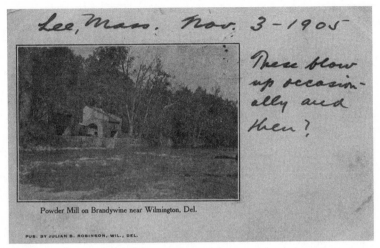

Lee, Mass. Nov. 3 – 1905

These blow up occasion-ally and then?

Powder Mill on Brandywine near Wilmington, Del.

PUB. BY JULIAN B. ROBINSON, WIL., DEL.

Figure 8.1

from a single exposure offered by traveling photographers—was already commonly slipped into the letters of all classes of patron.

An offshoot of the trade card, the first illustrated "post cards" were advertisements for a trade, perhaps illustrated with famous landmarks in the city where the company's business was located. By the time cheap postal rates were introduced in England, the United States, and elsewhere, postal authorities needed to decide how to regulate this popular novelty, which in the United States was already starting to be used by private companies. Early cards allowed patrons to write on a small strip on the picture side (figure 8.1), with the address appearing on the obverse (figure 8.2).

By 1907 in the United States, the post had evolved into the "divided-back" card, with the writing space for your message on the address side and the obverse filled with the picture image—essentially the postcard we know today. The images ranged from the scenic, the early color-saturated

Figure 8.2

images, to comic images (known to collectors as "saucy" postcards). Messages were by design short, often a quick update on the traveler's status, not too different in content from a Twitter "tweet," as in this 1917 card from the Smithsonian collection:

> Arrived here O.K. two hours late. Leave tonight 7-35 pm. Bright & cool today. Overcoat feels good but I wouldn't be back in St. Pete. Everybody talking war. Hope you have a safe journey home. You will find soldiers guarding all buildings
>
> Harry D.

Some postcards were perhaps never meant to be sent. The erotic postcard by definition was illegal to mail, existing solely to be collected, unsullied, unlike the more popularly collectable postage stamp, by a cancellation mark. Others, such as the Christmas and Valentine's Day card, were certainly meant to be sent if not actively collected, sometimes saved for the address on the envelope in the case of the former and for its sentimental value in the case of the latter.

The Christmas card's history goes back far earlier than the postcard. People in pre-Christian Egypt and Rome gave each other mass-produced scent flasks and oil lamps that were stamped with seasonal messages, in this case for winter festivals and the new year. For various reasons, the prominence of Christmas waxed and waned throughout history—sometimes overshadowed by other Christian holidays, sometimes banned because of a concern that it would be linked to pagan holidays and the reckless partying that went along with them. Between Queen Victoria and her German husband's public celebration of the holiday season and the publication of Charles Dickens's *A Christmas Carol,* Christmas was literally reinvented in a few short years, along with the production of the first preprinted Christmas card in 1843, in close proximity to the dropping of the postal rate. The queen started the tradition of the "official" Christmas card shortly thereafter, a practice followed by royalty and other heads of state ever since.

If the queen sends out an official card each year, what about the rest of us? Early cards left little room for a message, but later designs provided an opportunity to add a personal message and perhaps some news. If the family Christmas card is meant to represent the Smith family in the same way that the Queen's card represents her family, considerable thought must be given not only to the message but to the recipients. Enter the "Christmas card list" and the "Christmas letter." The first ensures that no one who sent a card last year is bypassed—a reason to save those envelopes from last year—and the second is, in theory, a hand-cramp-reducing timesaver. For most people, the Christmas card list is revisited annually in a winnowing process that feels like a passive "unfriending" on Facebook—"Did we get a card from Aunt Joyce last year?" "Do we still want to send a card to your old boss?" Once the painful threshing has separated the wheat from the chaff, one now needs to decide if one can call up the stamina necessary to write personal, touching, and witty messages to every individual on the entire list (on the average, twenty-six, according to a greeting card trade group), or if one will resort to the use of a general, one-size-fits-all form letter that sums up everything that you would have wanted to say to each of those twenty-six people. The end result is, as one columnist put it, "the family version of a corporation's annual report." The result can sound just as stilted. Every corporation wants to shine a light on the flattering events of the previous year, glossing over that little accounting fraud issue that the newspapers were all atwitter about, and a Christmas letter can paint an image of a perfect family that, unlike your actual family, is just a little smarter and more successful than your neighbor's. Cynics argue that the only people who seem to enjoy Christmas letters are, at most, the people who write them. Members of the nuclear family may be forgiven a lack of enthusiasm:

> Dad used last year['s letter] to explain what I was doing—or not doing—in Seattle: "Rumor has it that a phone may be installed this week. Who knows? A job may not be far behind."

Those that receive them may be miffed that they didn't rate the handwritten version or that such an epistle-general is either too boastful or too whiny. But considering that the first Christmas card was created to save time, the impulse to mass-produce your sentiment may actually be a Christmas tradition, and even as some writers take the job of crafting a letter of this sort as a serious exercise in giving domestic peculiarities a general appeal, so their recipients may have the dual satisfaction of being brought up to date on these homely details about people of whom they are genuinely fond with at least a modicum of charm, wit, and benevolence.

The paper Christmas card may be in decline as the popularity of the e-card increases. Once limited and somewhat cheesy, modern e-cards can now personalize content with images, audio, and video content. As a U.K. proponent of the e-card notes:

> Whilst it is still of course special to receive a Christmas card, the impact a personal video message from a granddaughter or grandson has on the recipient can't be underestimated.

If there is social pressure associated with the giving and receiving of Christmas cards, the stakes are even higher when it comes to the Valentine's Day card. Referred to by some as "Singles Awareness Day" because it tends to highlight those who are not in a relationship, Valentine's Day isn't a happy time for everyone. (Of course, Christmas isn't either, but that's another story.) Whatever you call it, the day has a complicated history, part religious, part commercial, which has gone from an "often forgotten, easily neglected Old World saint's day to an indigenized, not-to-be-missed American holiday," according to Harvard Divinity School's Leigh Eric Schmidt, who describes the commercialization of the day as "an early exemplar of how an emergent consumer culture transformed traditional holidays." Two hundred years earlier, diarist Samuel Pepys notes that while "little Will Mercer" has "brought [Mrs. Pepys's] name writ upon blue paper in gold letters, done by himself," the ever-penurious Sam adds that it will cost him £5 to be his wife's valentine as well. By the end of the 1840s, commercially printed cards were all the rage. Children have been a part of the celebration, making their own cards or giving commercial ones as part of grade-school curricula. In contemporary society, giving cards is now considered insufficient, and in America alone, "total spending this year [2008] is estimated to top $16.90 billion, with the average consumer spending nearly $120 on the holiday" and with men "expected to spend more than $156." Apparently, we will no longer settle for a handful of heart candy with upbeat sentiments as a suitable accompaniment to the card.

The flip side of Valentine's Day would have to be the "Dear John" letter, which appears to be a product of the Second World War's long-distance relationships and hasty marriages (though the first hit song by that name, by Ferlin Husky and Jean Shepard, dates from 1953, the year of the Korean War armistice). While the popular usage may have existed for some time during the war, the first published reference appears in a 1945 issue of the Rochester, N.Y., *Democrat and Chronicle*:

> "Dear John," the letter began. "I have found someone else whom I think the world of. I think the only way out is for us to get a divorce," it said. They usually began like that, those letters that told of infidelity on the part of the wives of servicemen... The men called them "Dear Johns."

While not as formal as "Dear Mr. Smith," the neutral salutation "Dear John" from one's sweetie might have served as a signal that what was to follow would be all business and no pleasure.

FROM SNAIL MAIL TO E-MAIL (AND BEYOND)

To help speed the flow, letters and cards needed to be a fixed, recognized size, and most industrial countries have developed some kind of sorting system similar to the

American ZIP code system to expedite routing and delivery. Each postal code originally represented a fixed geographical location; it was usually easier to read than a handwritten address and could be optically scanned and sorted with the aid of a computer as improving technology permitted.

The assumption that a piece of mail with enough stamps affixed to it can go anywhere is in fact limited by postal treaties between countries, as we are reminded in Heinrich Harrer's account in *Seven Years in Tibet* of mailing a letter that is at once modern and Roman:

> ...we had to use the complicated Tibetan post, sending our letters to the frontiers in double envelopes, the outside one bearing a Tibetan stamp. At the frontier we arranged for a man to remove the outer envelope, put an Indian stamp on the inner one and post it on. With luck it took only a fortnight for a letter to get to Europe. In Tibet the post is carried by runners who work in relays of four miles each. Along all the high-roads are huts in which relays wait ready to relieve the runners as they arrive. Postal runners carry a spear with bells attached as a sign of their office. The spear can, if necessary, be used as a weapon and the bells serve to frighten off wild animals at night. Stamps are printed in five different denominations and are on sale in the post offices.

From Tibet to cyberspace, even e-mails share a structure with Heinrich's letters home. Each e-mail has an electronic address for the sender and intended recipient, and if you make a mistake when addressing your message, it is unlikely ever to arrive, held instead in a computer equivalent of a "dead letter" office. Like most things on the Internet, e-mail has its origin in military's ARPANET, and most of the components of an e-mail from 1971 would look the same as a message sent yesterday, with the "from" and "to" indicated with a username, an "@" sign, and the name of your host computer system. An "envelope" of a kind serves as a "wrapper" to indicate, like a ZIP code, how to route the message, as well as information about what's inside the envelope digitally as an aid in rendering the content on the other end. Technically, you can send your message to as many people as you want, though bulk mailing is typically throttled by your service provider to 100 or fewer at a time to control the load on the system.

The ability to send a single message to multiple recipients at a single go is one of the handy features that distinguishes e-mail from paper mail, as are the Reply and the sometimes treacherous Reply to All options in most e-mail systems. Another is the BCC (blind carbon copy) function, the source of some etiquette concerns, since it enables you to send mail to several people at once without each individual's being able to see (or reply to) any of the other recipients. Some etiquette guides suggest that the BCC function is a courtesy that preserves the anonymity of the other recipients, while others feel that BCC senders can seem a little like creepy crypto-spammers.

Perhaps because e-mails are so easy to send, we are faced with a couple of issues: mistakes caused by sending them too quickly, and recipients getting overwhelmed with the volume of mail. First, most guides to writing professional, readable e-mail suggest techniques for slowing the process, advising the writer to review an e-mail before sending it to make sure that the addresses in the recipient fields are correct (and the recipients are all and only the ones you intend), the grammar and spelling are accurate, the tone is appropriate (sarcasm doesn't e-mail well, and, as with paper mail, there are no facial or intonational cues you can offer by way of clarification, though in some cases an emoticon can help), and the text is in bite-sized blocks of text and not loaded with CAPITAL LETTERS before you click the Send button. In your personal life you may send off an e-mail when you are, let us say, not in full possession of your faculties—in other words, "drunk mailing." One of the largest e-mail providers, Google, has a solution: "Mail Goggles." In this system, during a preset time frame (by default, weekend nights between 10 P.M. and 4 A.M.), you must answer five basic math problems in sixty seconds before the "Send" button will work. You can change both the time frame and the difficulty of the math (assuming, that is, that you are compos mentis).

As for e-mail overload, one cause is that once it is in your inbox, each e-mail appears like every other e-mail: We can't immediately tell the difference between mail we care about, mail we must act on immediately, mail that we wish to read but can open at our leisure, and mail we wouldn't read if we were paid to do so. Some software solutions include restricting our inbox to only those people we have already sent mail to, and so-called smart solutions that scan our inbox and make an attempt at prioritization. Other systems allow the sender to flag the importance of the mail with an icon to appear next to the item in the recipient's e-mail list.

Unlike third-class junk mail, "spam," or junk e-mail, used to be hard to spot before the development of smart filters, but since spam costs almost nothing to send, it is likely to continue to seek our electronic mailboxes for the indefinite future. Spam comes in a variety of flavors, some of which are simply paper-mail genres adapted to cyberspace while others are extensions of the oral tradition. Among the former may be counted plain old advertising and the chain letter, which in its paper version has traditionally offered good luck and quick money only if forwarded, either retyped or photocopied, and sent to some number of individuals (sometimes with cash). The e-mail version tends to be less about money than good wishes or petitions for good causes. Extending the oral tradition of rumor and urban legend, e-mail offers an excellent medium for spreading misinformation quickly and widely, giving rise to such sites as snopes.com, which has become hugely popular by listing and debunking the latest e-mail chain you should take with a grain of salt or, less often, take as gospel. An example of the former:

> Claim: Gang members all over the country are spreading a deadly mixture of LSD and strychnine on pay phone buttons.
> Status: *False.*

The site then sources the origin of the claim, and in a method similar to the one used in the *Urban Legends* series of books, researches the claims and when possible, debunks the myth associated with the e-mail.

TWEET!

A newcomer to the messaging world is the social networking tool Twitter. With this product, users can send and read short messages known as "tweets." Tweets are strictly text-based and can consist of up to 140 eight-bit characters for a message comparable to what you can put on a postcard or in a short message service (SMS) text. The message is displayed on your profile page and is either delivered to your inner circle of subscribers (followers) or is allowed to be read by anyone. You can send and receive tweets through the Twitter website or by using your cell phone's SMS texting feature. The function of Twitter is ostensibly to answer the question "What are you doing?" For people who feel the need to be connected to their friends and to know what they are doing throughout the day and also need to share that same level of detail, Twitter is

a godsend. When a group of hackers caused a temporary out-
age in 2009, users reported that they felt completely adrift
without the interconnection that Twitter provided:

> "You know how you pat your pockets for your cell
> phone and your keys? Well it's that same kind of phan-
> tom [limb] with Twitter," she said. "It's like, 'I can't
> update! I can't update!' It's just one of those bugs that
> gets in you."
>
> She added: "I was pretty upset, actually. It feels like
> a lifeline for me…Pretty much everyone knows almost
> every detail of my life by what I'm doing on Twitter."

This kind of dependency isn't for everyone. While the number of new Twitter users has grown dramatically, according
to the Nielson rating people, most folks don't come back:

> Currently, more than 60 percent of U.S. Twitter users
> fail to return the following month, or in other words,
> Twitter's audience retention rate, or the percentage
> of a given month's users who come back the following
> month, is currently about 40 percent.

Facebook, the other major social networking site, seems to
retain users at a higher rate, perhaps because in addition to
short status messages, users can also share other content,
such as photos and comments. With both sites, users can
control to some extent who can view their content, though
questions have been raised about who "owns" the content—
the user posting it or the company hosting it. The many
questions revolving around the issue of advertising on both
Facebook and Twitter are still being hashed out.

And, as always with new technology, questions of social
impact and etiquette arise, not least with the concept of
"friending." Are we desperate enough to have friends that
we accept people we barely know as Facebook "friends?"

What if you have a tight circle of friends on Facebook and you enjoy discussing your social life, and your boss asks to be your friend: Do you say no and risk your career, or "friend" him and take down the pictures of you dancing naked on tables? One solution is to maintain multiple accounts—one for "real" friends and another account for "work" friends or your painfully hip parents.

Surely there must be something more basic at work here than the desire to have the latest gadget—are there "parallels between online social networks and tribal societies?" As Alex Wright notes:

> Still, the sheer popularity of social networking seems to suggest that for many, these environments strike a deep, perhaps even primal chord. "They fulfill our need to be recognized as human beings, and as members of a community," Dr. [Lance] Strate says. "We all want to be told: You exist."

9

IN AND OUT OF TROUBLE

Warnings, Excuses, and Remedial Work

"HEADS UP!" "UH-OH...." "SORRY." AVOIDING TROUBLE, realizing that you *are* in trouble, and extricating yourself from it are all processes that have short forms of communication associated with them. Indeed, the first situation often mandates terseness on the part of those who would warn unaware others about impending catastrophe: the air raid or tornado siren, or cries of "Duck!" "Timberrrrr!" "Low bridge!" This is particularly true of danger from above (*catastrophe* itself comes from *kata-*, 'descending from higher up,' plus *strophē*, 'turn,' the idea being that such misfortunes fall from celestial or at least Olympian heights); since our gaze is normally in a horizontal orientation, signs such as "Phone Workers Overhead" and "Falling Rock Zone" are conveniently placed more or less at eye level.

We don't always heed warnings—who knew that the safety cone labeled "piso mojado" said "wet floor" on its other face and that this was in any case not an admonition to refrain from tracking mud on the newly cleaned floor but rather to be careful not to slip and break one's neck, or that if you got caught zooming through the crosswalk (so many pedestrians, so little time), you might indeed have to pay that $100 fine threatened by the preceding traffic sign? Of course, sometimes there is no warning to heed: Mother Nature fails to warn us of the lightning strike, the manufacturer neglects to mention that the article of kiddie clothing is flammable, or the maker of Snippo Scissors assumes that no reasonable person should need to be told in writing not to run with the product. But however we get into it, trouble is sooner or later sure to let us know where we are, whether in the form of an overdue notice in the mail or the flashing blue light that announces the imminent arrival of a ticket for that moving violation. Then we can turn our attention to trying to control the damage as quickly and as gracefully as possible.

HEADS UP!

Warnings are designed to raise our consciousness, if not outright alarm. The French sign reading *"Danger de mort! Défense absolue d'entrer!"* ('Deadly danger! Absolutely no admittance!') both warns us off and tells us what might occur if we disregard it and barge in. "Keep Off! 100,000 Volts!" more explicitly identifies the source of the peril while being less informative as to why it's a problem; implicit is that everyone knows what a volt is, and that a lot of them at once can cause a serious shock. Such signs presuppose, however, not merely a certain fluency in their actual language but some cultural literacy as well (at least enough to recognize a hazard to life and limb much greater than would be indicated by parodic warning signs saying *"Danger des petits-fours!"* or "Keep Off! 100,000 Dollars!"

A difference between a warning and a threat is that while both advertise danger, a warning simply tells you that a bad thing may happen ("Harmful if swallowed"), whereas a threat is often associated with the person giving the notice ("Be home before midnight or I'll take away your teddy bear"). The sense of *warn* has changed little since the Middle Ages: 'to inform, especially in such a way as to put one on one's guard and take precautions.' *Threat* is from Old English *préat,* which originally meant '(a) press (of people), crowd, or throng,' a Germanic import from Latin *trūdere* ('to press,' the *-trud-* or *-trus-* of *extrude, protruding,* and *intrusive*). According to the *Oxford English Dictionary,* it also came to mean "painful pressure," "compulsion," "vexation," and "danger," and by extension "a denunciation to a person of ill to befall," the root sense being "pressure applied to the will by declaration of the harm that will follow noncompliance."

To be sure, we sometimes say "That's not a threat; it's a promise," to underscore the seriousness of our intentions. Forensic linguist Bruce Fraser distinguishes nicely between the two: Whereas a threat announces an "intention to act," a promise is a "commitment to act." Even more fundamental is that a threat is "an unfavourable act intended to instil fear" while a promise is "a favourable act intended to promote good feeling. It follows from the first distinction that sanctions may be imposed for a broken promise, while no such redress is permitted for a broken threat." A warning thus more closely resembles a threat than a promise, as when a sentry calls out "Halt or I fire!"

One can, of course, combine promise and threat, like the overseer who tells the slave child, "Your daily quota is 100 pounds of cotton. For every pound over that, you'll get a penny; for every pound less, a swat from my stick." But for a mere warning to become a threat, Frasier says, the speaker must not merely be "bring[ing] to the addressee's awareness a state of the world...the addressee should want to avoid" but be the actual agent through whom something bad will befall the addressee. Moreover, there must be at least some intention to intimidate; even if my tutor tells me that if I fail to make at least three Cs and a D he'll have little choice but put me on probation next term, this may merely be a neutral or even friendly advisory that my academic career is in some danger, and hardly a threat as such. (*Danger* comes from medieval French *dangier*, which meant 'power over [someone],' derived from Latin *dominārium*, 'power to dominate,' in turn from *dominus*, 'lord, master;' the modern English and French sense of *danger* as 'peril' dates from the fourteenth century.)

Drugs have been touted since time immemorial as cures for troubles (and the source of others: Odysseus's crew twice had to be rescued from the latter, first in the Lotus-Eaters' Land and again when turned to pigs by the sorceress Circe's spiked honeyed wine). With few exceptions, the illegal ones come without any textual embellishments, but the prescriptions on the over-the-counter sort often bear characteristic labeling, including standard warnings such as "Do not drive or use heavy machinery" or "Do not take with alcohol." (So do containers of alcohol itself, from easily concealed one-ounce nips on up through champagne magnums and beyond, which caution about possible effects on the future children of pregnant drinkers, while tobacco labeling—whether cigarettes, pipe shag, or snuff—cycles through a variety of the Surgeon General's warnings, there being more dire consequences than can fit on a single label with legible type.)

Such warnings seem to fall into two categories: those that are government-mandated as a matter of public health policy and those that are intended to head off litigation for negligence should the consumer behave other than as directed. The latter sort can be taken to extremes, as when a fast-food restaurant's disposable coffee cup warns you that the contents may be awfully hot; but behind a printed warning that one supposes only a fool would need is not infrequently someone who was indeed foolish enough to incur injury from an obvious hazard but smart enough to hire a ruthless lawyer after the fact, plus a deep-pocket corporate defendant willing to settle out of court. (Whence such real-life label warnings as "May irritate your eyes" on a can of pepper spray, "Do not ignite in face" for a cigarette lighter, and "Do not drop out of window" for an air conditioner.)

Auto accidents are of course a rich source of litigation as well: Trivial fender benders are less of an issue now that most states have some form of no-fault insurance, but accidents are still a fertile vineyard for personal-injury attorneys, insurers being understandably reluctant to pay claims for harm whose gravity or connection to their client is unsubstantiated. The scandalous percentage of car accidents, injuries, and fatalities resulting from drunk driving has prompted extensive advertising and stiffer punishments—Ohio's special yellow license plate for people convicted of driving under the influence arguably combines the two—as well as do-it-yourself breathalyzers that allow you to check whether you're over the legal limit before you go driving, with even a version for hooking up to your car's onboard computer that will not let you start the car if you're too sozzled.

Indeed, the proliferation of safety devices built into our cars has caused some drivers to grumble about the car as nanny: bells that bong incessantly till your door is really closed or your passenger fastens the seat belt, air bags that explode if you bump the car in front too hard while trying to wriggle out of the space its driver parked you into, too-sensitive break-in detectors that cycle through five irritating siren variants until your neighbors loathe you enough to pray your car *will* be broken into, and even talking dashboards. Some of these are no more than just clever examples of what our technology allows us to add to the old flivver in newfangled features (or bugs, when they malfunction); others, such as bumpers designed to collapse on impact, cushioning the force over distance (compare the '39 Plymouth's springy steel strips), mitigate real trouble when it's unavoidable.

UH-OH...

Cars have a way of breaking down in inconvenient places. While having your radiator boil over in the middle of stalled traffic on a hot day can be a great nuisance, at least you can usually count on a neighborly push to the side of the road. On superhighways, a breakdown lane is conveniently provided for emergencies, though trying to change a flat tire with tractor-trailers whizzing by just a few feet away can be an unnerving experience at best.

If the problem is more serious, there are several conventions for indicating that you are stopped and in trouble: the handkerchief tied to your driver's seat doorknob, the folding window shade whose other side reads SEND HELP, the flashers on your taillights, and at night, magnesium flares, which truckers routinely carry, as well as folding orange-triangle reflective signs which they can set up on the roadway behind their disabled semitrailers. Such signifiers will sooner or later attract the attention of the highway patrol, meanwhile decreasing one's chances of getting slammed into while waiting for help to arrive. Thanks to the advent of cell phones, it is also now possible to dial police directly, with some highways posting signs bearing a special star-prefixed two- or three-digit number for on-the-road assistance. (This is one of several ways in which cell phones provide a way of reaching out beyond your zone of trouble to those outside it who may be able to help you—or failing that, at least to hear your good-byes, as was poignantly demonstrated at the World Trade Center on Sept. 11, 2001.)

Compliance with a police order of "Hands up!"—or in Britain, "Hands on head(s)!"—is both a ready sign to observers that you are already in trouble and a way of avoiding more of it by showing that those hands are empty. To be sure, there are counterexamples: During the Second World War, a Japanese officer on Iwo Jima, ostensibly surrendering with his hands in the air, suddenly reached behind to draw the samurai sword still strapped to his back, and with one blow split from crown to belly the American soldier facing him before being gunned down by his other captors. But even here the ploy would not have worked without a presumption that hands up meant no more fighting: Displaying an open hand with no weapon in it is by default a gesture of peaceful greeting, or at least is so understood throughout much of the world.

In the power-exchange games of consenting adult participants in the BDSM (short for bondage/discipline–sadomasochism) demimonde, limits are theoretically guaranteed by means of a *safeword,* the "magic word" you and your partner agree in advance will function as a red flag signifying trouble that stops your as-if scene in its tracks as soon as it is uttered. Experienced players suggest that patently incongruous utterances such as "pickles!" or "Basingstoke!" work a lot better as safewords than "ouch," "stop," and "mercy," which too closely resemble the kind of thing one is *supposed* to say while engaged in acting out dominant/submissive scenarios of the "Now, my proud beauty, you are in my power!"/"Oh please don't thrash me till I moan" variety.

"Stop thief!" presents no such potential for misreading, being instantly recognizable as hue and cry (one of those legal doublets, hue being from French *huer,* 'shout, cry, make a noise like an owl') and demanding every honest citizen's assistance in apprehending the malefactor. For the thief, it is a warning that trouble is now in hot pursuit. "You have the right to remain silent...," "The defendant will rise," and "Abandon All Hope, Ye Who Enter Here" tell us we're in trouble too, of course, but for the most part we already know it once matters have progressed that far, unless we are really stupid or else in very deep denial.

Parking and traffic tickets serve such notice as well, the former generally in our absence, the latter almost always at the conclusion of a conversation in which, if we are lucky, we may adduce mitigating circumstances that persuade the officer to let us off with a warning instead. If we're less lucky, our traffic citation constitutes a summons to appear in court to pay our fine (Latin *citāre* meant 'to move, excite, summon,' as did *summonēre,* a compound of *sub-* plus *monēre,* 'to warn'), though depending on the offense one can sometimes skip the court appearance and send the money in the post instead. Parking tickets are routinely paid by mail, and there's an end to it—unless, of course, one fails to pay enough of them, in which case sooner or later one will find one's car with one wheel immobilized by a Denver boot (so called from one of the first cities to make extensive use of it; compare the concrete lane separators called *Jersey knees*).

A *ticket* was originally a *stick:* Old French *estiquet*—whence *etiquette*—was a Germanic borrowing originally meaning a branch or switch stuck in the ground as a target for practice shots but later taking on the meaning of 'note, label.' It came into English as *tiket* in the early sixteenth century with the sense of 'written certification,' 'short written notice,' or 'publicly posted notice.' Its modern meanings are suggestive of an elongated rectangular printed format: 'political slate,' 'piece of paper that entitles the bearer to something,' 'summons for a traffic violation,' *Tickety-boo,* as any fan of Danny Kaye's *The Court Jester* knows, means marvy (though the origin of *tickety* is uncertain—the OED offers Hindi *ṭhīk hai* 'all right' as a possibility while inviting the reader to compare the use of "ticket" in the expression "that's the ticket.").

A summons might be considered pretty good evidence that one was in some sort of trouble. It shares with the subpoena the implicit threat of a bailiff coming after you if you don't turn up when you're supposed to. In the case of some legislative hearings, most notoriously those of the House Un-American Activities Committee, or HUAC, during the 1950s, the very fact of being called to testify was trouble on its face. To be sure, the Fifth Amendment protected witnesses from having to incriminate themselves, and not a few of them answered questions about their former involvement with the Communist Party by invoking it. Not so easy to choose between ratting out someone else or being jailed for contempt, and in any case those in the film industry who were subpoenaed often found themselves sacked and obliged to work under assumed names for outsider film and television companies. (Old enough to remember watching the TV series *Robin Hood, Sir Lancelot,* or *The Buccaneers* as a kid? All three shows employed blacklisted ex-Hollywood people under fake names.)

But it is the courts that are the ideal theater for tropes of trouble, teased statement by statement from plaintiffs, defendants, and witnesses and summed up by attorneys for both sides in a long tradition of forensic histrionics. One of the earliest court transcripts we have is from the corruption trial of Kushshiharbe, mayor of the Hurrian city of Nuzi in northern Mesopotamia, around 1400 B.C.E. And in the twilight of the Roman republic, the eloquent senator Cicero made his reputation working as a defense attorney, in which capacity he obtained acquittals for at least two accused murderers (one certainly guilty and the other probably so) through the brilliance of his rhetoric, a batting average many a lawyer of today might envy.

On the other hand, sometimes it's a fair cop, and not even a combination of Clarence Darrow and Perry Mason could get us off the charges. Hence, at a sentencing hearing, defendants may do well instead to acknowledge the error of their ways in hopes that a show of contrition will lighten the sentence. (*Confess* is from Latin *confitērī*, 'to acknowledge,' and *error* from *errāre*, 'to wander, stray.' We shall have more to say about confession below.) Unfortunately for those just convicted, their victims will, if allowed to speak (as is increasingly the case), take the opportunity to ensure by their testimony that the defendant gets as hard a sentence as possible, so that they may have the cathartic experience of seeing justice done, even unto the uttermost farthing. Moreover, the judge may use the occasion to deliver a homily on how the gravity of the crime warrants a punishment of condign severity, not just explaining to defendants what sort of trouble they are in but rubbing their nose in it. All of this may be duly reported by the press, so that the public has the vicarious (and voyeuristic) pleasure of wallowing in someone else's troubles at second hand.

No such separation attends computer error messages, by which we certainly know we're in trouble, and to a certain extent what sort of trouble it is. The quest for user-friendly interfaces has been so successful (good-bye DOS, hello Windows) that it is easy for us to imagine that the box telling us "WidgetWorks has encountered an error at module r2d2 and the program will now terminate" was posted there by an actual demon inside our terminal, but no: Such messages are there because some programmer put them there—that is, wrote them into the source code that will make your computer hardware do what is necessary to make the appropriate stuff appear on your screen and respond to your keystrokes. (There are also code comments, which are statements that a programmer inserts into a program's source code for future reference. The compiler ignores them, with the result that they do not become part of the object code and are inaccessible to the executable program. Let's pretend they're not there for now.)

In theory, of course, one could write such a program in machine language, the strings of 0s and 1s that actually correspond to the on and off states of binary switches in the computer's vacuum tubes, transistors, or chips. In practice, nobody does this, because programming languages from FORTRAN and COBOL to C++ and Java allow us to write commands in code that looks something like a rather peculiar sort of English. Translating such code into assembly language, which will in turn generate the machine code of 1s and 0s, is done by a type of program called a compiler. The application programmer's job is to write code that will actually compile.

Faulty source code can generate errors when it's run through the compiler. Even good (i.e., executable) code can generate errors at run time when, for example, a working program tries to perform an operation on faulty input (garbage in, garbage out). It's up to programmers to include error-trapping code in their applications, and to deal with such errors by doing an end run around them where possible—and, where not, signaling the error by sending a message to the effect that something untoward has occurred. Error messages are sometimes sent to an error log (i.e., a file that keeps a record of the errors encountered when the compiler or compiled program runs); sometimes such a message is sent to the screen.

Once upon a time, in the early mainframe days, when you wanted information about the meaning of an error message (or, for that matter, how to write an application in the first place), you might ask a long-suffering colleague for help and receive the oft-repeated advice "RTFM" ("Read the effing manual"). As like as not, the FM was a behemoth of a tome in a bulky three-ring binder that came with the software. The three-ring binder was a practical economy: If the product that its contents described was to enjoy subsequent releases with new features and enhancements requiring documentation (not to mention, in passing, corrections to the existing documentation), the company could save some money by issuing "change pages," that is, new pages to replace the old, the new or changed text often being flagged with change bars to call attention to itself.

Never very popular with users, change pages and the unwieldy ring binders gradually came to be replaced by bound books as the audience for software expanded beyond a relatively small number of techies to a broader market of application end users. This now meant that the installation guide, user's manual, programmer's reference manual, getting-started guide, quick reference card, license agreement, and other documentation for a software application aimed at a general audience needed to fit in a box that could sit on a retailer's shelf, along with the after-market guides that inevitably followed on a successful product's heels.

Meanwhile, as computer memory became cheaper and software companies sought to rein in the increasing costs of printing their ever-growing documentation sets (which, with the demise of change pages, now had to be completely reprinted with each new release of the product), more and more information about the product and how to use it came to be offered in electronic form, online Help being the most immediate. Indeed, there has been a trend toward replacing freestanding user guides and reference manuals by "chunking" their contents into bite-sized online Help messages with links to related topics and examples for the full story, allowing you to simulate riffling a book with Back and Forward buttons or links to let you to keep fingers between pages.

Paragraph 1194.22 of the 1998 amendment to the Rehabilitation Act of 1973—a.k.a. Section 508—has mandated an additional form of Help to assist in making Web-based applications with their graphical user interface (GUI) accessible to the visually impaired: "A text equivalent for every non-text element shall be provided (e.g., via 'alt', 'longdesc', or in element content)." In other words, if you want your application to be compliant with Section 508 (mandatory if you want to do business with the federal government), to describe each graphic element in the application on the screen you need to provide hover Help (see page 6 above) or a link to a text file readable by a text-to-speech screen reader.

In the early days of the computer industry, error messages tended to be short and often somewhat opaque because (a) the format of the files in which error messages were typically stored and the way in which their contents were accessed imposed severe constraints on the number of characters an error message could contain, and (b) they were generally written by programmers who were apt to be more fluent in programming languages than in the niceties of polished prose. In more recent times, professional writers have been engaged to provide documentation to help users understand the workings and misworkings of computer applications, where "users" can run the gamut from application programmers to data entry workers. Often, however, error messages remain the jealously guarded children of the programmer rather than the wards of the tech writer.

And there is more than a hint of Zen in the suggestion from the author of an after-market user guide to a popular

American spreadsheet program of the 1980s: "Now that we've told you how to use the help screens, we would like to caution you not to use them too much. What we mean is that guessing (and experimenting) is a *very* powerful tool by itself. [Our] menus are designed to be self-explanatory and to work intuitively. If a choice seems like the appropriate one, try it even if you aren't sure." And then, somewhat alarmingly, "You will occasionally do damage this way. However, the damage you do will be trivial relative to the amount of learning time you will save."

Words to live by, perhaps, but cold comfort if everything you've been working on for the last three hours/days/weeks goes *frnk!* and disappears forever, leaving only the black Screen of Death on your monitor. Nowadays, however, *some* sort of error message is more likely, though it can at times be as gnomic as "No code is generated for a superfluous expression" or "Unsatisfied external references have been encountered"—actual compiler diagnostic messages that appeared on the screen of a programmer named Martin H. Booda, who was struck by "[t]he same terseness, the same mystical obscurity, the same vaguely threatening equivocation" one finds on the fortune slips in Chinese fortune cookies. "I almost expect the diagnostics to be followed by winning lottery numbers," Booda adds, proposing that programmers "come up with phrases which could be used equally well either as fortunes *or* diagnostics," such as "It is most unwise to build upon an undefined structure" or "Correct previous errors before persevering to gather objects."

SORRY

In the Christian church from its earliest days, the notion of confession as a way if not to correct previous errors at least to be forgiven for them has held much favor: That human beings are prone to sin is axiomatic, as is God's omniscience, and there is no wrongdoing we can commit so trivial or so well concealed as to escape divine cognition. We confess our sins, then, not so much to inform Heaven, which is already well aware of them, but to acknowledge that we know about them, are heartily sorry for them, and humbly repent of them, imploring God's mercy. (*Mercy* comes from the same root as *mercantile;* Latin *mercēs* originally meant "wages, fee, price, rent, bribe, commodity" and by extension got adopted into Old French in the sense of "heavenly reward, grace, pity.") Doing public penance both provided sinners a means of reconciliation with a God from whom their sin had alienated them and assured the community of their contrition; for children growing up Catholic in midcentury America, the Saturday ritual of confession to the priest and expiation in the pews afterward was a weekly reminder of how the power relations worked within the community of the faithful.

However, as Roger Shuy points out in *The Language of Confession, Interrogation, and Deception,* there is a substantial difference between the kind of confession one makes in church and what the police may be trying to elicit from a suspect down at the precinct house, for, as he writes, "persons from whom [law enforcement agencies] try to elicit confessions are unwilling to reveal all they have done." And for good reason, when the confessor is aware that his or her confession is correlated with some type of punishment. Moreover, while the sinner and congregation assume as a matter of course that God already knows their sins anyway, "[t]he real world of police confessions, despite the training of interrogators, often yields confessions that do not signify what the police may think.... Whatever the reasons suspects have for confessing, and whatever they choose to confess, the fact remains that the confession event is highly susceptible to interpretations that can cause considerable confusion."

Nevertheless, suspects do confess; indeed, in the courts of ancient China, according to Robert Van Gulik, it was "a fundamental principle…that no criminal [could] be pronounced guilty unless he confessed to his crime," and hence, he writes, torture was permitted "[t]o prevent hardened criminals from escaping punishment by refusing to confess even when confronted by irrefutable evidence." Of course, the evidence really did have to be solid, for should the accused be permanently injured or even die, not only the magistrate but his entire staff were held accountable and could even be executed, arguably as extreme as a public apology can get.

The history of public apologies in the West is also rich in examples, some accompanied by considerable ceremony. Eleven years after the Norman Conquest, the Holy Roman Emperor Henry IV humbled himself before Gregory VII by standing barefoot in penitential garb in the courtyard of that pope's palace at Canossa, whence "going to Canossa" became synonymous with eating crow. Occasions of public amends could be played for irony as well, as in the (undoubtedly apocryphal) story in which when two brothers reached the end of their career as robbers on the gallows at Tyburn in the eighteenth century, the first to die waived the customary privilege of the condemned and delivered no speech at all before being hanged. When his brother was about to follow him, the crowd naturally expected more of a performance, and got it: "Good people," said he, "my brother hangs before my face, and you see what a lamentable spectacle he makes; in a few moments I shall be turned off too, and then you'll see a pair of spectacles!"

Paul Slansky and Arleen Sorkin provide a cornucopia of modern-day apologies in their aptly entitled book *My Bad,* ranging from the abject "I was a real jerk, I was greedy. I want to apologize to anyone who ever did business with me" (from a travel agent who had bilked his many customers of a whopping $800,000) to the understated, not to say weaselly, passive-voice "Judgments were made regarding the assignment of John Geoghan which, in retrospect, were tragically incorrect" (from a former archbishop of Boston's quasi-apology after years of archdiocesan cover-up for a pedophile priest by deftly moving him from parish to parish).

Weasel words are those aptly named utterances which, as the OED nicely puts it, are so "equivocating or ambiguous" as to sap "the force or meaning of the concept being expressed." The earliest citation in the OED is from a short story by Stewart Chaplin in the *Century Magazine* of June 1900, in which a character named Harris St. John explains that weasel words "suck all the life out of the words next to them, just as a weasel sucks an egg and leaves the shell." What is so offensive about weasel words in place of a bona fide apology is their failure to square accounts. This is the purpose of what sociologist Erving Goffman calls "remedial work," rooted in the widespread assumption that people ought to treat each other with a reasonable degree of fundamental fairness. When we transgress, we do not do so in a vacuum, but within a society whose norms expect us to make good when we do something bad, in apologies, penance, and restitution perceived to be proportional to the harm we did.

This can be as simple and self-contained as saying "Oops, sorry" when we accidentally bump the next person in line, or as complex and recursive as Germany's efforts to compensate victims of the Third Reich. It can entail extensive reframing of events, as when a person who has just recovered from a manic episode of wreaking havoc on his or her social surround now asks for absolution on the grounds that "I was not myself." The conceptual problem here, as

Goffman points out, is that "mental symptoms are willful situational improprieties, and these, in turn, constitute evidence that the individual is not prepared to keep his place." Hence "the offense is often one to which formal means of social control do not apply." This contrasts with the normal scenario of remedial ritual work, in which "the offender tries to show that the offense is not a valid expression of his attitude to the norms. The impiety is only apparent; he really supports the rules."

Newspapers, as we have mentioned in chapter 6, are prone to error; breaking stories, like breaking waves, do not always turn out in retrospect to break quite the way everyone thought they would, inevitably necessitating a certain amount of cleanup after news has been printed that wasn't quite so. With a few sterling exceptions, the usual place for this remedial work is a correction box, generally on the second page below the fold.

The subtitle of Craig Silverman's book *Regret the Error* argues that inaccuracies in the media "pollute the press and imperil free speech." This is rather a strong indictment, but his examples make a good case, such as the *Newsweek* fact-checker's out-of-the-blue guess at how many soldiers were in the Sudanese army, which became enshrined as the official count at the Sudanese embassy itself.

Correction boxes, at least, allow a newspaper to set the record straight, though, as Silverman points out, this does not automatically mean that one can stop the metastasis of an untruth once it has gotten online. Still, one does what one can in print; thus, the *Baltimore Sun* revealed: "Because of incorrect information provided to the *Sun,* an article...reported that Precious the Skateboarding Dog had recently gone 'to the great skateboard in the sky.' Precious is still alive."

Newspaper editors hope, of course, that with the correction the appropriate remedial work has been done and we can all move on, but it doesn't always happen that way. Thus the *Ottawa Citizen* and Southam News expressed their "wish to apologize for our apology to Mark Steyn, published Oct. 22. In correcting the incorrect statements about Mr. Steyn published Oct. 15, we incorrectly published the incorrect correction. We accept and regret that our original regrets were unacceptable and we apologize to Mr. Steyn for any distress caused by our previous apology." In this instance the text of the correction of the correction was dictated word for word by Mr. Steyn to the editor of the newspaper, whose first apology Steyn felt had inadequately addressed his concerns after one of its columnists allegedly libeled him.

It may be argued, of course, that the best way out of trouble is not to get into it in the first place. Some dangers, if properly foreseen, can be headed off, such as misunderstandings over payments and property; this is the essence of contract law, on which for centuries literally billions of words have been written and legions of attorneys and their families well and daintily fed. Since a wedding is an economic union as well as two hearts becoming one flesh, it is hardly surprising that marriage contracts have been of considerable importance in almost every society in the world. But only within the last few decades has the prenuptial agreement come into its own.

Unlike traditional marriage agreements (generally between the parents' generations in both families), a prenup commitment regarding their separate estates is made by the prospective bride and groom themselves, a defining of what shall be mine, thine, and ours. Such a contract may be of particular importance in situations where the marriage is a second one for one or both parties and the couple lives in a common-property state, one in which the default division of property in the event of divorce is an even split.

Let us suppose that Ms. Highbracket, having previously divorced Col. Rovingeye (the father of her two grown children, Bunny and Hartwell), now wishes to marry the more interesting but poor Prof. Farthingsworth. Highbracket comes to the altar with a net worth of some $750,000, including her home, her car, and her grandfather's antique highboy; Farthingsworth's TIAA-CREF retirement fund amounts to about $80,000, he owns no real estate, and his other assets amount to about $5,000 on a good day.

Reluctant though they both are to imagine that the marriage mightn't be for keeps, Highbracket follows her financial advisor's counsel: An agreement is drawn up that in the event of divorce, Farthingsworth will walk away with the same $85,000 he brought to the marriage, plus (over his present pious objections) an additional payment of $50,000 to him by Highbracket in lieu of division of any presumed jointly owned assets acquired during the marriage, the understanding being that this disproportionate division will trump the default statutory 50–50 that their state's laws would require if no such prearrangement between the couple were in place.

Nine years later, Farthingsworth experiences a massive midlife crisis ending in the arms of his comely teaching assistant, Ms. Wiley. Thanks to the prenup, after the divorce Farthingsworth is now worth $135,000, a good deal more than he brought to the marriage. (He is also, unless she has been named as a corespondent, free to marry Wiley, should he be so foolish.) Highbracket, sadder but wiser, still manages to keep more than 90 percent of her capital safe for Bunny and Hartwell to inherit in the fullness of time. By such means may many a nasty post-breakup financial squabble be avoided in our litigious age, thus steering clear of a certain kind of trouble before anyone even thinks of starting it.

10

IN THE END

Last Words

GOOD-BYE. FAREWELL. ADIEU. THERE ARE MANY WAYS to signal that all has been said that's going to be said and that it's time to go. "Finis" or "The End" tells us that we've reached the end of the book or the movie. "That's all, folks" marks the end of the cartoon (and now, engraved on his tombstone, the passing of Mel Blanc, the voice of Bugs Bunny, Porky Pig, Daffy Duck, and a host of other animated Disney characters). XXX (or -30-) flags the end of a newspaper column for the compositor, while XOXO, SWAK [sealed with a kiss], Love, Sincerely yours, and bfn [bye for now] are but a few of the ways to end a message sent by mail.

Some closers can be used by both the person leaving and the person being left—*farewell, good-bye,* and *adieu* were all originally addressed to the departing (much as we might say "Safe journey" to speed you on your way) but are now appropriate for both parties to say at the end of an encounter.

Some gestures can serve as greetings as well as partings. For example, the handshake, the wave, and the military salute can come at either the beginning or the end of a social transaction; Italian *ciao* and, regionally, French *adieu* can be either "Hi" or "Bye," depending on the circumstances, reflecting, perhaps, the fact that a salutation—the expression of a wish for someone's good health and safety—can go just as well on either end of a get-together. Or consider, as a further wrinkle, Ernout and Meillet's gloss on the Latin greeting *ave*, "[which was] also used on tombs to force the passer-by who read the inscription aloud to greet [*saluer*] the deceased," who had presumably long since said his last good-bye (in Latin, *vale*, literally, 'be strong, vigorous,' perhaps most famously paired with *ave* by Catullus, whose moving elegy on the death of his brother ends with the words *frater, ave atque vale* 'brother, hail and farewell').

Not all good-byes are meant to be final, of course, a fact underlined in the refrain to "Prends Ton Manteau," a song made famous by Kate and Anna McGarrigle: "cet *adieu* ce n'est qu'un *au revoir*" ('that *farewell* is just a *see you later*'). This chapter, what with its being the last in the book, will restrict itself to leave-takings of the permanent variety—specifically, to those surrounding that most permanent of partings, death.

LAST WORDS OF THE DECEASED

Why do we place so much value on the last words someone utters? Actually, we mostly don't unless the someone is famous: Christ's last words have remained prominently in the public ken for centuries (in the different gospels and in a variety of musical settings), while Joe Blow's have generally had as little staying power as the first words he uttered as a toddler.

Collections of last words of the famous are a relatively recent phenomenon, gaining popularity only in the middle of the nineteenth century, before which, as Karl S. Guthke

(1985) put it, "there were only rather specialized antholo-gies of dying words, limited to martyrs, criminals, or infi-dels." Each type of anthology was basically instructional in purpose: The dying words of the martyrs and infidels exem-plified the do's and don'ts of living the good life and dying the good death. Whether criminals were to be classed with martyrs or infidels often depended on one's political per-suasion. And whether or not one shared the then common belief that a dying person's words were likely (a) to be the truth and (b) to rest on an unencumbered clarity of vision was also up for grabs.

In a more secular age, collections of the last words of the dying are sometimes said to reveal something about the age in which the speaker lived, some useful social history, but this is a bit like saying that you only subscribe to *Playboy* for the interviews. The fact is that we are fascinated by the famous, and we are especially fascinated by the famous when they say something pithy. In the case of dying words, we are sometimes willing to help the famous to be more pithy than they might in fact have been as they drew their last breath, though we will sometimes settle for something as mundane as "I'm dying," said to be the last words of Luis Buñuel and Leonhard Euler (*"Me muero"* and *"Ich sterbe,"* respectively), if the famous are famous enough and the words don't seem to be out of character—we prefer last words to fit our pre-ferred myths of the deceased.

Mark Twain (1889) cautioned that "[a] distinguished man should be as particular about his last words as he is about his last breath. He should write them out on a slip of paper and take the judgment of his friends on them. He should never leave such a thing to the last hour of his life, and trust to an intellectual spirit at the last moment to enable him to say something smart with his latest gasp and launch into eternity with grandeur. No—a man is apt to be too much fagged and exhausted, both in body and mind, at such a time, to be reliable," advice of which Pancho Villa was apparently either unaware or unmindful, his last words to witnesses as he expired being widely reported as "Don't leave it that I finished like this. Report that I said something." ("*No dejen que acabe así. Cuéntenle que he dicho algo.*")

Does anybody follow Twain's advice? Probably not in real life, with the result that, as a physician of our acquaintance put it, "there's not much poetry" at death. (She could only recall one instance, during her hospital residency, where she heard last words at all, namely: "I'm not afraid.") But who knows? We'd like to think that hotelier Conrad Hilton really did say "Leave the shower curtain on the inside of the tub," that John Maynard Keynes said "I wish I'd drunk more champagne," and Anton Chekhov said, "Champagne!" as they shuffled off their mortal coil. Were Humphrey Bogart's last words "I never should have switched from scotch to martinis," or Alexander Graham Bell's "So little done, so much to do"? Maybe not, though more memorable, perhaps, than "Hurry back" (which Bogart was said to have said as his wife left to run an errand) or "No" (which Bell is said to have replied in sign language to his wife's request that he not leave her).

Suicide Notes

Suicide notes constitute a special kind of last words. Like the last words of the dying, they are supposed to be true, and to reveal something epitomic about the writer's character and life, though their actual meaning is by no means always clear to either the suicide's survivors or the army of suicidologists who study those words to try to learn what leads people to kill themselves and to use that knowledge to prevent others from doing so. Such studies have identified a number of characteristics.

First of all, suicide notes themselves are relatively rare. Most studies agree that fewer than 15 percent of suicides leave notes, though that figure is probably low, as some notes are hidden or destroyed by, or at the behest of, the suicide's survivors (for a variety of reasons). Further, the person who attempts but fails to commit suicide may also fly under the radar. However, many of those suicide notes that do survive share some notable features.

They are typically short, like the following examples cited by Schneidman and Farberow:

Honey. I am sorry this is the only way I know. I am all wrong. I love you very much.

Bill

or, even more succinctly,

I hope this is what you wanted.

There are, of course, exceptions: The English historical painter and writer Benjamin Robert Haydon kept a detailed daily diary for almost fifty years which, according to Thomas Mallon, "reads like a lifelong harangue from Speaker's Corner in Hyde Park, the complainant never pausing long enough to catch his breath, or take a sip of water," all of which could be considered a preamble to the final entry, written shortly before he took his life:

God forgive me—Amen
Finis
of
BR Haydon

If the length of such messages is perhaps not particularly remarkable, since notes of all sorts are by definition short, there appear to be some significant, characteristic differences between the language of suicide notes and that of other kinds of note that one might address to a family member or friend, from the

Sweetie, Had to go out. Back soon. XOXO

or the possibly disingenuous

Dear Grandma, Thank you for the paisley necktie...

to the pseudo-suicide note that suicidologists have asked test subjects to write imagining that they (the subjects) were about to commit suicide. The differences appear in vocabulary, syntax, and general organization, and in the sometimes subtle semantics underlying the message. For example, Osgood and Walker found that, among other things, the vocabulary of suicide notes tended to exhibit lower Type-Token Ratios (TTRs) than other kinds of notes. (A low TTR, generally taken by forensic linguists as an indication of truthfulness, occurs when the number of different words in a text divided by the total number of words in that text is low—the more repetition in vocabulary, the lower the TTR.) In addition, the ratio of adjectives and adverbs to nouns and verbs was lower, and the use of so-called *allness terms* ("terms that permit no exception, e.g., *always, never, no one, no more*") was greater. As far as general structure was concerned, suicide notes tended to be more disorganized than the other notes studied as well.

On the semantic plane, the ambivalence often revealed in a suicide note is remarkable:

Dear Betty,
I hate you.
Love,
George

and

Ted, Darling I loved you more than life itself. Forgive
me I love you. You should have been better. I love you.
    Nancy

Beside ambivalence, outright denial of obvious circumstances is also common. (As Ronald Maris put it, "Schneidman and Farberow have observed that while one may expect
people to write pure poetry before their suicides, what is
usually found are banal, pragmatic notes indicative of the
high level of denial apparently necessary to end one's life.")
A social or financial scandal that is clear to everyone else
may go unmentioned or be denied completely in a suicide
note, as in the case of Dr. Paul Kammerer, a scientist who
challenged Charles Darwin's evolutionary theories with his
own and, when it was discovered that he (or his lab staff)
had been systematically faking test cases and that financial
ruin was imminent, took his own life. In his suicide note,
however, he admitted no wrongdoing, but suggested a way
in which his body could be disposed of:

> Perhaps my esteemed colleagues will find in my brain
> a trace of the qualities they found missing from the
> expression of my intellectual activities while I was alive.

Nowadays, suicide notes may appear in a variety of media:
from the traditional handwritten farewell scrawled on a
scrap of paper to the neatly word-processed document, the
audio recording, the e-mail message, and, with the advent
of the Internet, the Web site posting, where your note can
garner a wide audience of the morbidly curious, and where
a quick search reveals not only notes left by others but
also hints and tips on how to write your own should you
be at a loss for words. When you leave your note on, say,
your MySpace page, comments from your online friends
become a virtual funeral home guest book in which you can

be eulogized by people who never met you in the physical world. Indeed, posting an online suicide note can result in coverage of the event beyond one's wildest dreams. For example, a Google search for, say, Paul Zolezzi, who posted a suicide note on his Facebook page ("Paul Zolezzi is born in San Francisco, became a shooting star over everywhere, and ended his life in Brooklyn...And couldn't have asked for more.") yields 72,000+ hits; and a search on Christian Mogensen, whose final blog posting, before he killed his wife and then himself, consisted of a wedding picture of the couple accompanied by their dates of birth and death, returns nearly a hundred thousand.

Fortunately, the virtual reality that the Internet embodies has come to offer the possibility of virtual suicide, a much more benign and surely less final gesture than the real thing. Since Facebook first appeared on the Internet, hundreds of thousands (by one estimate) have struggled with the disappointments of online life only to end it all by deactivating their accounts. As one woman who found major disappointments with her online existence remarked, "It was hard to kill the profile I'd spent so long creating, but I felt it was the only way out...."

FAREWELL FROM THE LIVING

The dead never really have the last word: Final farewells are inevitably left to be spoken—or written—by the living. Relatives or a stranger on the newspaper staff may write your obituary as a public send-off to be witnessed by the reading public in hard copy or, increasingly, online; a family member, friend, or member of the clergy may deliver a eulogy to celebrate your life and mourn your passing; attendees at your funeral may sign the guest book after the ceremony (or go online to post a message at the funeral home's Web site); and, finally, someone will probably see to it that your existence is permanently called to memory by a labeled stone, plaque, or other public marker for passersby to see and reflect upon.

The Obit

Obituaries are one of the best-read sections of the newspaper, often close to the sports page in readership. So why do we read them, especially since, in most cases, they refer to people we have never known? The old joke has it that it's a sign of aging when you start the day by checking the obits to see if you've been written up before you turn to the front page with your morning coffee. Con men and urban apartment seekers scan them for opportunities. According to Marilyn Johnson's *The Dead Beat*, we read them with the hope that they will "tell me the secret of a good life." Many people read them simply because they are short, often well-written accounts of interesting lives whose details are left to our imagination to fill in.

Almost as old as printing, the first obituaries date to the 1500s. In the late 1800s the London *Times* began featuring obits that were more elaborate than simple death notices. They began to include, to popular acclaim, short biographies, prayers, and short poems for the deceased. Obituaries remained popular in the Victorian age, if tending toward the morbid, as evidenced by this gem:

> Within a short period of a year she was a bride, a beloved wife and companion, a mother, a corpse.

Over time, the form became more or less standard, with an increasing tendency to cover only the officially famous. Today, the divide continues in most newspapers between detailed feature obituaries for the famous and infamous and shorter death notices for ordinary people. Formats vary accordingly from the minimalist to the feature-length. At the far end of the scale, a death notice in the newspaper lists (often by town) the name of the deceased, generally accompanied by the date of death and sometimes by the name and location of the funeral home and the visiting hours, for example:

Cambridge, 7/14, Backlund, James A., Wednesday 2–7 pm, O'Sullivan Funeral Home, South Boston.

A rather different take on the minimalist death notice was offered by the epigrammatic journalist Félix Fénéon, whose specialty was the reduction of an item of (usually lurid) news, such as a death, to a succinct three lines of text, as in the following example:

Falling from the scaffolding at the same time as the mason Dury, of Marseille, a stone crushed his head.

Marilyn Johnson describes the structure of the more conventional, medium-sized obituary as "a swift, economical description of the person who died, a few short stories from the life or work, and the list of survivors trailing behind." This can be set out diagrammatically, using Johnson's terminology:

1. The "tombstone" is the lead sentence in which the deceased is identified, for example, "JOHN SMITH, 89…"
2. The "tombstone" contains, in addition to the name of the deceased, "the bad news," as in "John Smith…died of a stroke on Wednesday." In American papers the bad news appears at the end of the sentence, while the British prefer to place it in the middle, if they include it at all. Traditionally, the

British press tends not to mention "the bad news," especially the actual cause of death. (The American press has become more forthright about cause of death, increasingly eschewing such euphemisms as "after a long illness" for "cancer" or leaving us to suspect AIDS from other details.) Longer obituaries often don't get to the bad news until the third or even fourth paragraph.

3. The "song and dance," the details of the person's life, are laid out, preferably avoiding what is called the "desperate chronology," a seemingly endless list of life events. Some papers avoid the desperate chronology by putting these sometimes dry facts in a separate boxed list.

4. A list of survivors (optional), which Johnson calls the "lifeboat."

5. Also optional, a short quotation providing a final, positive note.

To this is typically appended information concerning the funeral or memorial service, the burial, and the organization to which one is invited to make a contribution in lieu of flowers.

Thus, for example, the hypothetical obituary of the equally hypothetical John Smith:

1. John Smith, 89, a grocer and inventor who popularized the frozen fish stick,

2. died at home on Wednesday.

3. An avid golfer, devoted husband and father, he was founder of the Smith Fish Stick Company in 1952.

4. He is survived by his children, John, Jr. and Sally.

5. Sally remembered him often remarking: "If only all of life could be preserved like a fish stick."

6. A Mass of Christian Burial will be celebrated in
St. Bridget Church, Waltham, on Monday, June 20.
Interment will be private. Donations in John's memory
may be made to the Friends of Fish. For directions and
guest book, visit feakefuneralhomes.com.

The foregoing example, while made up, reflects an important trend in obituary writing that began in the 1960s and
has by now become well established, namely, the promulgation of the notion that portraits of ordinary people can be as
important culturally and historically as those of the famous.
With the loosening of the constraints on the types of person
seen as appropriate subjects for an obituary in this increasingly egalitarian era has come a loosening of the constraints
on the style and format considered to be appropriate. Thus,
with the calamitous events of September 11, 2001, the *New
York Times* began a series of brief portraits of all the dead from
the World Trade Center labeled "Portraits of grief" and for-
matted like feature shorts rather than standard obituaries.
    Creative leeway in style and subject matter has its limits,
of course, but is, unfortunately, in no way an immunization
against the obituary writer's two greatest fears: getting the
facts wrong and—the worst of all possible errors—reporting a death prematurely. Getting certain facts wrong is a
fairly common occurrence and is often the result of families' misstatements, misrecollections, or repetitions of a
cherished family legend as fact, especially when it comes
to the deceased's military background—evidently, everyone
thinks Dad served in Patton's army. Caveat scriptor.
    More embarrassing is the perpetration of what Craig Sil-
verman has termed "obiticide," or "death by media," the publication of a death announcement for a person who is still very
much alive. While Mark Twain's often misquoted "The report
of my death was an exaggeration" was a response to a rumor

rather than to an actual obituary, instances of actual obiticide abound, one of the most widely disseminated in recent times having been the inadvertent Internet posting of the obituary outlines that CNN, like other news organizations, keeps on hand to update quickly when a person of note dies. The obituary of the Queen Mother was used as a template, so the outlines for such notables as Ronald Reagan, Fidel Castro, and Dick Cheney appeared with links to such topics as "Life as the Queen Consort," "UK's favorite grandmother," and "A love of racing." Castro's premature obituary comes with the lead-in to what should have been Ronald Reagan's.

Aside from providing entertainment for the reading public, obiticide, whether in print or by word of mouth, can also prove a source of enjoyment for the victim, as suggested by the words of Lux Interior, founder of the band The Cramps, quoted in his (legitimate) obituary in the *Boston Globe:*

> In 1987, there were widespread rumors of his death from a heroin overdose, and half a dozen funeral wreaths were sent to Poison Ivy [Lux's wife].
>
> "At first, I thought it was kind of funny," Mr. Interior told the Times, "but then it started to give me a creepy feeling."
>
> "We sell a lot of records, but somehow just hearing that you've sold so many records doesn't hit you quite as much as when a lot of people call you up and are obviously really broken up because you died."

While making sure they have their facts straight, obituary writers today also need to be careful lest their words inspire undesirable actions by others. One study suggests that the insensitive reporting of deaths can adversely influence suicidal individuals. Thus, the American Foundation for Suicide Prevention (AFSP) has created guidelines for media suggesting, among other things, that obituary writers avoid using the word "suicide" in the headline and omit details on the method of death.

This doesn't mean that negative details of a life are completely off-limits. For example, in the notice published in the *Boston Globe* for reputed mobster Frank "The German" Schweihs, not a single positive aspect of his seventy-eight years is mentioned, and the photograph used was an unflattering, scowling mug shot. Where one might expect to find details of hobbies and interests, we find:

> Federal law enforcement officials said that Mr. Schweihs specialized in beatings and murders and that they had hoped to put him in prison for life.

One way to try to control what is said about you after your death is to write your own obituary, possibly following one of the many templates posted to the Internet, such as Don Fry's "Want to Live Forever? Write Your Own Obit" at Poynter.org. No less a literary light than Norman Mailer proposed his own obit, taking pardonable liberties with the facts:

> Novelist Shelved
> By Norman Mailer
>
> Norman Mailer passed away yesterday after celebrating his fifteenth divorce and sixteenth wedding.
>   "I just don't feel the old vim," complained the writer recently.

In fact, Mailer died after having been married a mere six times.

The Guest Book

Life offers many occasions for awkward moments in personal communication—the first day at a new school, the blind date, the job interview, and, perhaps most awkward of all, the receiving line at the funeral home.

Sorry for your loss.

at least euphemistically avoids a starker reality:

It's too bad your mom died.

but even the ritual condolence hardly trips off the tongue.

A step removed from the funeral home receiving line (with its eerie resemblance to the receiving line at a wedding) is the funeral home guest book and its high-tech offspring, the online memorial guest book.

Usually placed at a slight remove from the proceedings, the book allows for a brief written expression of grief in a semiprivate setting. Guest book comments tend to be triggered by the first comment, or at least by the comment above the vacant line. One funeral home staff member notes that "they tend either to be directed to the deceased or to the family."

You'll get to see granddad in heaven.

and, perhaps more personally,

I'll be seeing you in heaven someday.

The online version of the guest book allows for an even more comfortable setting for composition, often with longer and more thoughtful entries, although they still address two different audiences:

Dad, you lived a good long life with many adventures. Thanks for surviving Pearl Harbor to have me. Great Grandma Julia, Granny, Grandpa and all the others are waiting for you. See you on the other side.

or

To the Smith family: Just want to send my sincerest sympathy to each one of you! I have many fond

> memories of the fun family on the Pleasant Street.
> Mary, I think of you often and wonder how you are
> doing. Take Care!

with the latter entry sounding a little like a Christmas card
from an almost forgotten relative. Advantages of the online
guest book are that comments can come from loved ones
at a distance, the book remains continuously available, and
entries can continue to be added long after the funeral has
passed, creating a kind of extended grieving community in
which immediate family members can regularly check in
not only to reread comments but to see if new discussion
has been added.

The online possibilities can also extend beyond the
guest book that the funeral home provides. Several Internet entrepreneurs have founded pay sites such as Legacy.
com, Memory-of.com, and Mem.com. These sites sell the
tools survivors need to customize their memorial pages for
a permanent site. You can view the obituary and a biography, make an entry in the guest book, and then visit the
gift shop, either to send flowers to the family or to create
an attractive, personalized bound memorial book. For a
younger demographic, there is MyDeathSpace.com, a sort
of bulletin board focused on deceased members from the
teenage social networking site MySpace.com.

However, the anonymity of the Internet provides new
challenges. Not only can complete strangers leave comments, but internal family squabbles and the occasional
comment from mistresses previously unknown to the family
(the surviving family, that is) can create a less than thera-
peutic setting for the grieving process. On the pay memorial sites, administrators try to filter the profane, political,
and commercial entries (yes, spam in the afterlife), but stay
out of family arguments, leaving the person that paid for

the site to remove comments as they see fit, which is not an option with a hard-copy guest book.

R.I.P.

The desire to perpetuate the memory of the dead is one of our most natural impulses. The physical realization of this desire can take a number of forms, a gravestone being perhaps the most familiar, though by no means the only, means of calling the attention of passersby to the prior existence of the deceased.

Epitaphs

Liddell and Scott gloss Greek *epitáphios* (ἐπιτάφιος) as "(ἐπί, τάφος), *on, at, belonging to a tomb…esp.* ἐπ. λόγος, *a funeral oration* or *eulogy*, such as was spoken at Athens yearly over the citizens who had fallen in battle."

Táphos originally referred to the ceremony of burial and subsequently came to designate the place at which the ceremony took place and the remains were buried, hence the grave or tomb. (The Romans made a distinction between the *bustum*, the place where the body was cremated and buried, and the *ustrinum*, the place where the ashes of the deceased were buried when the cremation had occurred someplace else.)

That the *grave* of *gravestone* and that of *engrave* come from a common root (meaning something like 'scrape, dig') is satisfying. As for the containers to which epitaphs are applicable, *sarcophagus* comes from Greek and means, literally, 'flesh eater,' the term having been applied to the limestone believed to consume the bodies encased in the burial containers made of it; *urn* comes from Latin *urna* ('jar vessel'), which is of obscure origin but is probably not related to the verb *ūrere* ('to burn'); and *tomb* is ultimately from Greek, from an Indo-European root meaning something like 'heap, mound' and referring to the place where a body was burned and buried.

The earliest extant carved burial markers in the Western world are found on the sarcophagi of ancient Egypt and usually feature a prayer to a deity, typically Osiris or Anubis, on behalf of the deceased, whose name, familial descent, and office are then noted. By the Third Dynasty, however, a burial for the well-to-do, emulating pharaonic practices, could involve inscriptions not only on the outside of one's sarcophagus but on the inside, on the coffin that the sarcophagus held, and on the walls of the tomb that housed the sarcophagus. These inscriptions contained not only biographical information but prayers, spells, and other texts, profusely illustrated.

The Greeks, perhaps holding that less is more, scaled back on the text, raising the epitaph to an art, as exemplified by the poet Simonides's memorial to the fallen Spartan soldiers at the battle of Thermopylae in 480 BCE:

> *ô kseîn', angéllein Lakedaimoníois hóti tếde*
> *keímetha toîs keínōn rhếmasi peithómenoi.*

('Stranger, tell the Spartans that we lie here, obedient to their words.') The idea was that travelers on their way from Thermopylae to Sparta should report the fate of the fallen when they arrived. Cicero translates this epitaph in his *Tusculanae quaestiones* (usually translated as *Tusculan Disputations*):

> *Dic, hospes, Spartae nos te hic vidisse iacentes,*
> *dum sanctis patriae legibus obsequimur.*

('Say in Sparta that you saw us lying here, as we obey the sacred laws of our fatherland'). It is echoed in the "Kohima Epitaph," written to memorialize the British soldiers who died at the battle of Kohima in 1944:

> When you go home tell them of us and say
> for your tomorrow we gave our today.

Typically, Roman inscriptions on the funeral urns or tomb-stones of ordinary people tended to be somewhat more pro-saic (urn inscriptions being written in the third rather than the first person). For example, the funeral urn dedicated to Serullia Zosimenes, who died at age 26, by her son Pros-decius bears the following inscription:

D. M.
SERVLLIAE ZOSIMENI
QVAE VIXIT ANN XXVI.
BENE MEREN. FECIT
PROSDECIVS FILIVS

[To the shade of
Serullia Zosimenes
Who lived to the age of 26.
This memorial to her is well deserved.
Her son, Prosdecius]

Note that Prosdecius gets his name on the urn, thereby, so to speak, killing two birds with one stone, memorializing both his mother and himself. How he managed to do this if his mother was only twenty-six when she died is unclear unless he was an unusually precocious child. In any case, the inscription begins with the letters D.M. (sometimes

D.M.S.), short for *Diīs Mānibus* (*Diīs Mānibus Sacrum*), the standard invocation of the *Mānēs,* the spirits of the dead. The invocation is followed, conventionally, by the name of the person whose ashes are enclosed in the urn and the person's age at death. This information, as was common, is followed by the name of the person who provided the urn to the well-deserving (*bene merentī*) deceased.

The final Roman resting place for the ashes of loved ones was usually by the side of one of the several roads leading into Rome, such as the Via Appia and the Via Flaminia, and not in the city itself. If you were to travel into or out of Rome, you would have passed miles and miles of an almost unin-terrupted procession of markers, inscribed with either *Siste Viator* ('Stop, traveller') or *Aspice Viator* ('Behold, traveller,' 'Ponder, traveller'), which is still echoed 1,500 years later in many an old parish churchyard in Britain as *Stop Passenger*. In contrast, William Butler Yeats's epitaph urges you not to:

> Cast a cold Eye
> On Life, on Death.
> Horseman, pass by.

The influence of Roman Empire funeral rites and tradi-tions was strong across its former colonies in Europe and Britain. The earliest existing British epitaphs belonged to the Roman period and are written in Latin in the simple Roman form. The first known markers in Britain are for the remembrance of the legions of soldiers of the occupying Roman forces, but native Britons soon adopted this familiar, succinct Roman form. Long after both the Roman Empire and the Roman epitaph format were history, Latin contin-ued to be the favored language in funeral markers, espe-cially for the rich and famous of a more public character. This may suggest perhaps a form of literary class snobbery, but also some kind of lineage and linkage to a glorious past, bespeaking more permanence and stolidity, as "Rule Britannia" recalls. This high-toned practice has gradually faded in Britain, giving way to epitaphs in the deceased's native tongue, even for the high and mighty.

Back in the day, however, Latin was still the nearly sole literary language, and certainly the de facto official language of the church, so it was natural to use it for inscriptions. Almost every British epitaph extant from the eleventh and twelfth centuries is in Latin. Again, as in their Roman forebears, the format is restricted to simple terms, in this case the words *Hic iacet* ('Here lies') and the name and rank of the deceased, with rare exceptions, again, for the rich and famous.

Although her own epitaph was modestly short ("E.S."), the reign of Elizabeth I, (1533–1603), was to signal a sea change in the composition of epitaphs. More poetic and longer inscriptions began to appear, and for the first time in native English to boot. For the first time, contemporary literary luminaries, both as critics and contributors, get into the act. For example, Alexander Pope contributed this epitaph for Isaac Newton:

> Nature and nature's laws lay hid in night;
> God said, "Let Newton be!" and all was light.

and for the Hon. S. Harcourt:

> . . .
> Who ne'er knew joy but friendship might divide,
> Or gave his father grief but when he died.

In the same period in the young United States, a combination of tradition, pioneer do-it-yourself spirit, and the harsh realities of the New World led to some unique changes to the epitaph. It has been said that in colonial times marriages were early and widowhood was brief. Infant mortality was high, physical danger could be constant, and conditions were difficult. For example, of the influential Cotton Mather's three wives and fifteen children, only his last wife and two children survived him. Epidemics, hostile neighbors, multiple wars, and harsh weather conditions contributed to a realistic and stoic attitude about death. "Sudden and awful" death was common from these early days well into the nineteenth century. For example (cited by Mann and Greene):

> Soloman Towslee, Jr.
> Who was killed in Pownal, Vt. July 15, 1846
> while repairing to Grind a scythe on a stone
> attach'd to the gearing in the Woolen
> Factory; He was entangled. His death was
> sudden and awful.

Often the epitaph had a poetic flourish:

> Soldier rest, thy work is done:
> Sharp the contest, fierce the strife.
> The battle's fought, the victory won;
> Thy sure reward, Eternal Life.

or

> Affliction sore long time I bore
> Physicians skill was vain.
> Then God did send Death as a friend
> To ease me from my pain.

The turn of the twentieth century brought with it a trend toward pithier epitaphs, however, signaling the demise of an era in which poetry, beyond tombstone verse, was a popular form of expression familiar to all literate Americans, a daily feature of the front pages of many newspapers as well as a standard component of every child's primary education. Of course, the cost of labor may have been a factor both here and in Europe—for example, while the survivors of First World War casualties in Britain could get a grave marker dedicated to their loved ones for free, epitaphs cost 3½ pence a letter or space.

This is not to say either that terse gravestone text is a novelty or that poetry has completely disappeared from the cemetery (or the newspaper, for that matter). While stones bearing only initials or a kinship term—Brother, Mother— are less common than in the past (as is the family plot itself in our increasingly crowded world), the couplet and the one-liner have largely replaced the quatrain or the more discursive epitaph. The purveyor of headstones (monuments or memorials) may offer a selection of couplets from which to choose an epitaph, as may your local newspaper for placement in a memorial notice on the obituary page, as

> Till memory fades and life departs
> You live forever in our hearts.

though contemporary newspaper memorial notices, like gravestones, are more likely to be in prose:

> IN MEMORIAM
> In loving memory of
> Rusty Smith
> Lie down with the lamb and rise with the bird

We love and miss you,
From the family

As with last words, the epitaphs of the famous hold a fascination for us, and like last words, some are apocryphal, though, unlike last words, they can be verified if one troubles to go look at the stone as Elaine McCarthy did, publishing documentary photographs in her book *Morbid Curiosity: Celebrity Tombstones Across America*. Armchair travelers can learn there, for example, that Margaux Hemingway's tombstone bears her given name (Margot Louise Hemingway, accompanied by a heart containing the word "Love" next to her dates and the inscription "Free Spirit Freed") but Norma Jean Mortenson's simply reads

Marilyn Monroe
1926–1962

The reader also discovers that Erma Bombeck's tombstone, contrary to urban legend, does not contain the epitaph "I told you I was sick." (Indeed, the stone, a boulder imported from her home in Arizona, bears no text at all.) Ascribed to Dorothy Parker and believed by some (wrongly) to have been inscribed on her grave, "I told you I was sick" does in fact appear verifiably on a number of tombstones of the nonfamous in locations as different as Florida, California, New Hampshire, and Massachusetts (in Concord's Sleepy Hollow cemetery, where another unconventional epitaph—"Who the hell is Sheila Shea?"—caused a local ruckus).

Not recorded in the book *Morbid Curiosity* (because the stone is in Père Lachaise Cemetery in Paris) but well documented is that of the late leader of The Doors, Jim Morrison.

ΚΑΤΑ ΤΟΝ ΔΑΙΜΟΝΑ ΕΑΥΤΟΥ

This short line has kept the Lizard King's fans puzzled for years. Often misinterpreted to mean something like "According to his own demon," "Fighting his own demons," or the like, the stumbling block has been the word *daímōn* (accusative singular *daímona*), from which the English word *demon* is indeed derived, but which in Classical Greek originally designated a spiritual being of a somewhat lower order than a god (comparable in some respects to the Roman *mānēs*) and took on a more personal sense. Socrates, for example, speaks at his trial of having an internal spirit that told him right from wrong, which he refers to as his *daímōn*. So, when he composed the inscription, what Morrison's erudite father probably had in mind was more along the lines of "Following his inner spirit," or, as Frank Sinatra (whose gravestone bears the inscription "The best is yet to come"), might have said, "He did it his way."

Descansos

The author of *Ecclesiasticus* (44:9) notes that "some there be, which have no memorial; who are perished as though they had never been; and are become as though they had never been born."

In the United States, the roadside markers known as *descansos* offer something of a compromise. Literally, 'rests,' that is, 'resting places,' they have their origin in the Southwest as spots where the coffin bearers and mourners could stop and rest as they made their way from the church to the cemetery in an era in which that journey was made on foot over uncomfortable terrain. Today, descansos mark the place of a fatality involving an automobile (or some other form of motorized transport) and are found along highways and byways in every state of the union. (In some urban areas, fatal accidents involving a bicyclist are marked by a white bicycle or "ghost bike," chained on or by the site of the accident.)

Some descansos are makeshift and ephemeral, "created," as Anaya, Chávez, and Arellano put it, "out of love in a time of pain and wonderment," while others are government-sanctioned and built to last. Some identify the victim(s) by name, while others shroud the deceased in anonymity. Some are simple markers, while others may incorporate a photograph, notes from the bereaved, and other items reminiscent of the offerings to the dead customary in ancient times.

Descansos have not been without their critics. According to Anaya et al., descansos were officially banned in New Mexico in the 1700s because "there were so many that travelers who stopped to pray for the souls of the departed became easy targets for the Indians roaming the nearby hills." Nowadays a more politically neutral objection has been that they are a distraction and therefore a driving hazard. More politically charged is the objection by some to the use of religious iconography on public property, a complaint that the state

Figure 10.1

of Florida attempted to resolve by replacing its Christian crosses with secular plain white circles to mark the sites of highway fatalities. Policy varies in other states, though most do have rules (not always rigorously enforced) concerning the amount of time a makeshift, unofficial descansos (figure 10.1) may be allowed to rest in peace.

ACKNOWLEDGMENTS

WE ARE DEEPLY INDEBTED TO THE FOLLOWING PEOPLE whose inspiration and help made writing *Short Cuts* such an enjoyable adventure: Henry Alford, Karen Alkalay-Gut, Martha Birnbaum, Jill Blanchard, Sharon Bogue, Elizabeth Bowling, Jonathan Brandon, Jane Cates, the Rev. Mike Clark, Paul DeVore, Malcah Yaeger Dror, the Rev. Christine Elliott, Sheila Fischman, John Flynn, Arden Ford, the Rev. Ann Franklin, Bruce Fraser, Angus Gillespie, the late Col. H. W. Gleason, Edward Goldfrank, Janice Goldfrank, Betsy Handley, Eric Handley, David Hildebrand, Laurence Horn, Andrea Humez, Jean Humez, Leslie Edwards Humez, Andrew Joslin, Denise Lee, Tanya H. Lee, Don Leslie, Jane P. Lord, Gail Marcinkiewicz, Susanne McAdam, Chris McArdle, the Rev. Devin McLachlan, Rosamund Moon, Robert Nowicki, Kat Powers, Luise Pusch, Daud Rahbar, Yoram Ramberg, Louis D. Ureneck, Pat Washburn, and Robert Wilfong.

We are especially grateful to our editors at Oxford University Press—Steve Dodson, Keith Faivre, Brian Hurley, and Peter Ohlin—for their unflagging encouragement and support.

Our heartfelt thanks to you all.

BIBLIOGRAPHY

The following is a list, organized by chapter, of the works that we have cited, alluded to, or otherwise found especially informative in writing *Short Cuts*. The validity of each URL has been verified as of the access date shown, but the usual disclaimer applies: We cannot guarantee that each is still in existence or that its content has not changed at the time you are reading this.

PREFACE

Schmandt-Besserat, Denise, "The Earliest Precursor of Writing," *Scientific American* 238:6 (June 1977), pp. 50–58.

CHAPTER 1. IN THE EYE OF THE BEHOLDER

Budge, Sir E. A. Wallis, *Egyptian Language: Easy Lessons in Egyptian Hieroglyphics* (London: Routledge & Kegan Paul, 1966; reprint of the 1910 original).

Carr, Steven, *City Signs and Lights* (Cambridge, Mass.: MIT Press, 1973).

Castleman, Greg, *Getting Up: Subway Graffiti in New York* (Cambridge, Mass.: MIT Press, 1982), pp. 134–157.

Cobley, Paul, and Litza Jansz, *Introducing Semiotics* (Duxford, U.K.: Icon Books, 1999), pp. 4–5.

Cooper, Martha, and Henry Chalfant, *Subway Art* (New York: Henry Holt and Company, 1984).

Donno, Elizabeth Story, *Harington's Metamorphosis of Ajax* (New York: Columbia University Press, 1962), pp. 96–97.

Eisner, Will, *Comics and Sequential Art* (Tamarac, Fla.: Poorhouse Press, 1985), pp. 46, 62.

Goffmann, Erving, "Response Cries," in *Forms of Talk* (Philadelphia: University of Pennsylvania, 1983), pp. 78–123.

Gordon, Cyrus, *Forgotten Scripts* (New York: Basic Books, 1982).

Grant, Francis J. (ed.), *The Manual of Heraldry* (Edinburgh: John Grant Booksellers, 1948), p. *v*.

Gwynn-Jones, Peter, *The Art of Heraldry* (New York: Barnes and Noble, 1998), pp. 15–17, 122, 124.

Hora, Mies, interviewed by Steven Heller at http://www.aiga.org/content.cfm/navigating-today-s-signs-an-interview-with-mies-hora (accessed Feb. 27, 2009).

Lee, Tanya, personal conversation (Fall 1966) [MBTA "T" logo].

McCloud, Scott, *Understanding Comics* (Northampton, Mass.: Kitchen Sink Press, 1993).

Pierce, C. S., quoted in "Icon," *The Century Dictionary and Cyclopedia* (New York: The Century Company, 1895, Vol. IV), pp. 2970–2971.

Renner, Timothy, class handout for "Reading Roman Graffiti: From Poetry to Platitudes," lecture delivered at Classics Day, Montclair (N.J.) State University, October 2001.

Sampson, Paul, personal e-mails (March 22 and 26, 2008) [Skywriting technique].

Schein, Jerome Daniel, and David Allen Stewart, *Language in Motion: Exploring the Nature of Sign* (Washington. D.C.: Gallaudet University Press, 1995), p. 183.

Skrobucha, Heinz, *Introduction to Icons* (Recklinghausen, Germany: Aurel Bongers, 1961), p. 16.

The Slang Dictionary (London, Chatto and Windus, n.d. [1873]), pp. [ii], 29, 31.

Tai, Kaihsu, "Panneau arrêt au Québec," at http://en.wikipedia.org/wiki/File:Arret.jpg (accessed March 4, 2010).

Walker, Mort, *The Lexicon of Comicana* (Lincoln, Neb.: iUniverse.com, 2000).

Williams, R.E. (ed.), *A Century of Punch Cartoons* (New York: Simon and Schuster, 1955), p. 239.

http://blogs.orlandosentinel.com/features_orlando/2007/04/the_message_fro.html (accessed March 10, 2008) [skywriting evangelist].

http://en.wikipedia.org/wiki/File:Stop_sign.jpg (accessed March 4, 2010) [Israeli Stop sign].

http://forum.atlasrr.com/forum/topic.asp?TOPIC_ID=51735 (accessed Feb. 19, 2009) [railyard worker signs].

http://glossographia.wordpress.com/2009/03/ (accessed Sept. 30, 2009) [Québécois Stop signage].

http://mechanicrobotic.files.wordpress.com/2007/07/4_1_fig_signs3–450w.gif (accessed Feb. 19, 2009) [uniform travelers' icons].

http://mutcd.fhwa.dot.gov/sitemap.htm (accessed Feb. 27, 2009) [U.S. road sign standards].

http://www.backtoclassics.com/artists/janvaneyck/annunciation.php (accessed Feb. 27, 2009) [Van Eyck *Annunciation*].

http://www.blackbeltjones.com/warchalking/community/ steveroadknight/my_wibo_marks.jpg (accessed Feb. 20, 2009) [Matt Jones's expanded list of warchalking signs].

http://www.blamblot.com/grammar.shtml (accessed Feb. 14, 2009) [Nate Piekos's *catalogue raisonné* of comic book dialogue balloon and caption box styles].

http://www.cockeyed.com/archive/candy_code/candy_code.html (accessed Feb. 21, 2009) [trick-or-treaters' chalk signs].

http://www.jiwire.com/i/fig_wc1.1.gif (accessed Feb. 20, 2009) [warchalking].

http://www.loc.gov/exhibits/religion/f0304.jpg (accessed Feb. 27, 2009) [1769 political cartoon].

http://www.loc.gov/rr/scitech/mysteries/skywriting.html (accessed March 10, 2008).

http://www.nytimes.com/1994/05/29/weekinreview/the-world-balkan-road-signs-this-way-to-chaos.html (accessed Sept. 30, 2009) [Balkan road signs].

http://www.rosieairads.com/airplanes.htm (accessed March 26, 2008) [skywriting smoke].

http://www.skywriter.info (accessed March 10, 2008) [hearts in the sky].

http://www.tomorrowsthoughtstoday.com/fast/wp-content/ uploads/2008/07/chalking.jpg (accessed Feb. 19, 2009) [British hobo sign page from "Homeless City Guide"].

www.tomorrowsthoughtstoday.com/fast/wp-content/uploads/2008/07/ hobo-signs.jpg, (accessed Feb. 19, 2009) [American hobo signs].

www.turntojesus.net/home.html (accessed March 10, 2008) [skywriter evangelism].

www.valleyofthegeeks.com/Features/Images/vc_warchalk.jpg (accessed Feb. 20, 2009) [Silicon Valley warchalking parody].

www.victorynetwork.org/ArtFile/HoboSigns1.gif (accessed Feb. 20, 2009) [American hobo signs].

CHAPTER 2. IN THE DICTIONARY

Adams, Douglas, and John Lloyd, *The Deeper Meaning of Liff: A Dictionary of Things There Aren't Any Words for Yet—But There Ought to Be* (New York: Harmony Books, 1990).

Alford, Henry, "Not a Word," *The New Yorker*, August 29, 2005, p. 32 [Ghost words and Mountweazels].

Bailey, Nathaniel, *An Universal Etymological English Dictionary...* (London: Printed for J. Darby et al., 3rd ed. 1726).

Basso, Alberto (ed.), *Dizionario Enciclopedico Universale della Musica e dei Musicisti* (Torino: Unione Tipografico—Editrice Torinese, 1988) [Ugolino de Maltero].

Baumgartner, Alfred, *Alte Musik von den Anfängen abendländischer Musik bis zur Vollendung der Renaissance* (Salzburg: Kiesel Verlag, 1981) [Baldini].

Béjoint, Henri, *Tradition and Innovation in Modern English Dictionaries* (Oxford: Oxford University Press, 1994), pp. 17ff.

Besseler, Heinrich, *Bourdon und Fauxbourdon: Studien zum Ursprung der niederländischen Musik* (Leipzig: Breitkopf & Härtel, 1950).

————, "M. Ugolini de Maltero Thuringi 'De cantu fractibili': Ein scherzhafter Traktat von Hugo Riemann," *Acta Musicologica* vol. 41 (Jan.–June, 1969), pp. 107ff.

Bierce, Ambrose, *The Collected Writings of Ambrose Bierce* (New York: The Citadel Press, 1946).

Boisson, Claude, Pablo Kirtchuk, and Henri Béjoint, "Aux origines de la lexicographie: les premiers dictionnaires monolingues et bilingues," *International Journal of Lexicography* vol. 4, no. 4 (1991).

Brinkmann, Reinhold, "The Art of Forging Music and Musicians: Of Lighthearted Musicologists, Ambitious Performers, Narrow-Minded Brothers, and Creative Aristocrats," in Ryan, Judith, and Alfred Thomas (eds.), *Cultures of Forgery: Making Nations, Making Selves* (New York: Routledge, 2003), pp. 113–115.

Burgess, Gelett, *Burgess Unabridged* (New York: Frederick A. Stokes, 1914).

Dahlhaus, Carl (ed.), *Riemann Musik Lexikon, Ergänzungsband II* (Mainz: B. Schott's Söhne, 1975) [Ugolino de Maltero].

Di Gennaro, Richard, "Baldini, Guglielmo," in Sadie, Stanley (ed.), *The New Grove Dictionary of Music and Musicians* (London: Macmillan, 1980).

Evans, Ivor H. (ed.), *Brewer's Dictionary of Phrase and Fable* (London: Cassell, 14th ed. 1989).

Fallows, David, "Spoof Articles," in Sadie, Stanley (ed.), *The New Grove Dictionary of Music and Musicians* (London: Macmillan, 2001).

Finscher, Ludwig (ed.), *Die Musik in Geschichte und Gegenwart: Allgemeine Enzyklopädie der Musik, begründet von Friedrich Blume, Personenteil 2* (New York: Bärenreiter, 1999) [Baldini].

Galfridus Anglicus (Galfridus Grammaticus), A. L. Mayhew (ed.), *The Promptorium Parvulorum: The First English-Latin Dictionary C. 1440* A.D. (Boston: Elibron Classics, 2006 replica of the 1908 edition published by Kegan Paul, Trench, Trübner & Co.).

Gilliver, Peter, "When is a Word Not a Word?" *VERBATIM* XXXI, No. 3 (Autumn, 2006), pp. 6ff.

Gove, P. B., "The History of 'Dord'," *American Speech*, vol. XXIX, no. 2 (May 1954), pp. 136ff. ["dord"].

Green, Jonathan, *Chasing the Sun: Dictionary Makers and the Dictionaries They Made* (New York: Henry Holt and Company, 1996).

Gurlitt, Wilibald (ed.), *Riemann Musik Lexikon, Ergänzungsband I* (Mainz: B. Schott's Söhne, 1972) [Baldini].

————, *Riemann Musik Lexikon, Personenteil A–K* (Mainz: B. Schott's Söhne, 1959) [Baldini].

————, *Riemann Musik Lexikon, Personenteil L–Z* (Mainz: B. Schott's Söhne, 1961) [Ugolino de Maltero].

Hall, Rich, *Sniglets (snig'lit): Any Word That Doesn't Appear in the Dictionary, But Should* (New York: Macmillan, 1984).

Hall, Rich, and Friends, *More Sniglets* (New York: Macmillan, 1985).

Harris, William H. and Judith S. Levey (eds.), *The New Columbia Encyclopedia* (New York: Columbia University Press, 4th ed. 1975) ["Mountweazel"].

Leibowitz, René (trans. and ed.), *Un Traité inconnu de la technique de la variation (XIVme siècle)* (Liège: Editions Dynamo, 1950) [Ugolino de Maltero].

Mathews, M. M., "Of Matters Lexicographical" *American Speech*, vol. XXVIII, no. 4 (December 1953), pp. 289ff. ["dord"].

Moon, Rosamund, "Objective or Objectionable: Ideological Aspects of Dictionaries," *ELR Journal (New Series)* vol. 3 (1989), p. 63 et passim.

Murray, Sir James. A. H., *The Evolution of English Lexicography: The Romanes Lecture 1900* (Oxford: Clarendon Press, 1901), pp. 6ff.

————, "Ninth Annual Address of the President to the Philological Society," *Transactions of the Philological Society, 1880–1* (London: Trübner & Co., 1881), pp. 126ff.

Oestreich, James R., "Words on Music, 25 Million of Them," *New York Times,* Jan. 21, 2001 [review of *The New Grove Dictionary of Music and Musicians*].

Phillips, Edward (John Kersey, ed.), *The New World of Words: or, Universal English Dictionary…* (London: Printed for J. Phillips, sixth edition 1706).

Riemann, Hugo, "M. Ugolini de Maltero Thuringi…De cantu fractibili…," in *Präludien und Studien: Gesammelte Aufsätze zur Aesthetik, Theorie und Geschichte der Musik, III. Band* (Leipzig: Hermann Seemann Nachfolger, 1901), pp.185ff.

Room, Adrian (ed.), *Brewer's Dictionary of Phrase and Fable* (London: Cassell & Co., 16th ed. 2000).

Skeat, Walter, "Report upon 'Ghost-words,' or Words Which Have No Real Existence," The President's Address for 1886, *Transactions of the Philological Society (1885–7)* II. (London: Trübner & Co., 1887), pp. 35off.

Tomaszczyk, Jerzy, "Dictionaries: Users and Uses," *Glottodidactica* vol. XII (1979).

http://cd.ciao.co.uk/G_Baldini_Madrigals_Bk_2_6188931#productdetail (accessed Sept. 30, 2009) [Don't get your hopes up].

http://en.wiktionary.org/wiki/WT:CFI (accessed Sept. 30, 2009) [criteria for Wictionary: inclusion].

http://german.about.com/library/blmus_deutschland.htm (accessed Sept. 30, 2009) [German national air].

http://home.graffiti.net/hidemann/texte/guglielmo.htm (accessed Sept. 30, 2009) [Baldini].

http://online.wsj.com/article/SB120303234117369959.html (accessed Sept. 30, 2009) ["borrowed" blog blurbs].

http://www.boston.com/ae/celebrity/articles/2008/03/29/sox_ing_it_to_la/?page=2 (accessed Sept. 30, 2009) [Meat Loaf interview].

http://www.facebook.com/topic.php?uid=33546937517&topic=4968 (accessed Feb. 27, 2010) [furnidents].

http://www-users.cs.york.ac.uk/~susan/joke/essay.htm (accessed Sept. 30, 2009) [Hugh Gallagher's "College Essay"].

CHAPTER 3. BY THE GREAT CRIKES!

Brown, Margaret Wise, *The Runaway Bunny,* ill. Clement Hurd (New York: Harper and Row, 1942).

Child, Francis James (ed.), *The English and Scottish Popular Ballads,* vol. 1, Part 1 (Boston: Houghton, Mifflin and Company, 1882), p. 217.

Diderot, Denis, *Paradoxe sur le comédien,* ed. Ernest Dupuy (Paris: Société française d'imprimerie et de librairie, ancienne librairie Lecène, Oudin, 1902), p. 121.

Donahue, Charles, *Law, Marriage, and Society in the Later Middle Ages* (New York: Cambridge University Press, 2008).

Erard, Michael, *Um . . . : Slips, Stumbles, and Verbal Blunders, and What They Mean* (New York: Pantheon Books, 2007).

Ernout, A[lfred], and A[ntoine] Meillet, *Dictionnaire étymologique de la langue latine: histoire des mots* (Paris: Librairie C. Klincksiek, 1959), p. 586.

Gabelentz, Georg von der, *Die Sprachwissenschaft, ihre Aufgaben, Methoden, und bisherigen Ergebnisse* (Leipzig: T.O. Weigel Nachfolger, 1891), pp. 238f.

Goffman, Erving, "Response Cries," in *Forms of Talk* (Philadelphia: University of Pennsylvania Publication in Conduct and Communication, 1983), pp. 78–123.

———, "The Territories of the Self," in *Relations in Public* (New York: Harper Colophon, 1971).

Hamblin, William James, *Warfare in the Ancient Near East to 1600 BC* (New York: Routledge, 2006), pp. 415–417.

Harmetz, Aljean, *The Making of the Wizard of Oz* (New York: Dell, 1977).

Heaney, Seamus (trans.), *Beowulf* (New York: Farrar, Straus and Giroux, 2000).

Huizinga, Johan, *The Waning of the Middle Ages* (Garden City, N.Y.: Doubleday Anchor, 1954), pp. 162–163.

Humez, Nick, "Whatsisnames and Thingamajigs," *VERBATIM* XXIX, No. 2 (Summer 2004), pp. 26–29.

———, "Words of Power," *VERBATIM* XXX, No. 2 (Summer 2005), pp. 27–31.

Kurtzman, Harvey, and David Wood, "Book! Movie!" *MAD Magazine* #13 (July 1954).

LeGoff, Jacques, "The Marvelous in the Medieval West," in *The Medieval Imagination*, tr. Arthur Goldhammer (Chicago: University of Chicago Press: 1985), pp. 27–44.

Mellinkof, David, "History of the Language of the Law," in *The Language of the Law* (Boston: Little, Brown, 1963).

Oettinger, Norbert, *Die militärischen Eide der Hethiter*. Vol. 22 of *Studien zu den Bogazkoy-Texten* (Mainz: Akademie der Wissenschaften und Literatur, 1976).

Onion. C.T., ed., *The Oxford Dictionary of English Etymology* (New York: Oxford University Press, 1966) [bless and curse].

Pitard-Bouet, Capt. Jean-Christophe, "Avoir l'esprit d'escalier," *Les Carnets du Temps*, n° 42 (Novembre 2007).

Pollock, Walter Herries (trans.), *The Paradox of Acting* (London: Chatto & Windus, 1883), p. 41.

Pop, C. Snap, and Kid Rank, *Yo' Mama!* (New York: Berkley Books, 1995).

Quang Phuc Dong [James D. McCawley], "English Sentences Without Overt Grammatical Subject" in Zwicky, Arnold et al. (eds.), *Studies Out In Left Field: Defamatory Essays Presented to James McCawley on the Occasion of his 33rd or 34th Birthday* (Philadelphia: John Benjamins Publishing Company, 1992) [reprint of the original 1971 edition].

Randall, Jessy, *Dorothy Surrenders*, online at http://www.2river.org/chapbooks/jrandall/contents.html (accessed March 26, 2008).

Ripley, Robert L., *Ripley's Believe It Or Not* (New York: Pocket Books, 1941), pp. 93 and 97 [Bismarck's oath].

Schiffrin, Deborah, *Discourse Markers* (New York: Cambridge University Press, 1987), pp. 62–65, 312–326.

Thorpe, Benjamin, *Diplomatarium Anglicum Aevi Saxonici* (London: MacMillan, 1865), p. 483 [Anglo-Saxon wills].

Tiersma, Peter M., *Legal Language* (Chicago: University of Chicago Press, 1999), pp. 10–34.

Varro, Marcus Terentius, *De Lingua Latina I*, trans. Roland G. Kent (Cambridge, Mass.: Harvard University Press, 1958).

Wright, Sylvia, "The Death of Lady Mondegreen," *Harper's Magazine* (November 1954), pp. 48–51.

http://aixtal.blogspot.com/2007/05/lexique-une-prsidence.html (accessed Sept. 30, 2009) [*abracadabrantesque, mots ribonds*].

http://en.wikipedia.org/wiki/Oaths_of_Strasbourg (accessed Sept. 30, 2009).

http://en.wikipedia.org/wiki/Quebec_French_profanity#history (accessed July 27, 2009) [*sacres*].

http://www.cnn.com/2009/POLITICS/01/21/obama.oath/index. html#cnnSTCText (accessed Sept. 30, 2009) [Presidential oaths].

http://www.huffingtonpost.com/2009/01/20/justice-roberts-flubs-oba_n_159429.html (accessed Sept. 30, 2009) [Presidential oaths].

http://www.slate.com/id/2102964/ (accessed Sept. 30, 2009) [euphemism in the press].

http://www.stefanjacob.de/Geschichte/Unterseiten/Quellen. php?Multi=61 (accessed Sept. 30, 2009) [Strasbourg Oaths].

http://www.washingtonpost.com/wp-dyn/articles/A3699-2004Jun24. html [vice presidential oaths].

http://www.canoe.com/divertissement/tele-medias/dossiers/2006/ 10/20/2078568-jdq.html [*sacres* in the media].

CHAPTER 4. ON OR ABOUT YOUR PERSON

Arnold, David, "RMV Reads Between the Lines," *Boston Globe*, July 20, 2000, p. B1.

Batog, Jennifer, "Tiny Cards Make a Big Business Impression," *Boston Globe*, May 5, 2008, p. B5.

Bloch, Linda-Renée, "Mobile Discourse: Political Bumper Stickers as a Communication Event in Israel," *Journal of Communication*, vol. 50 (2000), pp. 48–76.

Chi, Lau Kin, "Samizdat and Designer T-shirts." *Index on Censorship*, Sept. 1992.

"Dog Tag (Identifier)," http://en.wikipedia.org/wiki/Dog_tag_ (identifier) (accessed July 16, 2009).

Edwards Humez, Leslie, personal conversation (July 2009) [scapulars and holy cards].

Exotic Expression, videotape (Quartz Hill, Calif.: California Star Productions, n.d.) [tattoos and piercing].

Fershleiser, Rachel, and Larry Smith (eds.), *Not Quite What I Was Planning: Six-Word Memoirs by Writers Famous and Obscure* (New York: HarperCollins, 2008).

Fuller, Gerald, O.M.I., *Stories for All Seasons* (New London, Conn.: Twenty-Third Publications, 1996) [Dr. Stein's *pro bono* tattoo removals].

Gleason, Col. Harold W., Jr., personal correspondence (letters to Alex Humez dated May 23, 1990, May 29, 1990, and June 1, 1990) [dog tags].

Goffman, Erving, *Relations in Public* (New York: Harper Colophon, 1971), chap. 2 ("The Territories of the Self"), chap. 6 ("Normal Appearances") and chap. 7 ("The Insanity of Place").

——, *Stigma: Notes on the Management of Spoiled Identity* (Englewood Cliffs, N.J.: Prentice-Hall, 1963).

Gutradt, Gail, personal conversation (June 2009) [Japanese business cards].

Handley, Eric, personal conversation (Fall 1965) [naughty license plate].

Klein, Lloyd, *It's in the Cards: Consumer Credit and the American Experience* (Westport, Conn.: Praeger, 1999), pp. 27–29.

"Letter Carriers' Uniform Overview," usps.com/postalhistory/_pdf/Letter_Carrier_Uniform_Overview.pdf (accessed July 16, 2009).

Marmion, Harry A., "Historical Background of Selective Service in the United States," in Roger W. Little (ed.) *Selective Service and American Society* (New York: Russell Sage Foundation, 1969), pp. 35–52.

Newman, John J., *Uncle, We Are Ready! Registering America's Men 1917–1918* (North Salt Lake, Utah: Heritage Quest, 2001).

Renner, Charlotte, "Dress Codes," Maine Public Radio broadcast essay, 1990.

Rio Grande Jewelers' Supply, *Gems and Findings* catalogue (Albuquerque: Bell Group, 2008), pp. 521 and 526.

Salamon, Hagar, "Ha'am in the Turbulent Discursive Sphere of Israeli Bumper Stickers," *Hebrew Studies* 46 (2005), pp. 197–234.

[unsigned], "Tattoos," *New York Times Magazine*, March 17, 1996.

Warren, Earl, majority opinion in *United States v. O'Brien*, 391 U.S. 367 (1968). Reprinted in Susan Dente Ross, *Deciding Communication Law: Key Cases in Context* (Mahwah, N.J.: Laurence Erlbaum Assoc., 2004), pp. 4.6–4.14.

Wilfong, Robert, personal conversation (Summer 1966) [fake IDs at Amherst bar].

http://sparklepony.blogspot.com/2007/11/breaking-news-poofter-wins-great.html, (accessed July 23, 2009) [vanity plates].

www.cosmeticsurgery.com/view_photos/cosmetic-surgery (accessed July 23, 2009) [cosmetic body enhancement].

www.cyborlink.com/besite/japan.htm (accessed July 18, 2009) [Japanese business card etiquette].

www.haitixchange.com/index.php/forums/viewthread/1276/P12/
#18604 (accessed July 18, 2009) [Haitian currency].
www.osb.org/gen/medal.html (accessed July 23, 2009) [crucifix and
St. Benedict medal].
www.washingtonpost.com/wp-dyn/content/article/2007/11/03/
AR2007110301111.html (accessed July 23, 2009) [vanity plates].

CHAPTER 5. ON THE LAM

Bader, Sara, *Strange Red Cow: And Other Curious Classified Ads from the Past*
(New York: Random House, 2005).
Cole, Simon A., *Suspect Identities: A History of Fingerprinting and Criminal
Identification* (Cambridge: Harvard University Press, 2001) [Bertillon].
Delafuente, Charles, "Terror in the Age of Eisenhower: Recalling the
Mad Bomber, Whose Rampage Shook New York," *New York Times,*
Sept. 10, 2004, pp. B1, B6 [Metesky story and quotations].
Demos, John, *The Unredeemed Captive: A Family Story from Early America*
(New York: Knopf, 1994).
Douglas, John E., and Mark Olshaker, *The Cases That Haunt Us: From
Jack the Ripper to JonBenet Ramsey, the FBI's Legendary Mindhunter Sheds
Light on the Mysteries That Won't Go Away* (New York: Scribner, 2000),
p. 170.
Ewing, Charles Patrick, and Joseph T. McCann, *Minds on Trial: Great
Cases in Law and Psychology* (New York: Oxford University Press, Inc.,
2006) [Metesky story].
Fass, Paula S., *Kidnapped: Child Abduction in America* (Oxford: University
of Oxford Press, 1997).
Fifer, Barbara, and Martin Kidston, *Wanted! Wanted Posters of the Old West*
(Helena, Mont.: Farcountry Press, 2003).
Fisher, Barry A. J., David R. Fisher, and Jason Kolowski, *Forensics
Demystified* (New York: McGraw-Hill, 2007).
Higdon, Hal, *The Crime of the Century: The Leopold & Loeb Case*
(New York: G. P. Putnam's Sons, 1975).
Madden, Mellissa Ann, "George Metesky: New York's Mad Bomber,"
online at http://www.trutv.com/library/crime/terrorists_spies/
terrorists/metesky/8.html (accessed Feb. 26, 2010).
Maggio, Edward, *Private Security in the 21st Century: Concepts and
Applications* (Sudbury, Mass.: Jones & Bartlett Publishers, 2009).
Norton, Mary Beth, *In the Devil's Snare: The Salem Witchcraft Crisis of 1692*
(New York: Alfred A. Knopf, 2002).
Ross, Christian K., *The Father's Story of Charley Ross, the Kidnapped Child:
Containing a Full and Complete Account of the Abduction of Charles
Brewster Ross from the Home of his Parents in Germantown, with the Pursuit
of the Abductors and their Tragic Death; the Various Incidents Connected*

with the Search for the Lost Boy; the Discovery of Other Lost Children, Etc., Etc. (Philadelphia: John E. Potter and Company, 1876).

"16-Year Search for Madman," *New York Times*, Dec. 25, 1956, p. 1 [Metesky story and quotation]

Solan, Lawrence M., and Peter M. Tiersma, *Speaking of Crime: The Language of Criminal Justice* (Chicago: University of Chicago Press, 2005), p. 117.

Zesch, Scott, *The Captured: A True Story of Abduction by Indians on the Texas Frontier* (New York: St. Martin's Press, 2004).

http://abcnews.go.com/TheLaw/story?id=5522209&page=1 (accessed Sept. 30, 2009) [fingerprint evidence in "Clark Rockefeller" kidnaping trial].

http://i.abcnews.com/US/story?id=7790834&page=1 (accessed Sept. 30, 2009) [kidnapping conviction of "Clark Rockefeller"].

http://archives.cnn.com/2002/LAW/08/05/ctv.alert/index.html (accessed Sept. 30, 2009) [AMBER alert system].

http://chnm.gmu.edu/courses/magic/plot/bertillon.html (accessed Sept. 30, 2009).

http://crimemagazine.com/04/leopoldloeb,0229.htm (accessed Sept. 30, 2009).

http://cyber.eserver.org/unabom.txt (accessed Sept. 30, 2009) [Unabomber's manifesto].

http://en.wikipedia.org/wiki/Impressment (accessed Sept. 30, 2009).

http://en.wikipedia.org/wiki/Percy_Lefroy_Mapleton (accessed Sept. 30, 2009).

http://en.wikipedia.org/wiki/Shanghaiing (accessed Sept. 30, 2009).

http://homicide.northwestern.edu/docs_fk/ homicide/5866/19240524tribo4.pdf (accessed Sept. 28, 2009) [Leopold and Loeb forensic evidence].

http://mainemostwanted.org/index.cfm?ac=casedetails&CaseID=2008 0037 (accessed Sept. 30, 2009) [wanted posters].

http://projects.exeter.ac.uk/RDavies/arian/current/howmuch.html (accessed Sept. 30, 2009) [changes in money value over time].

http://themediabiz.blogspot.com/2009/03/role-of-classified-advertising-in. html (accessed Sept. 30, 2009) [classifieds and decline of newspapers].

http://uv201.com/Radio_Pages/zenith_radio_nurse.htm (accessed Sept. 30, 2009).

http://www.boston.com/bostonglobe/ideas/articles/2008/07/20/ abducted/ (accessed Sept. 30, 2009) [a skeptical review of AMBER Alerts].

http://www.boston.com/bostonglobe/magazine/ articles/2009/03/12/1_man_3629_lies/ (accessed Sept. 30, 2009) [the many lies of "Clark Rockefeller"].

http://www.boston.com/news/local/massachusetts/articles/2009/02/
17/paid_sex_then_threats_bring_id_debate/ (accessed Sept. 30,
2009) [prostitute's text message].

http://www.enotes.com/forensic-science/lindbergh-kidnapping-
murder (accessed Sept. 30, 2009).

http://www.genealogytoday.com/guide/criminal-records.html
(accessed Sept. 30, 2009) [Bertillon].

http://www.innocenceproject.org/understand/Eyewitness-
Misidentification.php (accessed Sept. 30, 2009).

http://www.joshuarey.com/index.pl?Action=ShowArticle&ID=134
(accessed Sept. 30, 2009) [cut-out note generator].

http://www.klaaskids.org/printathon.htm (accessed Sept. 30, 2009)
[child safety/ID].

http://www.law.umkc.edu/faculty/projects/ftrials/Hauptmann/
Ransom.htm (accessed Sept. 30, 2009) [ransom note ascribed to
Bruno Hauptmann].

http://www.lindberghkidnappinghoax.com/ransom.html (accessed
Sept. 30, 2009) [Hauptmann ransom note alleged to be a hoax].

http://www.officer.com/web/online/Operations-and-Tactics/Cops-
Talk-Funny/3$40630 (accessed Sept. 30, 2009).

http://www.senatorwaugh.com/2009-press/0409/040109.htm
(accessed Sept. 30, 2009) [bank robbery notes].

http://www.usdoj.gov/usao/iln/osc/documents/libby_indictment_
28102005.pdf (accessed Sept. 30, 2009) [Lewis "Scooter" Libby
perjury trial].

http://www2.fbi.gov/wanted/topten/fugitives/bulger.htm (accessed
Sept. 30, 2009) ["Whitey" Bulger's wanted poster].

CHAPTER 6. IN THE NEWS

Bruthiaux, Paul, *The Discourse of Classified Advertising* (New York and
Oxford: Oxford University Press, 1996), pp. 90–131.

Cook, Guy, *The Discourse of Advertising* (London and New York:
Routledge, 2nd ed. 2001), pp. 36, 54–57, 123, 199.

"Crime Watch: Burglar Bogeys Golf Club Theft," *Watertown Tab & Press,*
May 22, 2009, p. 4.

Davis, Elizabeth A., "Small-Town Society Columns Hold Old-Fashioned
Charms," *Gaffney* [S.C.] *Ledger,* February 13, 2006, online at www.
gaffneyledger.com/news/2006/0213/LifeStyles/018.html (accessed
Aug. 6, 2009).

Fatihi, A. H., *The Language of Advertising and TV Commercials* (New Delhi:
Bahri Publications, 1991), pp. 36–61.

Forbes, R. J., *Studies in Ancient Technology,* Vol. II (Leiden: E.J. Brill,
1965), pp. 137–138.

Handley, Eric, personal conversation (Summer 1966) [4×5 newspaper photography].

Humez, Nick, "Wire Services," in *St. James Encyclopedia of Popular Culture,* Sarah and Tom Pendergast, eds. (Detroit: Gale Group, 2000), vol. 5, pp. 158–161.

Korzenik, Diana, *Drawn to Art* (Hanover, N.H.: University Press of New England, 1985) [wood engraving and the "art labor" movement].

Martin, Judith, *Miss Manners' Guide to Excruciatingly Correct Behavior* (New York: Atheneum, 1982), p. 309.

Vestergaard, Torben, and Kim Schrøder, *The Language of Advertising* (London and New York: Basil Blackwell, 1985), pp. 72–108.

White, E. B., "Irtnog," *The New Yorker,* Nov. 30, 1935, pp. 17–18.

Winchester, Simon, *Krakatoa* (New York: HarperCollins, 2003), pp. 189–194.

Wood, Cyndi, Bucksport Police notes, *Ellsworth* [Maine] *American,* July 2, 2009, p. I:4.

http://en.wikipedia.org/wiki/Ask_Ann_Landers (accessed Aug. 7, 2009).

http://en.wikipedia.org/wiki/Dorothy_Dix (accessed Aug. 6, 2009).

http://latimesblogs.latimes.com/thedailymirror/2008/08/us-drops-atomic.html (accessed Aug. 6, 2009) [*L.A. Times* issue of Aug. 7, 1945, including high-resolution .jpgs of pp. I:1–2 and II:8].

http://uxpress.com/dearabby/bio.html (accessed Aug. 13, 2009).

http://www.loc.gov/rr/record/nrpb/nrpb-2007reg.html (accessed Aug. 19, 2009) [Mayor LaGuardia reads the funnies on air].

CHAPTER 7. ON THE PHONE

Allen, Betty, *Behave Yourself! Etiquette for American Youth* (Chicago: Lippincott, 1937).

Baldridge, Letitia, *The Amy Vanderbilt Complete Book of Etiquette* (Garden City, N.Y.: Doubleday, 1978).

Benton, Frances, *Etiquette: The Complete Modern Guide for Day-to-Day Living the Correct Way* (New York: Random House, 1956).

Boettinger, H. M., *The Telephone Book: Bell, Watson, Vail and American Life, 1876–1976* (Croton-on-Hudson, N.Y.: Riverwood Publishers, 1977), p. 28.

Colvin, Jill, "Voice Mail Calls, but Do We Care?" Minneapolis-Saint Paul *Star Tribune,* June 3, 2009, online at http://www.startribune.com/lifestyle/46827897.html?elr=KArks7PYDiaK7DUHPYDiaK7DUiacyK UnciatkEP7DhUr (accessed Oct. 1, 2009) [youth's trend away from voice mail to texting].

Crystal, David, *Txtng: the Gr8 Db8* (New York: Oxford University Press, 2008).

de Sola Pool, Ithiel, ed., *The Social Impact of the Telephone* (Cambridge, Mass.: MIT Press, 1977).

Doskow, Art, "Signaling System 7 (SS7)," online at http://www.iec.org/online/tutorials/ss7/index.asp (accessed Oct. 1, 2009) [character storage].

Dumas, Daniel, "Be Mindful of Your Personal Space," *Wired Magazine*, July 15, 2009, online at http://www.wired.com/culture/lifestyle/magazine/17-08/by_personal_space (accessed Oct. 1, 2009) [impact of your electronic devices on others around you].

Elgan, Mike, "Should Cell Phone Jamming Be Legal?" *PCWorld*, Feb. 28, 2009, online at http://www.pcworld.com/businesscenter/article/160420/should_cell_phone_jamming_be_legal.html (accessed Oct. 1, 2009).

Francois, Nicole, "Is Voicemail Effective Communication?" April 3, 2009, online at http://www.allbusiness.com/media-telecommunications/telecommunications/12271285-1.html (accessed Oct. 1, 2009).

Gunn, Angela, "Everyone but You Is Being Rude with Their Mobile Gadgets," June 19, 2009, online at http://www.betanews.com/article/Everyone-but-you-is-being-rude-with-their-mobile-gadgets/1245410649 (accessed Oct. 1, 2009).

Harriman, Grace Carley, *Mrs. Oliver Harriman's Book of Etiquette: A Modern Guide to the Best Social Form* (New York: Greenburg, 1942), p. 67.

How to Use the Dial Phone (American Telephone and Telegraph Co., 1927), training film, online at http://www.youtube.com/watch?v=SACRoEoRsa4&feature=related (accessed Oct. 1, 2009).

Humphrys, John, "I h8 txt msgs: How Texting Is Wrecking Our Language," *Daily Mail*, Sept. 24, 2007, online at http://www.dailymail.co.uk/news/article-483511/I-h8-txt-msgs-How-texting-wrecking-language.html (accessed Oct. 1, 2009).

Lebedev, Artemy, "A Short History of Telephone Numbers," online at http://www.artlebedev.com/mandership/91/ (accessed Oct. 1, 2009).

Leshnower, Ron, "Don't Let Your Answering Machine Advertise the Fact You Live Alone," online at http://apartments.about.com/od/apartmentliving/qt/outgoingmessage.htm (accessed Oct. 1, 2009)

Martin, Judith, and Kamen, Gloria, *Miss Manners' Guide to Excruciatingly Correct Behavior* (New York, W.W. Norton & Co., 2005), p. 244.

Pilewski, Mike, "The Joy of Txt," interview with David Crystal, *Spotlight Magazine*, Nov. 2008, pp. 16–17, online at http://www.spotlight-online.de/files/spotlight/Magazine_content/Documents/1108text.pdf

Pollack, Andrew, "Next Office Revolution: 'Voice Mail,'" *New York Times*, Aug. 20, 1988, section 1, p. 1, online at http://www.nytimes.

com/1988/08/20/business/company-news-next-office-revolution-voice-mail.html (accessed Oct. 1, 2009).

Post, Emily, *Etiquette: The Blue Book of Social Usage* (New York, Funk & Wagnalls, 1960).

Post, Peggy, "Cell Phone Etiquette in Public," *Good Housekeeping*, March 2003, online at http://www.goodhousekeeping.com/family/etiquette/cell-phone-etiquette-mar03 (accessed Oct. 1, 2009).

Renshaw, Domeena C., "Coping with Obscene Phone Calls," *Psychiatric Times*, Oct. 1, 2008, online at http://www.psychiatrictimes.com/display/article/10168/1325936 (accessed Oct. 1, 2009).

Shaw, Carolyn Hagner, *Modern Manners* (New York: Fawcett Crest, 1958).

Stefoff, Rebecca, *Robots* (New York: Benchmark Books, 2007), p. 94.

Tchouaffe, Olivier, "Everywhere Means Nowhere: Cell Phones and the Reconfiguration of Space and Information," online at http://flowtv.org/?p=3938 (accessed Oct. 1 2009).

Weiner, Eric, "Our Cell Phones, Ourselves," essay broadcast on NPR on Dec. 24, 2007, online at http://www.npr.org/templates/story/story.php?storyId=17486953&ps=rs (accessed Oct. 1, 2009) [Leysia Palen quotation "...we have a generation..."].

Wilson, Margery, *The Pocket Book of Etiquette* (New York: Pocket Books, 1937).

Young, Doug, "Chinese Chatting Up with Numbers in Cyberspace," online at http://www.clta-gny.org/numbers.htm (accessed Oct. 1, 2009).

http://abcnews.go.com/Technology/PCWorld/story?id=4332957 (accessed Oct. 1, 2009) [cost of a cell phone, 1988–2008].

http://electronics.howstuffworks.com/cell-phone-jammer.htm (accessed Oct. 1, 2009).

http://en.wikipedia.org/wiki/E.161 (accessed Oct. 1, 2009) [E.161 keypad].

http://en.wikipedia.org/wiki/Freebie_marketing (accessed Oct. 1, 2009) [razor and blades business model].

http://en.wikipedia.org/wiki/Mobile_phone_jammer (accessed Oct. 1, 2009).

http://en.wikipedia.org/wiki/Motorola_DynaTAC (accessed Oct. 1, 2009).

http://japanese.meetup.com/7/boards/thread/4919994 (accessed Oct. 1, 2009) [texting in Japanese].

http://news.bbc.co.uk/2/hi/entertainment/1504053.stm (accessed Oct. 1, 2009) [cell phones drive pianist off stage].

http://news.bbc.co.uk/2/hi/uk_news/618065.stm (accessed Oct. 1, 2009) [BBC announcer hoaxed].

http://news.bbc.co.uk/hi/spanish/latin_america/newsid_7095000/7095670.stm (accessed Oct. 1, 2009) [Chávez ring tone].

http://pcworld.about.com/dbf/Dec242005id123950.htm (accessed Oct. 1, 2009) [answering machines].

http://query.nytimes.com/gst/abstract.html?res=9804E7DD133FE432 A25752C1A9629C946195D6CF (accessed Oct. 1, 2009) [telephone operators not yet obsolete].

http://reviews.cnet.com/4520-10779_7-5843439-1.html (accessed Oct. 1, 2009) [cell phone etiquette].

http://transcripts.cnn.com/TRANSCRIPTS/0209/15/lklw.oo.html (accessed Oct. 1, 2009) [Larry King interviews Prince Albert of Monaco].

http://www.fluther.com/disc/37682/do-americans-hang-up-on-the-phone-without-saying-goodbye/ (accessed Oct. 1, 2009).

http://www.metafilter.com/52273/Saying-goodbye-to-goodbye (accessed Oct. 1, 2009) [phone call closure].

http://www.msnbc.msn.com/id/7432915/ (accessed Oct. 1, 2009) ["First cell phone a true 'brick' "].

http://www.news.com.au/story/0,23599,22789713-13762,00. html (accessed Oct. 1, 2009) [teen texter breaks sms record—blindfolded].

http://www.retrobrick.com/moto8000.html (accessed Oct. 1, 2009) [Motorola DynaTAC 8000X].

http://www.3gpp.org/mobile-competence-centre (accessed Oct. 1, 2009) [SMS].

http://www.time.com/time/magazine/article/0,9171,853690,00.html (accessed Oct. 1, 2009) ["Robot Secretary" answering machine].

http://www.t9.com/us/learn/ (accessed Oct. 1, 2009) [T9 keypad text input].

http://www.tvsquad.com/2006/06/13/things-i-hate-about-tv-not-saying-goodbye-on-the-phone/ (accessed Oct. 1, 2009).

CHAPTER 8. IN THE MAIL

Adams, Stephen, "Traditional Christmas Card 'Set for Decline,' " *Telegraph*, Dec. 15, 2008, online at http://www.telegraph.co.uk/technology/3776875/Traditional-Christmas-card-set-for-decline. html (accessed Oct. 1, 2009).

Austin, Jane, *Persuasion* (New York: Oxford University Press, 1998 [1818]), chap. 16.

Buday, George, *The Mystery of the Christmas Card* (London: Spring Books, 1954), pp. 44–52.

"The Business of Valentine's Day," American Greetings Corporation, Winter 2007/2008, online at http://pressroom.americangreetings. com/archives/va108/valbiz08.html.

Campbell, Sarah B., *The Grammar of Email* (Somerville, Mass.: Grammar Guides, 2007) pp. 32, 105.

Cicero, Marcus Tullius, trans. W. Glynn Williams, *The Letters to His Friends, Vol. 1* (Cambridge, Mass.: Harvard University Press, 1965).

Forbes, R. J., *Studies in Ancient Technology*, vol. II (Leiden: E. J. Brill, 1965).

Gabriel, Richard A., *The Great Armies of Antiquity* (Westport, Conn.: Praeger, 2002), p. 9.

Greeting Card Association, "Christmas by the Numbers: 2008," online at http://www.greetingcard.org/userfiles/file/GCA 2008 Christmas by the Numbers.pdf (accessed Oct. 1, 2009) [holiday card statistics].

"Greeting from the Smithsonian: A postcard History of the Smithsonian Institution," online at http://siarchives.si.edu/history/exhibits/postcard/backs.htm (accessed Oct. 1, 2009) [World War I serviceman's postcard].

Harrer, Heinrich, "Seven Years in Tibet" (New York: Jeremy P. Tarchers/Putnam, 1953), p. 143.

Harris, William V., *Ancient Literacy* (Cambridge, Mass.: Harvard University Press 1991).

Henkin, David M., *The Postal Age: The Emergence of Modern Communications in Nineteenth-Century America* (Chicago: University of Chicago Press, 2006), pp. 17, 19–20.

Jones, Kyla, "In Defense of Christmas Letters," *New York Times*, Dec. 13, 2002, online at http://www.nytimes.com/2002/12/13/travel/rituals-in-defense-of-christmas-letters.html?scp=19&sq=Christmas%20 1etter&st=cse (accessed Oct. 1, 2009).

Lazarenko, Rebecca, "Be My Anti-Valentine: Rallying against Cupid's Corruption," online at http://media.www.brockpress.com/media/storage/paper384/news/2007/02/13/Culture/Be.My. AntiValentine.Rallying.Against.Cupids.Corruption-2716067. shtml?sourcedomain=www.brockpress.com&MIIHost=media. collegepublisher.com. (accessed Oct. 1, 2009).

Liddell, Henry George, and Robert Scott, *A Greek-English Lexicon, Based on the German Work of Francis Passow* (New York: Harper & Bros., 5th ed. 1861).

Martin, David, "Twitter Quitters Post Roadblock to Long-Term Growth," online at http://blog.nielsen.com/nielsenwire/online_mobile/twitter-quitters-post-roadblock-to-long-term-growth (accessed Oct. 1, 2009).

Martine, Arthur, *Martine's Sensible Letter Writer: Being a Comprehensive and Complete Guide and Assistant* (New York: Dick and Fitzgerald, 1866), pp. 18, 24, and passim.

McGrath, Alister, *In the Beginning: The Story of the King James Bible and How It Changed a Nation, a Language, and a Culture* (New York: Anchor, 2002).

Muir, John, *Life and Letters in the Ancient Greek World* (New York: Routledge, 2008), p. 31 [Letter from Apollonia and Eupous].

Pepys, Samuel, *Diary*, entry for Feb. 14, 1667, online at http://www.pepysdiary.com/archive/1667/02/14/ (accessed Feb. 26, 2010) [his wife's valentine].

Pool, David, *What Jane Austen Ate and Charles Dickens Knew* (New York: Simon & Schuster, 1993), p. 66.

Poster, Carol, and Mitchell, Linda C. eds., *Letter-Writing Manuals and Instruction from Antiquity to the Present: Historical and Bibliographic Studies* (Columbia: University of South Carolina Press, 2007), p. 322.

"Powder Mill on Brandywine near Wilmington, Del.," address side of postcard (Wilmington, Del.: Julian B. Robinson, n.d.), online at http://en.wikipedia.org/wiki/File:1905DuPontMillpcardback.jpg (accessed Oct. 1, 2009).

"Powder Mill on Brandywine near Wilmington, Del.," picture side of postcard (Wilmington, Del.: Julian B. Robinson, n.d.), online at http://en.wikipedia.org/wiki/File:1905DuPontGunpowderMill.jpg (accessed Oct. 1, 2009).

Procopius of Caesarea, trans. Richard Atwater, *The Secret History of Procopius* (New York: Covici Friede, 1927), online at http://www.fordham.edu/halsall/basis/procop-anec.html.

Ramsay, A. M., "The Speed of the Roman Imperial Post," in *Journal of Roman Studies* 15 (1925), pp. 60–74.

Schmidt, Leigh Eric, "The Fashioning of a Modern Holiday: St. Valentine's Day, 1840–1870," *Winterthur Portfolio*, Vol. 28, No. 4 (Winter 1993), pp. 209–245.

Staff, Frank, *The Picture Postcard and Its Origins* (New York: Praeger, 1966), pp. 9 and 13.

Stross, Randall, "Struggling to Evade the E-Mail Tsunami," *New York Times*, April 20, 2008, online at http://www.nytimes.com/2008/04/20/technology/20digi.html (accessed Oct . 1, 2009).

Suddath, Claire, "Testing Google's 'Drunk E-Mail' Protector," *Time*, Oct. 15, 2008, online at http://www.time.com/time/business/article/0,8599,1849897,00.html (accessed Oct. 1, 2009).

Sutter, John D., "Twitter Blackout Left Users Feeling 'Jittery,' 'Naked,' " online at http://www.cnn.com/2009/TECH/08/07/twitter.attack.reaction/ (accessed Oct. 1, 2009).

Trapp, Michael, *Greek and Latin Letters: An Anthology with Translation* (Cambridge: Cambridge University Press, 2003) [Letters from Mnesiergos and Apollonios].

U.S. Postal Service, "ZIP Code," online at http://web.archive.org/web/20031204074407/www.usps.com/history/his2_75.htm#ZIP (accessed Oct. 1, 2009).

VanArsdale, Daniel W., "Chain Letter Evolution, 1998, 2002, 2007," online at http://www.silcom.com/~barnowl/chain-letter/evolution.html (accessed Oct. 1, 2009).

Williams, James D., *The Teacher's Grammar Book* (Mahwah, N.J.: Lawrence Erlbaum, 2nd ed., 2005), p. 7.

Wright, Alex "Friending, Ancient or Otherwise," *New York Times,* Dec. 2, 2007, online at http://www.nytimes.com/2007/12/02/weekinreview/02wright.html (accessed Oct. 1, 2009).

Xenophon, trans. Walter Miller, *Cyropaedia, Book VII* (Cambridge, Mass.: Harvard University Press, 1914), pp.17–18, 419.

Young, John H., *Our Deportment: Or, the Manners, Conduct, and Dress of the Most Refined Society* (Detroit: F. B. Dickerson, 1882), p. 75.

http://openmap.bbn.com/~tomlinso/ray/firstemailframe.html (accessed Oct. 1, 2009) [the first e-mail].

http://twitter.zendesk.com/forums/10711/entries/15367 (accessed Oct. 1, 2009) [posting a Twitter tweet].

http://www.netmanners.com/email-etiquette/dont-brush-off-email-privacy/ (accessed Oct. 1, 2009).

http://www.snopes.com/horrors/mayhem/payphone2.asp (accessed Oct. 1, 2009) [urban legend: pay phone poisoning].

CHAPTER 9. IN AND OUT OF TROUBLE

Buchanan, M., "Identity and Language in the SM Scene," in Erin McKean, ed., *Verbatim* (New York: Harcourt, 2001), pp. 160–166.

Cathcart, Thomas, and Daniel Klein, *Aristotle and an Aardvark Go to Washington* (New York: Abrams Image, 2007), pp. 34ff. [weasel words].

Chaplin, Stewart, "The Stained-Glass Political Platform, *Century Illustrated Monthly Magazine,* June 1900, p. 305.

Cicero, M. Tullius, *Murder Trials,* trans. Michael Grant (Harmondsworth, U.K.: Penguin, 1975).

Crittenden, Jules, "Do Not Light This Paper on Fire and Stand in a Puddle of Gasoline," *Boston Herald,* Feb. 13, 1998, p. 16.

Fraser, Bruce, "Threatening Revisited," *Forensic Linguistics* 5(2) 1998, pp. 159–173.

Goffman, Erving, *Relations in Public* (New York: Harper Colophon, 1972), pp. 350–357.

Humez, Nick, "(S)wordplay," *VERBATIM* XXX:3 (Summer 2005), pp. 25–28.

Kuntz, Tom, "At Harvard, A Political Sex Scandal That's Not News, But Ancient History," *New York Times,* Oct. 18, 1998, section 4, p. 7.

Lee, Jennifer B. "Solving a Riddle Wrapped up in a Mystery inside a Cookie," *New York Times,* Jan. 16, 2008, online at www.nytimes. com/2008/01/16/dining/16fort.html, (accessed April 1, 2008).

Legge, James, trans. *I Ching: Book of Changes* (New York: Bantam, 1969), pp. 114–115.

Lomax, Alan, notes to "Poor Little Johnny," sung by Harriet McClintock and recorded in 1940, on *Negro Lullabies, Ring Games and Children's Games* (Library of Congress phonograph record, LC AAFS-20).

Marrus, Michael, *Some Measure of Justice* (Madison: University of Wisconsin Press, 2009), pp. 3–7 and 60–78.

Neale, Steve, "Swashbuckling, Sapphire, and Salt," in Frank Krutnik, Steve Neale, Brian Neve, and Peter Stanfield, eds., *Blacklisted Hollywood* (New Brunswick, N.J.: Rutgers University Press, 2007), pp.198–209.

Shuy, Roger W., *The Language of Confession, Interrogation, and Deception* (Thousand Oaks, Calif.: SAGE Publications, 1998), pp. 1–11.

Silverman, Craig, *Regret the Error* (New York: Sterling Publishing, 2007), pp. 123–124, 210, and 242–243.

Slansky, Paul, and Arleen Sorkin, *My Bad* (New York: Bloomsbury Publishing, 2006), pp. 33, 71, 99, and 168.

Tiersma, Peter M., "The Language of Law and Product Warnings," in Janet Cotterill, ed., *Language in the Legal Process* (New York: Palgrave Macmillan, 2002), pp. 54ff.

Van Gulick, Robert, "Postscript," in *The Chinese Bell Murders* (Chicago: University of Chicago Press, 1977), p. 284.

Walsh, William Shepard, *Handy-Book of Literary Curiosities* (Philadelphia: Lippincott, 1893), p. 715.

CHAPTER 10. IN THE END

Anaya, Rudolfo A., Denise Chávez, and Juan Estevan Arellano, *Descansos: An Interrupted Journey* (Albuquerque: El Norte Publications/University of New Mexico Press, 1995).

Brown, August, "Lux Interior, at 60; Founded NYC Horror-Punk Band The Cramps," *Boston Globe,* Feb. 6, 2009, p. B12.

Carpenter, Ronald H., "The Statistical Profile of Language Behavior with Machiavellian Intent or While Experiencing Caution and Avoiding Self-Incrimination," in Rieber, Robert W., and William A. Stewart, eds., *The Language Scientist as Expert in the Legal Setting: Issues in Forensic Linguistics* (New York: New York Academy of Sciences, 1990).

DeMillo, Andrew, "Roadside Memorials: Tributes or Hazards?" *Seattle Times,* June 7, 2000, online at http://community.seattletimes. nwsource.com/archive/?date=20000607&slug=4025369 (accessed Oct. 1, 2009).

Drelincourt, Charles, trans. Marius D'Assigny, *The Christian's Defence Against the Fears of Death: With Seasonable Directions How to Prepare Ourselves to Die Well* (Liverpool: Nutall, Fisher, and Dixon, 1810).

Ernout, A[lfred], and A[ntoine] Meillet, *Dictionnaire étymologique de la langue latine: histoire des mots* (Paris: Librairie C. Klincksieck, 1959).

Etkind, Marc, . . . *Or Not to Be: A Collection of Suicide Notes* (New York: Riverhead Books, 1997).

Fénéon, Félix, ed. Régine Detambel, *Nouvelles en trois lignes* (Paris: Mercure de France, 1997).

Flynn, John, personal conversation (Feb. 2008) [funeral home guest books].

"Funus," in Smith, William (ed.), *A Dictionary of Greek and Roman Antiquities* (London: John Murray, 1875), online at http://penelope. uchicago.edu/Thayer/E/Roman/Texts/secondary/SMIGRA*/ Funus.html (accessed Oct. 1, 2009) [Roman burial practices and terminology].

Guthke, Karl S., "Anthologies of Last Words: A Tour d'Horizon of a Literary Crypto-Genre," *Harvard Library Bulletin* 33:2 (Spring 1985), pp. 311–346.

———, *Last Words: Variations on a Theme in Cultural History* (Princeton, N.J.: Princeton University Press, 1992).

Howarth, Glennys, and Oliver Leaman, *Encyclopedia of Death and Dying* (London: Routledge, 2001).

Johnson, Marilyn, *The Dead Beat: Lost Souls, Lucky Stiffs, and the Perverse Pleasures of Obituaries* (New York: HarperPerennial, 2007).

Justice, Emma, "Facebook Suicide: The End of a Virtual Life," *The Times* [U.K.], Sept. 15, 2007, online at http://women.timesonline.co.uk/ tol/life_and_style/women/body_and_soul/article2452928.ece (accessed Oct. 1, 2009).

Larsen, Lyle, "Last Words of Famous Authors," online at http:// homepage.smc.edu/larsen_lyle/last_words_of_famous_authors.htm (accessed Oct. 1, 2009).

Leenaars, Antoon A., *Suicide Notes: Predictive Clues and Patterns* (New York: Human Sciences Press, 1988).

Mann, Thomas C., and Janet Greene, *Sudden & Awful: American Epitaphs & the Finger of God* (Brattleboro, Vt.: Stephen Greene Press, 1968).

Maris, Ronald W., *Pathways to Suicide: A Survey of Self-Destructive Behaviors* (Baltimore: Johns Hopkins University Press, 1981).

Maris, Ronald W., Alan Lee Berman, and Morton M. Silverman (eds.), *Comprehensive Textbook of Suicidology* (New York: Gilford Press, 2000).

May, Trevor, *The Victorian Undertaker* (Princes Risborough, U.K.: Shire Publications, 1996).

McCarthy, Elaine, *Morbid Curiosity: Celebrity Tombstones Across America* (Oceano, Calif.: Monagco Publishers, 2001).

Novak, Maximillian, "Defoe's Authorship of *A Collection of Dying Speeches* (1718)," *Philological Quarterly* 61:1 (Winter 1982), pp. 92–97.

Osgood, Charles E., and Evelyn Walker, "Motivation and Language Behavior: A Content Analysis of Suicide Notes," *Journal of Abnormal and Social Psychology* 59:1 (July 1959), pp. 58–67.

Rhees, Nigel, *I Told You I Was Sick* (London: Weidenfeld & Nicolson, 2005).

Roberts, Frank C. (compiler), *Obituaries from the Times 1961–1970* (Reading, U.K.: Newspaper Archive Developments, 1975).

Robinson, Ray, *Famous Last Words, Fond Farewells, Deathbed Diatribes, and Exclamations upon Expiration* (New York: Workman, 2003).

Schneidman, Edwin S., *Definition of Suicide* (New York: John Wiley & Sons, 1985).

Schneidman, Edwin S., and Norman L. Farberow (eds.), *Clues to Suicide* (New York: McGraw-Hill, 1957).

Silverman, Craig, *Regret the Error: How Media Mistakes Pollute the Press and Imperil Free Speech* (New York: Union Square Press, 2007).

Timmermans, Stefan, *Postmortem: How Medical Examiners Explain Suspicious Deaths* (Chicago: University of Chicago Press, 2006).

Twain, Mark, "Last Words of Great Men," *Buffalo Express,* Sept. 11, 1889, online at http://www.online-literature.com/twain/2848/.

Urbina, Ian, "Debating the Roadside Memorial," *New York Times,* Feb. 6, 2006, online at http://www.iht.com/articles/2006/02/06/news/road.php (accessed Oct. 1, 2009).

http://answers.google.com/answers/threadview?id=191570 (accessed Oct. 1, 2009) [Mark Twain's "Reports of my death"].

http://buscabiografias.com/ultimaspalabras.htm (accessed Oct. 1, 2009) [last words].

http://collections.iwm.org.uk/server/show/ConWebDoc.1261 (accessed Oct. 1, 2009) [the Kohima Epitaph].

http://colonial-america.suite101.com/article.cfm/health_problems_in_colonial_america (accessed Oct. 1, 2009).

http://itre.cis.upenn.edu/~myl/languagelog/archives/004787.html (accessed Oct. 1, 2009) [-XXX- origins].

http://parafernalia.lacoctelera.net/post/2008/10/27/ultimas-palabras-famosas (accessed Oct. 1, 2009) [last words].

http://webpages.charter.net/dnance/descansos (accessed Oct. 1, 2009) [David Nance's descanso photos].

http://www.afsp.org/index.cfm?fuseaction=home.viewpage&page_id=7852EBBC-9FB2-91-54125A1AD4221E49 (accessed Oct. 1, 2009) [American Foundation for Suicide Prevention "For the Media" page].

http://www.alsirat.com/epitaphs (accessed Oct. 1, 2009).

http://www.atheistactivist.org/Roadside.html (accessed Oct. 1, 2009) [anti-descanso page].

http://www.burmastar.org.uk/epitaph.htm (accessed Oct. 1, 2009) [the Kohima epitaph].

http://www.corsinet.com/braincandy/dying.html (accessed Oct. 1, 2009).

http://www.descansos.org/links.shtml (accessed Oct. 1, 2009).

http://www.dorothyparker.com/dot33.htm (accessed Oct. 1, 2009) [Dorothy Parker's actual epitaph].

http://www.eulogyspeech.net/ (accessed Oct. 1, 2009).

http://www.everlifememorials.com/v/headstones/epitaphs-inscriptions.htm (accessed Oct. 1, 2009).

http://www.gotquestions.org/seven-sayings-Christ.html (accessed Oct. 1, 2009).

http://www.mapping.com/words.html (accessed Oct. 1, 2009) [last words].

http://www.naghsr.org/html/publications/directions/2007/Spring/roadside.memorial.html (accessed Oct. 1, 2009) [governors on descanso pros and cons].

http://www.negenborn.net/catullus/text2/1101.htm (accessed Oct. 1, 2009) [Catullus's elegy].

http://www.porkjerky.com/free/suicide.php (accessed Oct. 1, 2009) [suicide note generator].

http://www.poynter.org/content/content_view.asp?id=99020 (accessed Oct. 1, 2009) [writing your own obit].

http://www.sofoca.cl/pebre/2007/10/28/ultimas-palabras-famosas/ (accessed Oct. 1, 2009) [last words].

http://www.stoa.org/hopper/text.jsp?doc=Stoa:text:2001.01.0012:section=3 (accessed Oct. 1, 2009) [epitaphs in antiquity].

http://www.thelatinlibrary.com/cicero/tusc1.shtml (accessed Oct. 1, 2009) [Latin text of Cicero's *Tusculan Disputations*].

http://www.thesmokinggun.com/archive/cnnobit1.html (accessed Oct. 1, 2009) [CNN's obiticide].

http://www.twainquotes.com/Death.html (accessed Oct. 1, 2009) [Mark Twain's "Reports of my death"].

http://www.usask.ca/antiquities/benemerenti/benemerenti_home.htm (accessed Oct. 1, 2009) [epitaphs].

http://www.well.com/~art/suicidenotes.html (accessed Oct. 1, 2009) [suicide notes].

INDEX

Italic page numbers refer to illustrations.